JEWS and
GENTILES

JEWS and GENTILES

MILTON HIMMELFARB

EDITED BY GERTRUDE HIMMELFARB

ENCOUNTER BOOKS
NEW YORK

Published by Encounter Books, an activity of Encounter for Culture and Education, Inc., a nonprofit, tax exempt corporation.

Encounter Books website address: www.encounterbooks.com

Manufactured in the United States and printed on acid-free paper.

The paper used in this publication meets the minimum requirements of ANSI/NISO Z39.48-1992 (R 1997)(*Permanence of Paper*).

FIRST EDITION

Library of Congress Cataloging-in-Publication Data

Himmelfarb, Milton
  Jews and Gentiles/Milton Himmelfarb
  p. cm.
  Includes a bibliography of the works of Milton Himmelfarb.
  ISBN 1-59403-154-1 (alk. paper)
  1. Judaism—20th century. 2. Jews—Intellectual life. 3. Jews—History—20th century. 4. Judaism—United States. 5. Religion and politics—United States. I. Title.
  BM565.H465 2007
  296—dc22   2006026359

10 9 8 7 6 5 4 3 2 1

Contents

Introduction

"HOW ODD / OF GOD / TO CHOOSE / THE JEWS." This dog-
gerel expresses one of the recurrent themes in this volume of
learned and provocative essays. Milton Himmelfarb traces its
source via the *Oxford Dictionary of Quotations* and the *Encyclopaedia Judaica*, meditates on the varied meanings that Christian and Jewish thinkers have attached to the "mystery" of the
Chosen People, and then reflects upon the "oddity" of that
choice: "the disproportion between how conspicuous certain
humans called Jews are and how few they are"—fewer than
25 in 10,000, he estimates. "Odder yet" is another fact: "that
the 99.75+ percent are called Gentiles because they are not the
.25 percent who are Jews." Theologians worry about the idea
of the Chosen People. For Himmelfarb, that idea is encapsu-
lated in the figures themselves, the dramatic evidence of
"Jewish disproportionateness and extraordinariness—the larger-
than-lifeness—through which I feel Jewish chosenness."[1]

More familiar is another oddity that has become Himmelfarb's trademark: his celebrated quip about Jews earning
like Episcopalians and voting like Puerto Ricans.[2] This aspect

---

[1] "What Do I Believe?" p. 162 below.
[2] In "Jews, Episcopalians, Puerto Ricans," the "anonymous aphorism," as Himmelfarb
described it (p. 211), refers to Hispanics rather than Puerto Ricans. In an earlier article
continued on next page

of Jewish "exceptionalism" is also supported by statistics, but it goes well beyond numbers in its implications, not only for electoral politics but for an ethos reflected in the largest issues of social policies and public affairs. American Jews are incorrigible liberals, or, as the title of one essay ironically puts it, "diehard conservatives"—conservative, that is, in clinging to habitual liberal values, often in spite of, and even to the detriment of, their economic, social, and religious interests.[3]

Again and again, Himmelfarb cites statistics (which are themselves, somehow, witty) demonstrating the "disproportionateness and extraordinariness" of Jews. Thus, "the number of Jews in the world is smaller than a small statistical error in the Chinese census."[4] Or, the annual excess of births over deaths in India is more then the population of "all the Jews in the whole world."[5] Or, the total number of Jews in the world is "fewer than two-thirds of the blacks in the United States, fewer than one-third of the Catholics in the United States."[6] In this sense, demography is truly destiny. The statistical error in the Chinese census, for example, appears in an essay on the Israeli war of 1967, giving the war a dimension and significance beyond that momentous event itself.

> Each of us Jews knows how thoroughly ordinary he is; yet taken together, we seem caught up in things great and inexplicable. It is almost as if we were not acting but were being acted through.... Yet we remain bigger than our numbers. Big things seem to happen around us and to us.[7]

---

making the same point, the reference was to Mexicans and Puerto Ricans ("Crisis" [1969] in *Jews of Modernity*, p. 91). He himself generally used the term Puerto Ricans, and it is in that form that the aphorism is now familiar.

[3]"American Jews: Diehard Conservatives," *Commentary*, April 1989.
[4]"In the Light of Israel's Victory," pp. 141–142.
[5]"A Haunting Question," in *Perspectives on Jews and Judaism: Essays in Honor of Wolfe Kelman*, ed. Arthur A. Chiel (New York: Rabbinical Assembly, 1978), p. 186.
[6]"A Plague of Children" (1971), in Himmelfarb, *The Jews of Modernity*, p. 135.
[7]"In the Light of Israel's Victory," pp. 141–142.

It is not only Jews who are defined by those small numbers and "big things." It is Gentiles as well. In the title essay of this volume, the "crude statistical fact" that "only 4 of 1,000 human beings in the world are Jews" gives Jewishness a qualitative as well as quantitative import, testifying to a people and a faith that have survived for so long against so many odds and in the face of so many near-fatal catastrophes. By the same token, the "providential uniqueness" of Jews defines "Gentiles" as well—"Gentile," according to the most authoritative dictionary, being "any nation [meaning 'people'] other than the Jewish." This, in turn, makes his subject "nothing less than the human race," which Himmelfarb takes as an invitation to range freely throughout antiquity and modernity, citing Scripture and Shakespeare, Tacitus and modern biblical scholars, English deists and German Marxists, a justice of the United States Supreme Court and a medieval Jewish commentator, and concluding with two versions of a Jewish travel prayer (one thoughtfully provided by El Al) read during a flight from New York to Tel Aviv.[8] Yet the whole adds up to a single theme, an illumination of that momentous "oddity" of Jews in a Gentile world.

■　　■　　■

So it is with the other essays in this volume—"occasional essays," as is said, written over a period of almost half a century, displaying the same depth and breadth of mind, the same erudition leavened by wit as well as wisdom. If they remain as pertinent today as when they were published, it is because they transcend the immediate occasions that called them into being, revealing a remarkable prescience and consistency. "In the Light of Israel's Victory," written in 1967, is more cautionary than that celebratory title might suggest. Indeed, the title

---

[8]"Jews and Gentiles," pp. 12–13.

has ironic overtones, for the essay ominously reminds us of an Israel that still confronts hostile neighbors who never recognized that "victory." It also describes an anti-Semitism in the West that comes, Himmelfarb foresaw (as few at the time did), more often from the Left than from the Right. He quotes the much romanticized Jewish socialist Rosa Luxemburg, who wrote to a friend from her prison cell in Germany during World War I: "Why do you pester me with your Jewish sorrow? There is no room in my heart for the Jewish troubles." "The sorrow and troubles of others," he comments, "had filled all the room in her heart."[9]

An essay that has become a classic in the literature of Nazism has the memorable title "No Hitler, No Holocaust." Written in 1984, it is the definitive rebuttal to the view then prevalent (and still held by many historians) that derides the "great man" theory of history as naive and simplistic. Himmelfarb recalls us to the terrible, deadly truth that history is, among other things, about the evil deeds committed by evil men. "Anti-Semitism," he declares, "was a necessary condition for the Holocaust; it was not a sufficient condition. Hitler was needed."[10] The essay also raises the still debated question of the extent to which Nazi anti-Semitism derived from pagan antiquity or from Christian antiquity. There was, and is, Himmelfarb argues, a form of Christian anti-Semitism, but it did not lead to the Holocaust. Hitler himself was "ex-Christian [Christian by birth] and anti-Christian," no more Christian than Stalin "the ex-seminarian."[11] Himmelfarb concludes with a warning that seemed bizarre at the time but that has since proved to be prophetic: "Jews now have more to fear from anti-Christians than from Christians, and from the Christian Left than from the Christian Right."[12]

---

[9]"In the Light of Israel's Victory," p. 120.
[10]"No Hitler, No Holocaust," p. 101.
[11]Ibid., pp. 107, 116.
[12]Ibid., p. 117.

The subject of paganism reappears in the discussion of the much controverted question of religion in public life. Again Himmelfarb addresses the issue boldly. The trouble is not that religion has too small a role, he insists. It is that a particular religion—"paganism, the de facto established religion"—has too large a role. And "Judaism," he asserts unequivocally, "is against paganism."[13] Yet Jews persist in holding to an exaggerated principle of the separation of church and state, an absolutistic secularism that is almost tantamount to paganism. This dogma of "separationism" is not only a violation of Judaism; it is against the best interests of all citizens, Jews included, because it would erect so high a wall between church and state as to exclude religion entirely from the public square, thus depriving everyone of the social and personal goods that religion contributes to the public. "Leave it to a poet," Himmelfarb concludes. "'Something there is that doesn't love a wall.'"[14]

It is a rich and eclectic combination of sources that Himmelfarb draws upon in each of these essays: facts and figures, authorities ancient and modern, an uncommon good sense and innate wisdom, and, no less compelling, personal experiences, reminiscences, and deeply felt sentiments. The most remarkable evidence of this variety is the earliest essay in this volume, written at the ripe age of thirty. "The Vindictive and the Merciful" is a bold exercise in historical revisionism, correcting—very nearly reversing—the age-old maxims about the merciful God of Christianity, the God of Love, in contrast to the Vindictive God of Judaism, the God of Wrath. The essay cites an impressive array of scholarly material—historical, theological, scriptural, textual. But it opens on quite a different note: childhood memories of attending synagogue with his father, the ways in which he gradually adapted the

---

[13]See essay of that title, pp. 61–65.
[14]"Church and State: How High a Wall?" p. 242. See also "Religion and the Public Square," p. 251.

conventional ritual for his own imaginative and spiritual purposes, and, most dramatic, a long Hasidic tale about a poor tailor's conversation with God on the eve of Yom Kippur, a
reckoning with the Almighty.[15] These are not afterthoughts,
not rhetorical attempts to personalize or humanize a difficult
subject. They are rather at the heart of the subject. The personal, for Himmelfarb, is, in a sense, the theological.

"Going to Shul," written many years later, when he was
saying Kaddish after his father's death, is more overtly and
more movingly personal. In the earlier essay he had confessed
to deviations from his father's observances: he read more often
than prayed from the prayer book, skipped repetitive passages,
and supplemented them with a "personal canon" from the
Bible and post-biblical poetry. The later essay, although critical of the physical appearance of some prayer books (type too
small to make the vowel signs legible) and of some editorial
excrescences (the word "insight" is particularly objectionable),
is more respectful of the content of the standard prayer book,
including its repetitions and *longueurs*. He even finds virtue
in a lengthy service, which, like a long poem, provides time
for "an alternation of high moments and moments less high,
of concentration and relaxation"; a short service, by contrast,
"tends to be of a piece, dull and tepid."[16] He is especially moving on the subject of the Kaddish, defending the twice-a-day
saying of the Kaddish in synagogue, even for those who do
not normally attend services. The Kaddish, he explains, spares
each Jew the need to devise a form of mourning at a time when
he is in no condition or mood to be inventive. Instead the
mourner has at hand traditional rituals, which are "appropriate almost by definition, because of their antiquity, their near-
universality, their publicness"—rituals, moreover, which can
be supplemented with whatever personal prayers or practices

---

[15]"The Vindictive and the Merciful," pp. 194–95.
[16]"Going to Shul," p. 173.

the mourner likes. "The Kaddish I now say for my father," Himmelfarb observes, "he said for his; and so back through a recession of the generations that exceeds what my imagination can grasp. Acting as my father acted, I become conscious that I am a link in the chain of being."[17]

It is appropriate that the last major essay Himmelfarb wrote, in 1996, on the subject "What Do American Jews Believe?" should have been the occasion for a statement of his own credo, lightened by his usual wit. Recalling Margaret Fuller's famous remark, "I accept the universe" (to which Carlyle had retorted, "Gad! She'd better!"), Himmelfarb commented: "I accept God. I hope He accepts me."[18] The final words of that essay may well serve as his own epitaph.

> "*Hatikvah,*" the Zionist and Israeli anthem, proclaims, "Our hope is not lost." That is in answer to the contemporaries of Ezekiel (37:11), who, more than 2,500 years ago, had despaired, crying, "... our hope is lost...."
>
> Hope is a Jewish virtue.[19]

■   ■   ■

I have reprinted these essays by my brother in their original form. (Unless otherwise noted, they first appeared in *Commentary* magazine.) It is tempting for an editor to edit, to clarify allusions, provide references, eliminate digressions and repetitions. But just as my brother paid his readers the honor of believing them capable of coping with complexity and subtlety, so I have chosen to honor him by respecting his wishes and his text. (The only liberty I took was to retitle a few of the essays, most of the original titles having been chosen by editors rather than by himself.) My great problem was that of selection. Given the limitation of space, I have tried to cover

[17]Ibid., pp. 166–67.
[18]"What Do I Believe?" p. 160.
[19]Ibid., p. 163.

most of the subjects upon which he has put his inimitable imprint.

I want to thank all those who made this volume possible: Neal Kozodoy, the editor of *Commentary*, who gave me valuable advice and encouragement, as well as permission to reprint the essays from that journal; David Billet, the assistant editor of *Commentary*, who did the onerous job of digitization with great skill and erudition; and David Singer, my brother's friend and colleague at the American Jewish Committee, who gave me leads to articles in other journals to include in the bibliography. I would also like to pay tribute to *Commentary* itself, under the editorship first of Norman Podhoretz and then of Neal Kozodoy, who were warm hosts to my brother over the years and receptive to a level of scholarship and boldness of thought characteristic of that journal.

Finally, this volume is dedicated to my brother's beloved wife, Judith, truly a "woman of virtue," and to their children, Martha, Edward, Miriam, Anne, Sarah, Naomi, and Dan, who were a source of great pride and comfort to him and who are the worthy bearers of his legacy.

Milton Himmelfarb (1918–2006),
alav hashalom

Gertrude Himmelfarb
March 2006

Judaism and Modernity

Jews and Gentiles

WE PRONOUNCE THE WORDS "Jews and Gentiles" trippingly on the tongue. They are a familiar dyad, like Frenchmen and Englishmen, Protestants and Catholics. All seem to go together, naturally and historically. In each couple, each member is tied to the other. The tie is as often one of hostility as of amity, but it is there.

Now, I am suspicious about things that we pronounce trippingly on the tongue, so I decided to look up "Jews" and "Gentiles" in dictionaries and encyclopedias. Or rather, I decided to look up "Gentiles" because, of course, everyone knows the answer to the question, Who is a Jew? "Gentiles" is the English translation—by way of Latin, by way of Greek—of Hebrew *goyim*. As one might expect, the best definition is in the best dictionary, the *Oxford English Dictionary*. As adjective "Gentile" means "of or pertaining to any or all of the nations other than the Jewish"; as noun it means "one of any nation other than the Jewish." (Note that in the state of Utah, in the United States, a Gentile is anyone who is not a Mormon. It has been suggested, unkindly, that the Jewish community of Salt Lake City is constituted of Jews who want in all honor to be called Gentiles without being apostates.) It follows from OED's definition that Gentiles plus Jews equal the human race. That being so, Jews and Gentiles must be of a different order altogether from Frenchmen and Englishmen or Protestants and Catholics. Jews and Gentiles must be more like men and women: men plus women equal the (adult) human race.

Nevertheless, the similarity is not complete. It breaks down over a crude statistical fact. If the Research Institute for Exobiology on the third planet from the sun Arcturus were to send an expedition to Earth, to take a random sample of 1,000 specimens of the human race, the odds are that the sample would consist of 500 males and 500 females, or 501 of one and 499 of the other—something like that. In the same random sample, the odds are that 996 of those 1,000 human beings would not be Jews. That is because in fact only 4 of 1,000 human beings in the world are Jews. When we speak of Jews and Gentiles, therefore, we speak of the 4 and the 996. As if that were not remarkable enough, the 996 are defined as not being the 4.

This is the empirical justification of the proposition that indeed there is a Jewish uniqueness that is different in kind from other uniquenesses. The Bulgarians can say that they are unique, because uniquely among the nations they speak Bulgarian and uniquely they have a capital called Sofia. Our uniqueness is more unique than that.

Let me tell you something about my adventures among the encyclopedias. The best thing for our purpose, a splendid bringing together of all biblical and most rabbinical references, is in the old *Jewish Encyclopedia,* dating from the early years of this century—more ample than the article in the new *Encyclopaedia Judaica.* In the *New Catholic Encyclopedia,* which is quite good, a Jew must be struck by how it explains the historic Jewish attitude toward Gentiles by explaining it away, apologizing for it, not using the discussion as an occasion for hostility to Jews. I think there are two reasons for this. The first is that Vatican II has happened. The second is that Christianity necessarily views itself as having grown out of the providential uniqueness of the Jews, which alone could have provided the soil for it.

A final report on my researches: I looked up *goy* in the *Encyclopaedia Hebraica.* The entry under *goy* is "see *nokhri* [alien]," so I looked that up. The entry under *nokhri* is "see *am Yisrael* [people of Israel]." I have not been able to look up *am Yisrael.* That volume is not yet in my library.

What all this amounts to is that my subject is nothing less than the human race—in a few hundred well-chosen words. I shall try not to be arbitrary.

With a great effort of will I am going to refrain from enlarging on pre-Christian, pagan anti-Semitism. For that I refer you to the documents collected in Théodore Reinach's *Textes d'auteurs grecs et romains relatifs au judaïsme,* now reprinted. I abstain from citing Tacitus, though it is tempting to cite him. Nor will I say anything about "a people dwelling apart" in Numbers 22:9, except to recall the noteworthy and possibly sinister fact that if we were asked to think of another verse in which *badad* figures quite so prominently, we would all think of Lamentations 1:1, "How *solitary* sits the city that was full of people!"

■   ■   ■

I will take as my text a verse from Scripture, but from an unusual book of Scripture, a *galuti* book, Esther. It is a verse that might almost have been written by a Jewish Thucydides, because uncharacteristically for the Bible, the author of this verse is able to put himself into the skin of the other and to express the idea of the other as well as the other himself could express it. (Contrast, for example, the standard "wood and stone" that Pentateuch and Prophets apply to pagan worship and art.) Reinach calls Esther 3:8 a concise, accurate summary of intellectual pagan opinion about the Jews and Judaism: "Haman said to King Ahasuerus: There is a certain unassimilated people dispersed among the peoples throughout all the provinces of your realm; their laws are different from those of any other people, and they do not keep your Majesty's laws; therefore it does not befit Your Majesty to tolerate them."

One of the least distorted statements of a Jewish point of view made by someone who was emphatically not a Jew occurs in what people think of as an anti-Jewish play, Shakespeare's *Merchant of Venice.* Talking to a Christian, to a Gentile, Shylock says, "I will buy with you, sell with you, talk with you, walk with you, and so following; but I will not eat with you, drink with you, nor pray with you."

Shakespeare omits only "nor marry with you"—surprisingly, because of what happens with Jessica later. Shakespeare was not unfair. A Jew under oath to tell the truth would say that. Let us make an effort of the imagination. Suppose someone tells you he will do business with you, talk with you, walk with you—presumably while you and he are doing business— but not eat or drink with you. You are not likely to be terribly fond of him. That is not an attractive or conciliating statement.

For brevity's sake, I will omit the specifically Christian— Church Fathers, New Testament, and so on—except to make one point, which implicitly I have already made by stressing the pagan origins of anti-Semitism: bad as Christianity has been toward Jews and Judaism, it has been less bad than paganism, whether ancient or modern. It is emblematic and symbolic that the oldest uninterrupted Jewish settlement on the continent of Europe is in Rome, the capital of Christianity. It is not as if Christianity were debarred by its own doctrine from murdering non-Christians. If Christianity had wanted to murder the Jews, it would have been very easy, and today no Jews would be left. No Albigensians are left, because Christianity did not debar itself from murdering Albigensians. Christianity did debar itself from murdering Jews. There were expulsions, there were pogroms, but Christianity debarred itself from the total destruction of the Jews. The traditional Christian doctrine is, We must let the Jews live, but not too well. What Jew would be happy with that? But what Jew would not have settled for it between 1939 and 1945?

I stress paganism because of contemporary relevance. What is dominant in the Gentile world today is no longer Christianity but paganism (which may also be dominant in the Jewish world). Let me tell you how my own curiosity was piqued in this matter. Not long after the Six-Day War, an article was published in the official Polish military journal by one Kazimierz Sidor, a high-ranking Communist. It was about Jews, Judaism, and Israel. Among other things, Sidor said that it is not true, as the Bible pretends, that Moses led forth the children of Israel out of the Egyptian house of bondage at God's command. What is true, he said, is that the Egyptians expelled the Israelites because the Israelites were lepers. The first one to say this was Manetho, about 280 B.C.E., and it was to become—as Sidor has shown—a staple of pagan anti-Semitism. It was repeated by Tacitus. But is Sidor such a scholar as to have read Tacitus?

There was something else that puzzled me. Sidor is a Marxist. If I were a Marxist and wanted to write something anti-Israel and anti-Jewish, why should I go to Manetho and Tacitus? I could be modern, scientific. I could cite modern scholarship to the effect that there was no Exodus at all, because the Israelites, or most of them, were never in Egypt. Since Marxists like to think they are scientific and up to date, I could not understand why Sidor relied on the ancient Egyptian priest Manetho. Later I understood. My eyes were opened by Samuel Ettinger's "Jews and Judaism As Seen by the English Deists of the Eighteenth Century" (Hebrew), which had been published in *Zion* (the journal of the Historical Society of Israel) in 1964.

■   ■   ■

The deists were not Christian, they were ex-Christian. Ettinger shows how they revived classical pagan anti-Semitism. This they transmitted to the French Enlightenment that followed them; and we know how in these things Marxism took over from the French Enlightenment by way of Bruno Bauer, Feuerbach, and so on. There is a chain of tradition that links Sidor in Warsaw today to Manetho in Alexandria 2,250 years ago.

We are indebted to Ettinger for a quotation from a book by a Thomas Morgan, an English deist, published in 1737, that gives us a foretaste of the Enlightenment's attitude toward the Jews. (As to Voltaire, the most recent treatment is by Jacob Katz in *Molad*, October–December 1973, "Jews and Judaism As Seen by Voltaire.") Morgan writes:

> And perhaps, one Reason why the Egyptian sorcerers could not create Lice, might be, because they had none about them, and the Israelites were better stock'd; for according to all Antiquity, Leprosy, Scabs, and Lice, were some of the Plagues with which these Shepherds, before their Expulsion had infested the Egyptians.

This is not Christian anti-Judaism. In the copious anti-Jewish literature of the Christians, this is not to be found. It is pagan anti-Semitism revived.

The great Marxist expert on the Jewish question was Karl Kautsky, the author of *Rasse und Judentum* (English translation of the second edition [1926], *Are the Jews a Race?*). Kautsky was so great a Marxist authority on the Jewish question that although Lenin and Stalin detested him, and though for Bolsheviks he was notorious as "the renegade Kautsky," they had to make his doctrine about the Jews the Bolshevik doctrine. The conclusion—the peroration, the call to action—of Kautsky's *Are the Jews a Race?* is as follows:

> The disappearance of the Jews will not involve a tragic process like the disappearance of the American Indians or the

Tasmanians.... It will not mean a mere shifting of domicile from one medieval ruin to another, nor a transition from orthodox Judaism to ecclesiastical Christianity, but the creation of a new and higher type of man.

The eminent historian George Mosse, in the *Leo Baeck Institute Year Book* for 1971, has an article entitled "German Socialists and the Jewish Question in the Weimar Republic." It is long and meticulously researched, but Mosse is able to summarize the entire matter in one sentence: "Revolutionary socialism desired to put an end to Jews and Judaism." Kautsky's book may have been the very first, and certainly was one of the first, to be published by the American Communist publishing firm, International Publishers. (Especially in those days, the American Communist Party was not exactly a *judenrein* organization.)

I shall turn soon to the Jewish side, but before I do that, and if only to savor a historical irony, I am going to quote from a speech made by a conservative justice of the United States Supreme Court. He is a Gentile who, because of the place where he was born and the schools he attended and the city in which he practiced, has known few Jews. His name is Lewis F. Powell, and his speech was made not long ago to the conservative American Bar Association:

> Today, we are being cut adrift from the type of humanizing authority which in the past shaped the character of our people. I am thinking not of governmental authority but rather the more personal forms we have known in the home, church, school, and community. These personal authorities once gave direction to our lives; they were our reference points, the institutions and relationships which molded our characters.... We gained from them an inner strength, a sense of belonging as well as of responsibility to others.
>
> This sense of belonging was portrayed nostalgically in the film "Fiddler on the Roof." Those who saw it will remember

the village of Anatoepka in the last faint traces of sunset on Sabbath eve. There was the picture of Tevye, the father, blessing his family, close together around their wooden dining room table. They sang what must have been ancient Hebrew hymns, transmitted from family to family through untold generations. The feeling of individual serenity in the common bond of family life was complete.

Sadly, this is not the portrait of contemporary American life. . . .

Who could have foretold it? When a conservative American Gentile wants to point to something wholesomely traditional and to be emulated, he must have recourse to Sholem Aleichem's Jewish Ukraine! How long is it since the one thing all conservatives agreed on was that the Jews poisoned the wells and gnawed at the roots? I will not belabor that. I will only contrast it to Kautsky.

■ ■ ■

From the Jewish side, as I have suggested, there is much to explain—which is to say, explain away. We know that there is not one Jewish attitude. There are Jewish attitudes, depending on historical period, milieu, and so on. Nevertheless, the central Jewish attitude is there in the Havdalah's distinction "between the sacred and the profane, between light and darkness, between Israel and the [other] peoples. . . ." Jews belong with the sacred and the light, Gentiles with the profane and the darkness.

To be sure, there are more ecumenical attitudes, too. A famous one, which apologists like to cite, is from *Tanna de-ve Eliyahu* (a Midrash both late and unknown to the great mass of Jews). Today it may be relevant because it has to do with what used to be known as the woman question. The exegete's problem is to account for Deborah:

What was it about Deborah that she should be Judge and Prophetess over Israel? Was not Phinehas son of Elazar still living?

(Which means: With a man available for the job, why choose a woman?) The answer is:

I call heaven and earth to witness against Me that whether Gentile or Jew, man or woman, manservant or maidservant . . .

(This last must be a mistake. On the evidence of structure, of the Morning Blessings, and of Paul in Galatians 3:28, it must be "bond or free.")

. . . [it is] all according to one's deeds, thus does the Holy Spirit rest upon him.

(Each of the last two clauses seems to be an alternative to the other.)

All this is very nice, but the ordinary Jew never heard of it. What the ordinary Jew knew was Rashi and Targum. The de facto theology of the Jews was what they picked up in Rashi and Targum—over and above Scripture itself and the prayer book.

In Jeremiah 1:5 we read, ". . . I have appointed you a prophet to the nations." Interpreting, Rashi bases himself on the Sifre to Deuteronomy 18:15 ("The Lord your God will raise up for you a prophet from among your own people, like myself. . . ."): "*a prophet to the nations [goyim].* That is, to Israel, who were behaving like pagans." Scripture declares Jeremiah appointed a prophet to the Gentiles, and Rashi denies the plain sense of Scripture! For Rashi, as for many before him, the Gentiles are not worth having a prophet appointed for them, so he twists *goyim* and makes it Israel. The Targum is worse: ". . . I have appointed you a prophet to give the peoples a cup of poison to drink." Or again, Isaiah 19:25—". . . blessed is My people Egypt, and the work of My hands Assyria

...."—where Rashi, following the Targum, is able to make Isaiah's Egypt and Assyria mean Israel.

■   ■   ■

I have written my share of ironical things at the expense of the modern sensibility, and relevance, and things of that sort, but this offends my sensibilities. In the Morning Blessings I do not say, "... for not having made me a Gentile"; I do not say, "... for not having made me a slave"; I do not say, "... for not having made me a woman." For the last, like many others, I say, "... for having made me in Thine image." For the first two, I am not sure I am going to say anything in future. I suspect that Paul, in polemizing with these three Morning Blessings, was able to capitalize on a pretty widespread feeling, in the Jewish community itself, that they were offensive. When Paul says, "There can be neither Jew nor Greek, there can be neither slave nor free, there can be neither male nor female," he is systematically saying no to these Morning Blessings.

Before my recent flight to Israel I had not known that El Al was going to give me a *tefillat ha-derekh,* a travel-prayer text, so I brought along my own *siddur.* When El Al gave me its versions of the travel prayer, joy! I could while the time away by comparing texts, its with mine. (By the way, El Al presents its travel prayer with the compliments of the United Mizrachi Bank.) As you know, there is an older, pre-aviation prayer for wayfarers that does not explicitly exclude Gentiles, though it uses phrases from older prayers whose rather clear intent is to supplicate the Holy One on behalf of His people Israel: "send a blessing upon the work of our hands," and so on. The El Al–Mizrachi Bank prayer for airline passengers beseeches Him to "guard and save us together with all airline passengers," etc. The text in my prayer book—which accords with "the instruction of the rabbinical tribunal in Jerusalem the Holy City," etc.—beseeches Him to "guard and save us together with all fellow Jews who are airline passengers," etc. The contemporary rabbinical tribunals in Jerusalem the Holy City, etc., want the modern flyers' prayer to be more explicitly anti-Gentile than the traditional wayfarers' prayer.

Two things must be said about this: that it is unattractive and that it is silly. Especially is it silly. When I fly from Chicago to Pittsburgh, I want everyone in my plane to be safe. The rabbis—e.g., R. Simeon b. Yohai in Leviticus Rabbah—would have been ashamed of a prayer that in essence says, "Please do not bore a hole under my seat in the boat." I am not sure what is more offensive, the narrowness or the folly.

It is not on Gentiles that this has the worst effect. Gentiles do not know about it. Besides, they really do not care. The worst effect this has is on Jews. It tempts Jews to ask themselves, "If these silly, nasty people are the upholders of Jewish tradition, then is not the tradition they uphold silly and nasty?" When my generation turned our backs on our parents' concern with Jewish things, there was a joke we liked to tell about an apocryphal headline in a Yiddish newspaper: "Terrible Train Wreck; Jew Dies." That justified us to ourselves.

I have spoken about *derekh,* "way," in connection with the *tefillat ha-derekh,* the travelers' prayer. In Proverbs (3:17) we are instructed, concerning Wisdom, that *derakheha,* its ways, are ways of pleasantness, and its paths all peace; and we chant that verse returning the Torah scroll to the Ark. Our literature tells us of rabbis whose behavior toward Gentiles was a hallowing of the Name, in that it led these to declare, "Blessed be the God of the Jews!" (In those days it was not yet thought unusually meritorious to induce Jews to bless the God of the Jews.) That verse from Proverbs, and the example of such rabbis, might be commended to those in our generation who have taken upon themselves the responsibility of speaking for the tradition, not to say personifying it.

(1975)

Modernity and Religion

WE ARE MODERN, OF COURSE, but what does that mean? How long have we been modern? When did modern begin? In the schools, modern history is generally understood to date from the years between 1450 and 1525—though Bury of *The Idea of Progress,* a professor of modern history, did his specifically historical work on the later Roman Empire. It isn't much of an objection to modernity beginning with the Renaissance and the Reformation that these entities may not be entities at all, that when one looks closely at them they seem to dissolve until almost nothing distinctively new is left. Granted that the scholars have long known about the twelfth-century renaissance and have long reminded us that there were reformations of various kinds centuries before the Reformation; whatever may be the microscopic view, when we step back there is a difference between Middle Ages and Renaissance, between Christianity before the Protestant Reformation and Christianity after. It is no disproof of the difference that students are examined on the medieval elements or survivals in Shakespeare. From 1450 to 1525 makes sense as the beginning of modernity. It was the time of Gutenberg, Copernicus, Machiavelli, Columbus, Luther. It was the time of the consolidation of nation-states as we know them, especially in Western Europe.

It was the beginning of the ascendancy of Western power and Western thought in the affairs of the entire world.

So much for beginnings. The more modern modernity, our modernity, is somewhat younger. It came into being in the seventeenth century—"the century of genius"—with the end of the wars of religion. Nowadays historians say that the Thirty Years' War had to do more with dynastic and imperial ambitions than with religion, but to deny that it had anything to do with religion would be presumptuous. The denial would be equivalent to saying not only that we understand the seventeenth century better than it understood itself—which may be so—but actually that we understand it completely and it understood itself not at all. The Thirty Years' War ended in religious stalemate, with a treaty establishing *cuius regio, eius religio:* a victory of practical secularity if not yet theoretical secularism. Responsible statesmen and sober citizens put religion in a position from which they were determined not to let it escape, to destroy the civic peace and ravage countries. Not that religious persecution ended completely: when Louis XIV abrogated the century-old toleration of the Huguenots, he made them choose between oppression at home and exile. But in retrospect that was a kind of last gasp of a former state of affairs in the West, just as intellectually the Quarrel of the Ancients and the Moderns was a last gasp of antimodernism.

Before modernity, to innovate in church or state was wrong on the face of it. In the Bible new things are good only when they are God's: "For behold, I create new heavens and a new earth" (Isaiah); "Behold, the days are coming, says the Lord, when I will make a new covenant with the house of Israel and the house of Judah" (Jeremiah); "A new heart I will give you, and a new spirit I will put within you" (Ezekiel). When the new things are men's, they are bad: "They sacrificed . . . to gods they had never known, / to new gods that had come in of late, / whom your fathers had never dreaded" (Deuteronomy). So reformers denied they were innovating. Whether in religion or in politics, they said and believed that they were only trying to restore pristine virtue and truth, cleansing it of later, newfangled, corrupt accretions.

It was the Royal Society, three hundred years old not long ago, that ratified the new respectability of newness. By charter the Royal Society was debarred from a concern with religion; even its papers were written in the new—plain, unadorned—style. Bacon was the Royal Society's grandfather, and the Society's mission was to cultivate Bacon's New Philosophy, science. Bacon had dared to draw attention to the newness of the things he said. He called his philosophy New, and his major work *Novum Organum*.

Today new is good, without question. Every detergent advertises itself as new and improved: "new" means "improved." President Kennedy, no revolutionary, told us that we must disenthrall ourselves from the past, which is to say, we must liberate ourselves from the bondage of the past. Pastness, nonmodernity, is bondage. Kennedy was repeating Bacon: the idols Bacon warned against included idols of the past.

Appropriately, therefore, the principles of modernity do not date from this year or last. One principle is expressed in the maximalist and yet normative slogan of Diderot: "Let us strangle the last king with the entrails of the last priest." Forcefully liberating ourselves from thralldom to the past, from mere tradition and from the guardians and beneficiaries of mere tradition, we shall come into our own. We shall be modern.

Diderot's predecessor was Spinoza, just as Spinoza honored Bacon as *his* predecessor. For our purpose it is less the Spinoza of the *Ethics* than of the *Tractatus Theologico-Politicus* who counts. That Spinoza is the first to speak explicitly for the secular, democratic state, in which the traditional religions will be subordinate to the state and to citizenship—a private matter, for landladies and others incapable of philosophy. The chief founder of modern biblical criticism, Spinoza undermines traditional religion. It isn't easy for someone who has read the *Tractatus* to continue believing that the Bible is the literal, inerrant word of God.

■   ■   ■

This brings us to the Jews, because Spinoza was or had been a Jew. More than Spinoza is a father of modernity, he is the father of Jewish modernity. There are only two reasonable dates for the end of the Jewish Middle Ages and the beginning of Jewish modernity: Spinoza's, and Moses Mendelssohn's a century later. I prefer Spinoza's. My friend Charles Liebman has shown me a passage from Etienne Gilson's *The Philosopher and Theology* in which Gilson remembers three striking things about the Jewish philosophers at the Sorbonne in the early years of this century: that there were so many of them; that in fact they weren't Jewish philosophers but philosophers who were or had been Jews; and that each of them had two philosophies, his own and Spinoza's. Hume the Scot and Jefferson the American said, approximately, that an enlightened man had two countries, his own and France. Spinoza is the modern Jew's second country.

Spinoza's secular state, in which the dominant principle is reason rather than tradition and the citizens' religions are irrelevant to the public life—that state is still our political ideal and passion. And Spinoza exemplified in his life the honor that has also been our ideal, if not always our actuality, insofar as we are modern. Having by reason proved to himself the unreasonableness of all traditional religion, Spinoza could not honorably be a Christian. He is the first man to have left the Jewish religious community without entering another—Christian, Muslim, or, in the ancient world, pagan.

If you wanted one theme around which to organize a modern Jewish history, honor could be that theme. Spinoza's immediate precursors in criticizing the Bible were Isaac de La Peyrère and Uriel da Costa—like him (or his parents),

Marranos. La Peyrère, not a Jew by religion, dubiously a Christian, has an exalted vision of the Jews resuming the elect status that God conferred on them long ago. This depends on their becoming Christians—Jewish Christians or Christian Jews. The Jews he reminds, in language that can only be called ecstatic, of the happy future God has in store for them. With the Christians he pleads to make Christianity more reasonable by purging it of its unnecessarily numerous and onerous dogmas. How can Jews *honorably* embrace Christianity, he asks, when the burden of Christian dogma is even more grievous than the burden of the Torah?

Da Costa turns from Christianity to what he thinks is Judaism because the Christian dogma of a future life terrifies him. When he discovers that the real Judaism has that dogma too, he ceases to be a Jew. He is contemptuous of religious martyrdom: since the most precious thing is life, what folly to sacrifice it by stubborn adherence to one religion and stubborn refusal to pretend to adhere to another! Contemptuous of martyrdom—and, one might therefore think, of honor—da Costa regards it as a high honor to be martyred for the real truth, the truth that knows both Judaism and Christianity to be false.

Spinoza is no longer of the Jewish community. Why doesn't he make a career for himself as a professor of philosophy by becoming or seeming to become a Christian? Perhaps for reasons of prudence; as a nominal Christian he would be exposing himself to unpleasantness about heresy. But above all, it is honor that keeps him from the baptismal font. He won't pretend to believe what he doesn't believe.

Moses Mendelssohn, we are told by an early biographer, would have welcomed the society favored by his friend Lessing, the Spinozist—a society in which there were neither Christians nor Jews. This side of Lessing's society, Mendelssohn despised apostasy—"for reasons of honor." Mendelssohn's son, when he had his children and then himself baptized, did it for expediency (his word), the opposite of honor.

For expediency Solomon Maimon, the first modern East European Jew, was once prepared to be baptized, but for honor he refused to subscribe to a Christian confession of faith:

> *Maimon:* The Jewish religion, in its articles of faith, comes nearer than Christianity to reason. But practically, the latter has an advantage....
> *German parson:* Don't you feel any inclination to the Christian religion apart from extrinsic considerations?
> *Maimon:* I would be lying if I answered yes....
> *Parson:* You are too much of a philosopher to be able to become a Christian. Reason has taken the upper hand with you.
> *Maimon:* Then I must remain what I am—a stiff-necked Jew....

Mendelssohn's disciple David Friedländer thought of becoming a Christian, again for expediency, but he couldn't entirely forget honor, and honor required that he insist on a unitarian rather than a trinitarian confession of faith. That wasn't enough for the Church. His children, giving even greater weight than he to expediency and even less to honor, became conventional Christians, or at least allowed themselves to be thought so.

■   ■   ■

Notoriously, Heinrich Heine was cynical about his baptism. He had contempt for the society that made baptism the price of ambition, and for himself and the many others who paid the dishonorable price. One of the others was his friend Gans. In a letter Heine says:

> ... Gans is preaching Christianity and trying to convert the children of Israel. If he is doing it out of conviction, he is a fool; if out of hypocrisy, a scoundrel.... I would much rather have heard Gans was stealing silver spoons.... If the law had allowed stealing silver spoons, I wouldn't have undergone baptism.

Everyone knows that Heine called the baptismal certificate the ticket of admission to European culture. In a less well-known mot, he put the blame for his having become a Christian on Napoleon's geography teacher, who failed to tell his pupil that in Moscow it's very cold in the winter.

Napoleon here is the embodiment of the French Revolution, which, if victorious throughout Europe, would have brought about the ideal society of Lessing and Spinoza. About a hundred and fifty years ago Richard Whately, a young man later to become an Anglican archbishop, wrote a brilliantly clever refutation-by-parody of Hume's kind of critique of the Bible, *Historical Doubts Relative to Napoleon Buonaparte*—a mock-critical analysis of a narrative, in biblical-sounding language, of the French Revolution and the Napoleonic wars. Names are reversed: France is Ecnarf, Louis is Sivol. Napoleon is Noelopan. Let us examine this Hebrew name No-el-opan, Whately's imaginary Humean critic says. It is not the name of an actual man, as so many foolishly suppose. Rather, the name personifies a process. *No* must be from the root *nw'*, which means "reducing to nothingness." (In Psalm 33:10, *heni'* is from that root: "He *maketh* the devices of the people *of none effect*.") *El* is "God." *Opan* (or *ophan*) is "wheel"—Ezekiel's "wheel within a wheel" is *ha-ofan be-tokh ha-ofan*—and by extension, "cycle," or "revolution." So *No-el-opan* can only mean "no-God-revolution": Godless Revolution. Heine was right.

As Gershom Scholem has shown, honor—of a sort—was the animating purpose of modern Jewish scholarship, the *Wissenschaft des Judentums*. Steinschneider wanted to give Judaism an honorable burial. The nineteenth century, the modern age, was the age of the death of all the positive-historical religions. Judaism, too, was dying. Like the others, it deserved to die. (He thought well of Ethical Culture, founded by modern Jews in America to be a meeting ground of honorable equality for ex-Jews and ex-Christians.) Nevertheless, it was the part of honor for Jews to give an honorable burial to the religion, culture, and tradition with which they and their ancestors had been immemorially identified, and by which they had been molded. In the future, through the efforts of the scholars, let men know that in the olden times of positive-historical religions, Judaism had been no mean thing. In the meantime, as any undertaker would be, Steinschneider was upset whenever the corpse showed signs of life—revived Hebrew, Zionism, and the like. He was severe about such things.

It is said of the founder of modern Jewish scholarship, Zunz, that someone once introduced to him a young Russian Jew who was a Hebrew poet. "A Hebrew poet?" Zunz is supposed to have asked the young man. "When did you live?" Like the undertaker, the necrologist is displeased with signs of life in the deceased.

Many Jews who allowed themselves to be baptized, expedientially, had first to convince themselves or allow others to convince them that what they were doing was honorable. At the turn of the century Franz Brentano, an Austrian philosopher and former priest, was another who had concluded that the age of the positive-historical religions was at an end. He tried to get his disciples into positions of influence from which to propagate his philosophy, the destined successor to those religions—that is, he wanted his disciples to be professors, especially in German-speaking universities. But many of his disciples were Jews, and those universities allowed few Jews to be professors of philosophy. Husserl was not the only one of Brentano's students persuaded by their master to be baptized. The argument was that it was their duty to do so—in other words, that it was the course of honor to do so—because scruples about baptism were unworthy of a philosopher. No more should a philosopher hesitate to change his formal religious affiliation, Brentano told them, than to change his clothes for a formal occasion. To Hugo Bergmann he once wrote that there was nothing morally wrong—or, as we may put it, dishonorable—about talented young Jews giving lip service to what they disbelieved. (Whatever philosophical reputation Brentano still has rests on what he published about truth.)

For other modern Jews, honor required that they formally remain Jews or that they proclaim themselves as without a formal religion, *konfessionslos*. Both honor and interest required that they should try to change the state or society in which it made a substantial political and social difference whether one was a Jew or a Christian. Temperament and circumstances determined whether they would work for that change in conventional or in revolutionary ways.

■　■　■

Closely related to the theme of honor is that of masculinity. Politically this expresses itself in the will to be a subject, not object, of history, active not passive. The ideal of masculinity was influential in the outlook and the political striving of nationalists and revolutionaries; actually, nationalism was one way of being revolutionary. The factor common to all Jewish modernity, hostility to traditional religion, was present with the Zionists and other Jewish nationalists, too; but in addition they thought the Jews needed autonomy or sovereignty, either as a substitute for the Spinozaic state or as a necessary condition for it. They differed from the older Jewish modernists in insisting upon a Jewish state, or Jewish autonomy. They agreed with them in insisting that that state, like any state, should be secular.

In Chaim Weizmann's autobiography we can see how close to the surface modernity could be even with traditional Jews. He says that his old-fashioned mother agreed neither with him that Zionism was "the solution to the Jewish problem," nor with his brother Samuel that a Russian revolution was the solution. She refused to take sides. Whoever is right, she said, it will be good for us. If Chaim is right we will have a country of our own, and if Samuel is right we will be able to live like human beings in Russia.

Here, too, the origins go back to Spinoza. Besides being the father of the secular, democratic state, he is also the first man to have set forth, if not the desirability, then at least the possibility of a secular Jewish state. What he says about this in the *Tractatus* has been known to get blurred in translation, so before it gets blurred here we may as well look at the exact words: "... *nisi fundamenta suae religionis eorum animos effeminarent, absolute crederem, eos aliquando, data occasione, ut sunt res humanae mutabiles, suum imperium iterum erecturos*"—"... since human affairs are changeable, if the foundations of their [the Jews'] religion did not make their characters feminine I would be convinced that, with an opportunity, someday they would reestablish their state." Not only is Spinoza talking of secular Jewish state building, he also is saying that establishing a state depends upon overcoming femininity, and that the Jews' religion effeminates them. No wonder Mr. Ben Gurion has called for lifting the excommunication that the Jewish community of Amsterdam imposed on Spinoza.

(Some years ago a scholar suggested that the Amsterdam Jews excommunicated Spinoza because they were afraid of irritating the Gentiles and endangering their tolerated status by a failure to dissociate themselves from a notorious unbeliever. I think that is farfetched. How else could the Jews of that time have dealt with a Jew who denied the God and the Torah of Judaism? There may be something, too, in the suggestion that the Amsterdam Sephardim, reverent about their ancestors' martyrdom and the continuing martyrdom of their Marrano relatives in the Iberian peninsula, couldn't forgive Spinoza's scoffing at the Judaism for the sake of which the martyrs gave their lives at the stake.)

To Spinoza and modern Jews since, what have masculine and feminine meant? To have a masculine character is to resist, to fight, to be active; to have a feminine character is to submit, to be resigned, to be passive. Masculine is brave, feminine is at best only obstinate. Masculine is modern, feminine is old-fashioned or traditional.

In our century, after the Kishinev pogroms it was the new Jewish Socialist Bund and the new Labor Zionists who organized self-defense units, acquired arms, and shot back; and it was the old-fashioned Jews whom Bialik (and others) raged against for their passivity. More recently, especially in Israel there has been insistent questioning whether the European Jews who died in Hitler's crematoria weren't showing again that old feminine passivity. Nor is this frame of mind political only. Both Freud—if I remember correctly—and Babel saw their fathers not standing up to Gentile ruffians; and both were affected by that sight, in intimate attitude and general outlook. The gifted Otto Weininger, that textbook case of Jewish self-hate, killed himself out of loathing for what he took to be the femininity of the people into which he had been born.

Was Spinoza justified in saying that the religion of the Jews made them feminine? No. He carefully blamed the very basis—"*fundamenta*"—of Judaism; for him Judaism was feminizing not accidentally or circumstantially but inherently and necessarily. Yet Rabbi Akiba, who certainly knew the basis of Judaism, had supported Bar Kokhba's entirely masculine rebellion against Rome, and had paid for that support with martyrdom. Again, Spinoza was a close student of Maimonides, and Maimonides—if only to calm the feverish messianic yearnings of his time—had selected from the complex rabbinical tradition that alternative which defines the Days of the Messiah as differing from ours in only one respect: that then we shall no longer be enslaved by foreign kingdoms. Maimonides wants the Jews to be interested in real politics, not eschatological fantasies. Spinoza must have known he was wrong. Spinozas are different from us. They don't make the innocent, ignorant mistakes we make.

Let us pause here for a moment. The deliberately prosaic character of the Maimonidean view is representative of much else in Judaism that Christian theology has traditionally decried as carnality—fleshliness—and contrasted to an infinitely superior Christian spirituality. Over the centuries many have gone over from Judaism to Christianity, in all honor and sincerity, because they have accepted the Christian valuation. Some months ago I heard Professor Yosef Yerushalmi read a fine paper about two Marrano brothers, Spinoza's contemporaries, who fled the Spanish royal court to return to full Judaism. The younger became a zealous follower of the false messiah Shabbethai Zevi, but the elder refused. Shabbethai Zevi cannot be the Messiah, he reasoned. These are not the Days of the Messiah. We are still enslaved to the foreign kingdoms. If we abandon that touchstone, why do you and I reject the Christian claim that Jesus was the Messiah? To this the younger brother gave an enraged answer, which showed how Christian doctrine had influenced even an anti-Christian Marrano: his brother's literalism—"the letter killeth"—and inability to see the messianic, spiritual grandeur that was all about them proved the mere carnality of conventional Judaism.

Let me risk being accused of what I have heard called Jewish triumphalism. Things are changing. The old spirituality is being devalued—by Christians. The things that count now are carnal, fleshly: racial equality, justice to the poor, peace. I have heard Protestant and Catholic theologians agree that this reversal is a wholesome return to a Jewish-biblical union of flesh and spirit. I have even heard them argue that "Incarnation" is from the same root as "carnal."

To return to Spinoza—if he was deliberately wrong about the passivity of Judaism, he wasn't completely wrong. Besides knowing what Maimonides had affirmed, Spinoza knew what Maimonides had passed over—including not only statements of feminine doctrine, which can be offset by masculine statements, but also the ritualization of feminine doctrine. Here is our holiday of Hanukkah, instituted to celebrate an earlier, more successful rebellion than Bar Kokhba's. For the Sabbath of Hanukkah the rabbis could have chosen a Prophetical reading about a victory over the enemies of Israel and its God, or else about reconsecrating a defiled Temple, or even about a miraculously prolonged supply of oil. Instead they chose Zechariah 2:14–4:7 (though it is also the Prophetical lesson after some Priestly chapters, 8–12, in Numbers):

> ...Then he showed me Joshua the high priest standing before the angel of the Lord.... And the angel of the Lord enjoined Joshua: Thus says the Lord of hosts: If you will walk in my ways and keep my charge, then you shall rule my house and have charge of my courts.... This is the word of the Lord to Zerubbabel: Not by might, nor by power, but by my spirit, says the Lord of hosts....

The Hasmoneans recapture and reconsecrate the Temple, and into the celebration of that glory the rabbis insert propaganda against the Hasmoneans' right to be high priests. Manly might and Jewish power triumph, and the rabbis make us read a text from a powerless time, which rationalizes powerlessness as if it were good in itself. The Jews win independence, and the rabbis implicitly prefer foreign rule: Zerubbabel was an agent of the Persian crown.

No more than Spinoza did can modern Jews approve those rabbis. We are glad he was wrong in equating their influence on the tradition with the very basis of the tradition. For us, manly honor is the truth. It is our truth. It makes sense of what we are, or what we want to be.

But there is another, adversary truth, and though two truths are hard to entertain at the same time, especially when we like one and dislike the other, let us make the effort. It will be easier if we think of the conflict between those truths in the history of India, rather than the history of the Jews. In the last century Tocqueville protested against the common notion that the Hindus were cowards. We think so, he said, because the many Hindus allowed the few Europeans in India first to conquer and then to rule them. But in the Hindus' recurrent famines they will die of hunger before violating the laws of their religion and eating beef. The difference between us and them is not the difference between honor and dishonor, masculine and feminine.

A preoccupation with manly honor can decline into the grotesque. I'm fond of those jokes about the Jewish duelist ("Don't wait for me if I'm late, shoot anyway"); but I think the duel—as fact, as impulse, and as ideal—is a neglected element in modern Jewish history. In the future Jewish state of Herzl's vision the duel was to be an institution. With the opera house, with the state itself, it would mark off the new, worldly, modern, erect Jew from the old, narrow, traditional, cringing one. In Horthy's Budapest, Jews fought duels against anti-Semites who had impugned their honor as Jews, or Jewish honor: I remember, respectfully, a former member of the Hungarian parliament who died here not long ago. In Vienna, the members of the anti-Semitic fraternities at the university, denying that Jews were *satisfaktionsfähig,* wouldn't duel with them; so Arthur Koestler and the others in the Zionist fraternity brawled with the anti-Semites in defense of Jewish honor and rights.

So far, so good (except for Herzl). But what about Ferdinand Lassalle? He was a socialist—the leader of German socialism—yet he was killed in a "feudal," silly duel. Honor and courage were important to him. As a boy he had dreamt of putting himself "at the head of the Jews, weapon in hand, to win them national independence."

And last, poor Jack Ruby. Uneducated and befuddled and disreputable, he was no less a modern Jew than we who are educated and rational and respectable. In his words, he shot Oswald to show that Jews have guts.

■　　■　　■

I began by saying that we are modern, "of course." But are we still modern? Aren't we coming to the end of modernity? Aren't we becoming postmodern, as some have long been insisting?

If I ask these questions, it is not because—like most people?—I am tempted to exaggerate the newness of the times. In these matters my own temptation has been to doubt newness since the *Commentary* symposium of the young Jewish intellectuals in April 1961. The most remarkable thing about it was what Norman Podhoretz noted in his introduction: how surprisingly little change there had been since the symposium of an earlier generation of Jewish intellectuals in the *Contemporary Jewish Record*, in 1944. The world had changed, America had changed, American Jews had changed—at least by the accepted standards of economics, sociology, and demography—but Jewish intellectuals had changed almost not at all. Is it likely that a change which failed to come about between 1944 and 1961—or, if we think of Western Jews generally, between earlier than 1800 and 1961—should have come about between 1961 and 1967?

There is much evidence that the modern world may indeed be moving toward something postmodern; except that the Jews, on the whole, remain conservatively attached to the old modernity of Spinoza. In this conservative attachment Jewish intellectuals differ little from nonintellectuals. At least in this they are all Jews together. All are more comfortable with modernity than with anything else.

Of the many things Romanticism was, one was an argument with modernity. Romanticism tends to make people respectful of religion, if not religious. Irreligious, even a Max Weber was not combative about religion in the classical modern manner. He said only, with the hint of a sigh, that he was religiously unmusical. For the eighteenth-century Enlightenment, "Gothic" was a term of abuse—the barbarian Goths had disappeared long before the later Middle Ages, when that style was invented—and Joan of Arc was the subject of bawdy jokes. Romanticism has taught us to think well of Gothic, of Joan, and of the religion and culture that produced them. Moderns who have been affected by Romanticism find it easy to think that while Christianity may not be true, at least one must say this for it, that it has had a powerful effect on culture and personality. Many Jews have gone over to Christianity because of that Romantic way of thinking, learned from teachers who were Romantic Christians.

Spinoza and the Enlighteners drew a clear distinction between society and state as the realm of the secular, on the one hand, and religion as a private matter, on the other. Romanticism was to discover that culture and national histories, not private but social, are entangled with religion—particularly Christianity in its various forms, or the memories and continuing influences of Christianity. In Poland and France, Marxist philosophers and literary scholars (including Jews) seem more attracted to seventeenth-century Christianity than to seventeenth-century irreligion. Fifty years after the Godless Revolution, the Soviet authorities will for the first time publish Bible tales for children.

The effect on Jews is best seen in art history, or rather in the history of art historians. A high proportion of the most significant art historians have been German Jews. As modern Jews they hold to Spinoza's primary ideals; as Germans they are especially influenced by Romanticism. This produces an unlikely or paradoxical state of affairs: modern Jews who are authorities on medieval and Renaissance Christian iconography. The paradox is compounded by the fact that the Jewish tradition—which made their ancestors who *they* were and which, though less directly and visibly, prolongs its influence into their own lives—is unimpressed by the aesthetic. Matthew Arnold knew what he was doing when he contrasted Hellenism and Hebraism; and Hebraism itself was aware of the contrast. Judah Halevi says, "Let not Greek thought [*hokhmat yewanit*] seduce you, for it bears no fruit, but only flowers."

Art historians who are Jews invest emotion, intellect, and career in something not immediately or unquestionably natural for people who are simultaneously non-Christians, irreligious, and Jews. The seriousness with which they have to take Romanticism—otherwise why be art historians?—is at odds with Spinozist purity.

■   ■   ■

It isn't news that the substitute religions deriving from the Enlightenment are dead, but some people who should know it don't seem to. In a university journal a professor of English publishes a lecture to the effect that the humanities humanize. Can he be serious? Does he still believe in the religion of culture? Arnold hoped that culture would make people humane, and we know that it doesn't. Lovers of Goethe and Beethoven ran Hitler's death machine. Apparently Nietzsche was right, after all: God having died, other deaths must follow.

If that defender of the culture-faith doesn't want to let uncultured reality in, he might at least listen to colleagues like Lionel Trilling and George Steiner. In the 1920s when clergymen preached sermons about the grounding of humane behavior in religion, Mencken's boys would laugh. When professors of classics preached about the grounding of humane letters (and mental acuteness) in the study of Latin and Greek, undergraduates would make remarks about old fogeys afraid for their jobs. Who will now say what needs to be said of anachronistic professorial sermons about the grounding of humane feeling in literature and art?

Not only do consumers or connoisseurs of culture fail to be made humane (or human) by the humanities, the very producers fail. The two greatest English-language poets of this century were Yeats and Eliot, reactionaries who at times were something worse; the oldest great living poet in English is Pound, the virulent anti-Semite who broadcast in wartime for

Mussolini; and Genet, whom Sartre has canonized as a saint, isn't exactly a spokesman for humanism.

Right-minded people know that society hounds the artist. Yet if Genet had been only a criminal who loved his profession and not also an artist, they wouldn't have let him out of jail. If Pound weren't an artist but a carpenter or merchant or veterinarian, first they wouldn't have let him take asylum in an asylum, and then they wouldn't have let him out.

Of all the religions prolific of cant, the religion of art and culture is most prolific. The hounded artist is a minor piece of culture-cant, life-enhancing art a major one. I think it was Berenson who taught us the syllogism: what is life-enhancing is good; art is life-enhancing; therefore, art is good. And contrariwise: if it isn't life-enhancing, it isn't art. Curiously, the Nazi death chiefs were most rapacious about precisely those works of art that Berenson held to be life-enhancing. Nor could he even give its plain meaning to "life": he was gloomily proud of not having children. *Fin de race,* end of the biological line, he said of himself.

The enhancement of life; creativity. "Create" is a biblical word, the first verb in the Bible. In the Bible, *bara'* ("create") can have only God as its subject. Only God creates. From the first verse in Genesis, in which He creates the heavens and the earth, "create" is a signal that something emphatic is being said about His self-definition in act and word. Its greatest frequency is in Deutero-Isaiah, especially Isaiah 45. "I form light and create darkness, / I make peace *and create evil*" (Isaiah 45:7). This is so bold that it had to be softened for liturgical use: in the first obligatory blessing of our morning prayers, immediately after *Barekhu,* we say, "Thou formest light and createst darkness, Thou makest peace *and createst all things.*" And Isaiah 45:18: "For thus says the LORD / who created the heavens / (he is God), / who formed the earth and made it / (he established it; / he did not create it a chaos, / he formed it to be inhabited): / 'I am the LORD, and there is no other.'"

Even in English, until well into modernity the various forms of "create" are apt to have a numinous feeling about them. "Creative" in an unambiguously human sense isn't much more than a hundred years old. "Creativity" is more recent still. It is a coinage of modern culture-religion, for which man is creator, especially man as artist. As we would expect, the *Oxford English Dictionary* gives as the first recorded use a statement about Shakespeare's "poetic creativity." I haven't found "creative art/arts" in OED, so I take this phrase to be a twentieth-century invention. Modern culture-religion made claims that even Hellenism didn't make: for classical antiquity, art is not creative but mimetic—imitative. A religious mood accompanied the modern contemplation of art, a ritual of pilgrimage and solemnity prevailed, and men hoped for salvation.

But the religion of creativity, frail to begin with, has become funny. First, every other college catalogue in America listed courses in creative writing—an art-sanctimonious name for helping students learn how to write fiction or poetry. Afterward, "creative man" was taken over as a technical term by the personnel directors of advertising agencies, on a par with "account executive." And now the inspirational literature of commerce hymns creative salesmanship.

A few years back I read a neofeminist's approving review of another neofeminist's book. The reviewer said she agreed with the author that for a woman, a career is more creative than being a mother. That puzzled me: without having given much thought to it, I had assumed that about the closest the human race can get to creation is when a woman bears a child, nurtures him, and cares for him. A little later I was looking through the racks in a drugstore and came across a specimen of a common subliterary genre—books for adolescent girls about a young heroine with an interesting/creative job/career. The title of the book was *Priscilla White, TV Secretary.* Then I understood. How can being a mother compare in creativity with being a TV secretary?

■   ■   ■

Political messianism was modernity's other substitute religion. Its obsoleteness is not news: *The God That Failed,* about the Revolution, preceded by ten years or so *The Death of God,* about traditional religion. (Each was addressed to the worshippers of the particular deity whose failure or demise it announced.) Yet in 1967 a book wins prizes and acclaim, and one would think that the last fifty years had never happened. At the end of Malamud's *The Fixer,* the hero Yakov speaks the author's moral or conclusion: "What is it Spinoza says?" (Always Spinoza.) "If the state acts in ways that are abhorrent to human nature it's the lesser evil to destroy it. Death to the anti-Semites! Long live revolution! Long live liberty!"

Whose revolution is Malamud thinking of, Kerensky's or Lenin's? Lenin's: a few pages before, Yakov daydreams that he kills the Czar. The historical reality behind Malamud's novel was the Czar's Beilis trial. Don't we remember any longer that just before Stalin died, he was about to stage a trial that would have been far more abhorrent to human nature? Under Stalin, the Jewish doctors—so they were universally referred to—wouldn't have been set free, as the Jew Beilis was under the Czar; and their conviction would have touched off a repression of Russian Jews worse than all the others they had had to suffer in those last Black Years of Stalin's life. Our ancestors would have seen the finger of God in Stalin's death at just that time, and would have celebrated a new Purim of thanksgiving. We have forgotten.

Czarism was abhorrent; and that revolution of Yakov's brought into being something more abhorrent still. "Death to the anti-Semites?" Anti-Semites are still in power in Russia. Stalin's daughter Svetlana Alliluyeva, asked about Judaism and Jews in the Soviet Union, answers that while she knows little about Judaism, she can testify as an eyewitness that Jews are discriminated against. Aside from Arabs, only Soviet representatives say anti-Semitic things in the United Nations.

So the occasional proclamation in the 1960s of revolutionary enthusiasms from before World War I isn't serious. Neither is a certain campus rhetoric of political messianism, nor much of the political rhetoric of the intelligentsia, with its apocalyptic shrillness. These only confirm again Marx's second most famous saying: when history repeats itself, it can reenact tragedy as farce.

■　　■　　■

Classical modernity is in decay. When Marx said religion is the opiate of the people—his most famous saying—both Marxists and religious people considered that to be a serious criticism, if true. Both agreed that opium was bad. Both agreed that life was real, life was earnest, life was purposeful. (The Yiddish word is *takhlis*.) Today, we are told, opium—in the broad sense: LSD, marijuana—is religion for the avant-garde. Timothy Leary, Allen Ginsberg, and Norman Brown are for "opium"—the thing itself and the symbol of inwardness and sensuality. These men aren't irreligious. The confrontation is between Brown and Marcuse (see *Commentary*, February and March 1967), between the new novelists and playwrights and Lukacs; and in this confrontation the classical modernists seem old-fashioned. The new young have been known to say: Freud was a fink. If Freud—because too repressive—why not Marx? Marx and Freud: in that *Commentary* symposium these great ancestors were invoked repeatedly, in the same breath with *their* ancestor, Spinoza.

This is not to say that Leary, Ginsberg, and Brown provide much comfort for upholders of the traditional religions. The new religiousness seems to be some kind of syncretistic paganism—syncretism is the polite word for mishmash—and the traditional religions will have to take its measure. But that paganism isn't what Peter Gay had in mind with his *Enlightenment: The Rise of Modern Paganism*. Gay meant atheism. For him, modern paganism is atheist. Then postmodern paganism is post-atheist; the hippies and even the angries, with their "God is love," can sound like fundamentalist evangelists.

Even the political young take religion more seriously than their elders did. A generation ago, who on the Left would have hoped for more from the churches than from labor? Who would have depended on marching or picketing nuns to be there when the going got rough? The change is hard for middle-aged moderns to accept. George Lichtheim, reviewing works blaming the Pope for what he did and failed to do in World War II, is impatient. What's the point of criticizing?, he asks. Who doesn't know better than to expect anything of an elderly gentleman and the large, complex organization he administers? That's just it. The very criticism of the young shows they expect something, and the expectation shows respect. Maybe that's because the popes of secularist modernity haven't done all that well, either.

No author would dare to contrive something so pat: in the fiftieth-anniversary year of the Bolshevik Revolution, Alliluyeva leaves Russia and says she believes in God and human decency, not in the dogmas of atheism and conflict she was brought up on. Voznesensky, the most highly regarded of the younger Soviet poets, says: "What is bad is when man, hypnotized by technology, becomes a technological object himself. . . . Theoretically, everything a man can do can be programmed into a machine and the machine will do it—everything except this: man's capacity for religion and poetry." Dialogues are held between Christians and Marxists—that is to say, between Christians and a combination of intellectuals and apparatchiks from Communist countries and mass Communist parties; and in the dialogue the Communists are less sure of their own rightness and the religious people's wrongness than ever before. The Communist Party of Great Britain issues a manifesto calling for a multiparty political system with legitimacy for parties opposed to socialism, insisting on the freedom of religion, and granting that religion can have progressive and beneficial as well as reactionary and evil effects.

■   ■   ■

Another thing Alliluyeva has said is that although she is generally rather than specifically religious, because she is Russian she has had herself baptized into the Russian Orthodox Church. The multiple irony of it: Alliluyeva, with her father and her training; religion after fifty years of unrelenting, official, monopolistic, persecuting, deriding, cajoling, "scientific" atheism; and not just religion, but the Russian Orthodox Church.

Is it only because I'm an ignorant outsider, a prejudiced son of Russian Jews, that I'm amazed? The Russian Orthodox Church! Of all the churches in Europe, the Russian Orthodox has always seemed—only to Jews?—the lowest. It is the church of the Beilis trial and of Rasputin. It excommunicated Tolstoy. In the first ten or fifteen years of this century, a few intellectually and morally superior men chose to identify themselves with it, but on the whole it is the church that an outsider would have thought least able to win the affection or even the nominal allegiance of intellectuals brought up in fifty years of official Dialectical Materialism and a hundred and fifty years of Russian literature.

The memoirs of pre-revolutionary Russia tell of the contempt that *gymnasium* students used to have for the official teachers of religion. Now the objects of that contempt are the official university lecturers in Dialectical Materialism—Diamat for short. (I understand that Russian students give to the Diamat lectures the name of the course in religion in the old days—God's Law.) Now all kinds of people are Russian Orthodox or pro–Russian Orthodox. Ten years ago a Soviet newspaper printed a complaint from a worker: he was under pressure from the other workers in his plant to have his children baptized in church. "You're Russian," they would tell him, "and Russians are Russian Orthodox." When the poet Akhmatova died last year, honored by the younger generation, her funeral

37

was Russian Orthodox. Stalin's cultural executioner, Zhdanov, had reviled her in good Stalinist fashion; a sign of her degeneracy, he said, was that one of her favorite haunts was the chapel. But she was of the pre-revolutionary generation. Among the intellectuals born or educated since the Revolution and pro–Russian Orthodox are Solzhenitsyn and Sinyavsky ("Tertz").

Yet that isn't the end of the irony—or, for Jews, the pain. The poet Pasternak, a good and brave man, the son of modern Jews, became Russian Orthodox in the Soviet Union—that is to say, after the Revolution. Or if he didn't become officially Russian Orthodox then, if—for the record is unclear—he was baptized earlier, his nominal Russian Orthodoxy became actual precisely in the days of the Godless Revolution. Of Joseph Brodsky, the young man sentenced to a killing term in the north for daring to write poetry without an official poet's license, one hears that he has a Russian Orthodox cross over his cot. Is that because he, too, is now Russian Orthodox, or is it because a cross is the only religious symbol this Jew can find? One also hears that some of the best young scientists in the Soviet Union are turning to Russian Orthodoxy, and that among these, in turn, are Jews.

Is that where Jewish honor has led? Surely that is not what modern Jews intended when they yearned for the creation of a state that would be neither Christian nor Jewish; surely what they wanted was a new Noelopan, who, subordinating every religion, wouldn't exact baptism as the price of a Jew's ambition and desire for equality; and surely the Soviet Union is the state that has done most to subordinate religion, and actually to repress it. In that state, to find not Spinoza's landlady but so many of the morally and intellectually best people religious or pro-religious is a shock. To find their religion or pro-religion expressing itself in the form not merely of Christianity or pro-Christianity, but actually of Russian Orthodoxy or pro–Russian Orthodoxy, is doubly a shock. How much more of a shock must it be to find that some of those best Russian Orthodox people are Jews? O Cunning of Reason!

In Israel the so-called oriental immigrants have taken the dominant Ashkenazim as models for how to be modern and up to date. One thing they learn quickly is that modern Israelis aren't religious, that to be religious is the best way not to be modern. I heard the following story from a professor at the Hebrew University, a German Jew who, influenced by Buber and Franz Rosenzweig, went up to Palestine in the 1920s as a *ba'al teshuvah,* a returner to Judaism from coldness and Jewish ignorance.

Military service integrates the Israeli population—as they say, it makes one nation out of many tribes. During military service this man's son became a noncommissioned officer, and with his new stripes he was assigned one afternoon to a new unit and barracks, where he was both senior and the only Ashkenazi. The next morning he put on his *tefillin* and prayed. The other soldiers stared, and a few began to cry. Later he discovered the reason. Here was their noncom, an Ashkenazi of the Ashkenazim, praying—and with *tefillin.* They had been deceived. All the sacrifice of habit and feeling and belief they had thought necessary was unnecessary. It was possible both to be *moderni* and to put on *tefillin.*

But at least Chaim Weizmann was right, and his brother Samuel wrong, in one crucial respect. In Chaim's Israel a Jew going from modernity to religion—either going back to it or advancing to it on a higher turn of the spiral—is rather more likely to go to Judaism and *tefillin* than to Christianity and the three-barred crucifix.

■   ■   ■

Most of what I know about da Costa and La Peyrère, and much of what I know about Spinoza, I owe to Leo Strauss's *Spinoza's Critique of Religion*—a book all the more impressive because the author was a young man when he wrote it, in

Weimar Germany. (I have also learned much from the chapter on the *Tractatus* in his *Persecution and the Art of Writing,* Free Press, 1952.) In 1965, Schocken published the English translation of *Spinoza's Critique,* together with a new preface by Professor Strauss. Above all, the preface is a personal document, about the author as a young German Jew who has to come to grips with Spinoza. Before him Hermann Cohen and Rosenzweig also have had to come to grips with Spinoza; more than Jews who are thinkers, these are Jewish thinkers. Strauss isn't the disciple of either. He is his own man and thinks his own thoughts, phrasing them with greater or lesser transparency, greater or lesser opaqueness, as he sees fit. In the new translation of his book about Spinoza's critique of religion he keeps the old dedication: "to the memory of Franz Rosenzweig."

(1967)

The Enlightenment:
Pluralism and Paganism

JEWS—MOST JEWS—ARE MODERN, enlightened. Judaism isn't. By Judaism I mean, for instance, the synagogue on Yom Kippur. Even of those of us who were in the synagogue on Yom Kippur probably few are all that different from the ones who stayed away. How many really believed what we heard, read, and recited then? We're too modern. And because we're modern, we're apt to be dubious about religion. Not for scientific or philosophical reasons—most of us aren't philosophers or scientists. You and I have neither the intellect nor the training to choose between Bertrand Russell and Father D'Arcy when they debate about God. What do you and I know about the ontological proof, let alone the history and present status of the argument over it? Of course we know that science is supposed to have disproved God, or religion; but then what do you or I say to an Orthodox Jewish physicist or biologist?

What you and I give weight to and feel confident about is the so-called anthropological argument, the argument from human nature and history. We judge religion by its human effects, and we don't like what we think it has done to men and women and to society. There are worse ways to judge.

What are those bad things that religion does? In antiquity Epicurus hated religion—the pagan religion he knew—for terrifying people and robbing them of peace of mind. The most complete extant statement of Epicureanism is the *De rerum natura* of the Roman Lucretius; and Professor Peter Gay, who admires the eighteenth-century Enlightenment, tells us that Lucretius was one of its two favorite classical authors. (The other was Cicero.) With ancient Epicureanism, the Enlightenment agrees that religion makes people unhappy and cruel. Lucretius lamented that *tantum religio potuit suadere malorum*, religion has been able to stir up so much evil; and the Enlightenment had its own confirming memories and experience. Additionally, the Enlightenment accused religion— Christianity, and the Judaism at its root—of despising reason, slandering human nature, and teaching a harmful sexual ethic.

Formally, at least, most of us haven't moved much beyond that bill of particulars. Yet for us the criticism has become less appropriate, less evidently a matter of good faith. What originated as criticism of religion can now be more validly directed against what is left of the Enlightenment in our late-twentieth-century hands. As with Epicurus's peace-of-mind argument, so with the later ones: the positions have been reversed. Only, after the reversals we still feel superior to religion.

For Epicurus, religion is bad because it robs us of peace of mind; if it gave us peace of mind, it would be good. For moderns, religion gives peace of mind, and therefore is childish. For moderns, religion stands in the way of a lucid maturity—our recognizing that the universe is indifferent or actually hostile to human needs, values, and yearnings. In Russell's "Free Man's Worship," the free man refuses to delude or beguile himself. Things are as they are, and they do not make for peace of mind. So much do we take all this for granted that the better class of religionists are embarrassed by Norman Vincent Peale and Joshua Loth Liebman—remember them?—and vie with the proudly despairing atheists in contempt for peace of mind.

Persecution, hate, division? To blame religion, now, is a feeble joke. We know what causes them: race, or nationality, or tribe, or caste, or class, or language, or ideology, or greed. Or simple bloody-mindedness.

The Enlightenment liked to say that Judaism invented intolerance, the mother of pious extirpations and burnings at the stake. At the same time, the Enlightenment greatly admired Rome, and the Latin authors more than the Greek. This wasn't only an inferior literary and intellectual taste. It was also political. The French Revolution had a cult of Roman republicanism.

The enlightened could blame the book of Joshua for teaching the West to kill unbelievers: if not for those dreadful Jewish examples in Palestine three thousand years ago, Europe would have been spared later horrors. None chose to remember the republican Romans' coldly expedient genocide of their kin, the Samnites, carried out in the full light of history. None thought to ask why not one Roman writer had ever expressed doubt or regret about that genocide—or, for that matter, why no European humanist had ever expressed doubt or regret. (Only in our time do the Romans seem to have first been indicted for the Samnite genocide. And—ironically—only the Bible criticism that arose after the Enlightenment knows that Joshua isn't very historical.)

For the eighteenth-century enlightened, the jealous Jewish God had to be blameworthy and the Romans' latitudinarian paganism had to be praiseworthy. For us, to the evidence from ancient pagan history can be added all those fine modern things that have happened in our own century, after the decline of religion. That makes no difference. We continue to blame religion.

■　　■　　■

Religion is the enemy of reason—so the Enlightenment taught and so we still believe. Or rather, we take the trouble to believe it in the part of ourselves that still honors reason. In the greater part of ourselves, reason bores us. Two hundred years after the Enlightenment, its heirs celebrate their independence not from rationalism—for the Enlightenment was as much empiricist as rationalist—but from rationality itself. The professors tell us that the campus rebels are the sweetest and most intelligent students of all, and maybe the French and German professors say that about their campus rebels. Of those heirs of the Enlightenment the implicit slogan is "logic, shmogic." In the old days the enlightened couldn't find language contemptuous enough for the religious *sacrificium intellectus*. Now the campus is as fertile in myth as any conventionally preliterate culture.

The distinction between reason and unreason is called artificial, and the very concept of insanity a gimmick for imprisoning spontaneity or vision. To some in the New Left, Rabbi Adler's murderer was not deranged and sick; he is a political hero, fallen in the struggle against bourgeois hypocrisy. Liberalism is fascism, permissiveness is repression—so says an elite of the intelligent and educated in the West. (In Prague and Warsaw the intellectuals are not amused.) As a certain comedian used to say, "You can't fool me, I'm too ignorant." Compared with some of the elite, the ignorant seem positively addicted to reason. In *The Religious Situation: 1968*, Professor Huston Smith writes:

> . . . as the weeks moved on . . . the students' true interests surfaced. . . . I cannot recall the exact progression of topics, but it went something like this: Beginning with Asian philosophy, it moved on to meditation, then yoga, then Zen, then Tibet, then successively to the *Bardo Thodol*, tantra, the kundalini, the chakras, the *I Ching*, karati and aikido, the yang-yin macrobiotic (brown rice) diet, Gurdjieff, Maher Baba, astrology, astral bodies, auras, UFO's, Tarot cards, parapsychology, witchcraft, and magic. And, underlying everything, of course, the psychedelic drugs. Nor were the students dallying with these subjects. They were *on* the drugs; they were eating brown rice; they were meditating hours on end; they were making their decisions by *I Ching* divination, which one student designated

the most important discovery of his life; they were constructing complicated electronic experiments to prove that their thoughts, via psychokinesis, could affect matter directly.

And they weren't plebeians. Intellectually they were aristocrats with the highest average math scores in the land, Ivy League verbal scores, and two-to-three years of saturation in MIT science.

I don't doubt it for a minute. Those weren't low-IQ types, in that Washington march last year, who performed their Tibetan rites of exorcism against the Pentagon. And those others in the march, who wouldn't be so gauche as to snicker, weren't low-IQ types either. If only I could forget how Paul Massing's *Rehearsal for Destruction* describes a group of the intellectual forebears of Nazism in the generation before World War I: emancipated, educated or semi-educated food faddists, naturists, spiritualists, lovers of conspiracy theories, *et hoc genus omne*. Massing's subjects were on the Right, while Professor Smith's (and Norman Mailer's) are on the Left. I know that should reassure me, but somehow it doesn't.

■   ■   ■

For two hundred years, liberals and radicals have agreed that traditional Christianity maligns human nature; and insofar as traditional Judaism has been thought of at all, it too has been judged guilty of lese humanity. Voltaire said that Pascal had taught men to hate themselves, whereas they ought to learn to love themselves. A generation or so later, in Boston, one of the Eliots—they are still prominently associated with Unitarianism—said to a relative of hers, in sufficient explanation of her departure from the old, Calvinist ways, and above all the doctrine of total depravity: "Eliza, do you kneel down in church and call yourself a miserable sinner? Neither I nor any of my family will ever do that." Yet today Voltaire's disciples are respectful about Pascal—less the Pascal who honored God. of course, than the one who was unimpressed by man.

Actually, it isn't clear how many descendants Voltaire has left. Sade probably has more. To say so may distress the proper members of the Enlightenment family, but Sade *is* in the genealogy. If it is true that the new young's philosophy of life can be summarized in the question, "Why not?", then Sade is the obvious ancestor. The God-is-dead theologians may not know it, but before Nietzsche it was Sade who declared (repeatedly, Professor Robert E. Taylor informs me), "God is dead, and anything goes": *Dieu est mort, et tout est permis.* In the contemporary theater there is a serious play that takes Sade seriously. From Sade descend *Story of O* and Genet and others as well. Does their idea about humanity teach us to love ourselves? Even Calvinism is likelier to do that than our art is (or our science). Calvinism insists that a human being is a miserable sinner. At least this can be said for a miserable sinner, that he has a soul and was created in an image of some dignity.

In these days, if any thinker tells us good things about humanity, he's probably religious: Reinhold Niebuhr, say, who in the *Religious Situation* speaks of a "religious expression of trust in the meaning of human existence ... recognizing and preserving the humanity of man." The irreligious will take this as further evidence of religion's childish shallowness—its unheroic evasion of the truth about man's total nullity.

■   ■   ■

On no point is there greater agreement than that puritanism—or religion simply—teaches a wrong and harmful sexual ethic. Commonly the argument against puritanism is the same as against chastity, or continence. Professor Gay calls the Enlightenment modern paganism, and a good bit of that paganism is rebellion against puritanism's twisting of our sexual nature.

It is a strong argument: Not only does puritan continence make us suffer, needlessly; not only does it impoverish our lives when they could be rich and fulfilled; but, as if that weren't enough, it also transforms an energy that could have rejoiced us into something sour and cruel and rancorous. Frustrated in the wholesome satisfaction of our needs, misled into feeling guilty about our natural desires, we do everything we can to make others equally wretched, enviously harrying men and women wiser and healthier than we. We make our society a prison, mirroring in the large the individual prison that each of us has allowed himself to be locked up in, or has actually built around himself. Delighting in death rather than life, we make misery and war the perverse expressions of the instincts we deny and suppress. Against such wicked folly the only useful counsel can be, "Make love, not war."

If any teaching of the intellectuals has become truly popular, it is this. One common theme of vicarage detective stories used to be the churchgoing voyeur, and another was the sanctimonious murderer. (We take it for granted that Jack the Ripper, who murdered prostitutes, must have been a victim of the puritan disease—indeed, take it for granted that prostitution itself is only a symptom of the puritan disease.) And just a year or two ago I was able to read a new detective story, set in Dutch Calvinist country, in which—I have forgotten the details—either the murderess or the writer of the poison-pen letters that touch off murder is a respectable, God-fearing woman, another victim of the puritan disease.

Professor Gay's *Party of Humanity* tells us:

> Diderot['s] ... *Supplément au Voyage de Bougainville*, written in 1772, ... may be taken as typical. Diderot seeks to integrate sexual life into the life of the community as well as the life of the individual—love-making is delightful in itself and socially useful. Diderot's Tahitians are noble, but they are not savages. They are genuinely civilized men, and they are genuinely free. Tahitian society, as viewed by and as reconstructed by Diderot, is a rational social order.
>
> "In our presence, without shame, in the center of a throng of innocent Tahitians who danced and played the flute, [the

47

young Tahitian girl] accepted the caresses of the young men.... The notion of crime and the fear of disease have come among us only with your [the Christians'] coming. I don't know what this thing is that you call 'religion,' but I can only have a low opinion of it because it forbids you to partake of an innocent pleasure to which Nature, the sovereign mistress of us all, invites everybody." ...

Christianity makes people miserable and criminal: "People will no longer know what they ought and ought not to do. They will feel guilty when they are doing nothing wrong."

Who that is modern, when he hears "Tahiti," can fail to see in his mind's eye an edenic existence—sun, and breeze, and waves, and handsome, happy people whose life outside the skin is continuous with the life inside? To a modern, what Diderot says is self-evident. I have read neither Bougainville's *Voyage* nor Diderot's *Supplément,* only what Professor Gay says about them. Whether it is a blessing or a curse I don't know, but I can't help being modern. Modernity is the station in history in which it has pleased God to set me. Tahiti can cast a spell on me, too.

Like the Maoris and the Hawaiians, the Tahitians are Polynesians. I became a bit uneasy about this Bougainville-Diderot-Gay picture of genuinely free and civilized men, and their rational social order, and their life harmonious with reason and a benign nature, when I remembered that except for "aloha" and "luau," the only Polynesian words I knew were "taboo" and "mana"—not quite the sort of words usually associated with freedom and reason. So I went to the encyclopedia (where I discovered I knew another freedom-and-reason Polynesian word, "tattoo"):

The Polynesians, because of their simple life and natural graces amid enchanting island surroundings, have long exercised a romantic appeal for the outside world.... The worship of the greater gods was in the hands of an organized priesthood, serving the ruling chiefs. Some of these gods required human sacrifices.... The chiefs, as descendants of the gods, possessed *mana....* All the land of the island or district under [a chief's] jurisdiction was his. Over the people he had absolute power.... In some of the islands, human flesh was included [in the diet] at times.

If the Tahitians were like the Maoris, they too had "slaves ... mainly prisoners of war [who] performed much of the menial labor."

So Diderot was mistaken about the happy consequences of paganism. And though Bougainville may have misinformed him about the Polynesians, he knew about Rome. Knowing about Rome, could he really believe that paganism, or pagan sexuality, is delightful in itself and socially useful? The one thing no one can say about the Romans, at least after the Punic Wars, is that they subjected themselves to the rigors of anything resembling a Jewish or Christian ideal of chastity. It wasn't puritanism that made the Romans what they were.

Even today it isn't pleasant to read about the gladiators. Gladiatorial combat wasn't a product of Roman corruption or decadence. It was well established long before the end of the Republic, when Augustus could boast that he had entertained the people by providing them with ten thousand gladiators to fight in the amphitheaters: butchered to make a Roman holiday. The Emperor Commodus—the son of Marcus Aurelius no less—personally engaged in a thousand gladiatorial duels, and staged fights between cripples. (Other examples are even more sick-making.) Only when the Roman Empire had been Christian for a hundred years could the gladiatorial shows be abolished.

As for Rome's treatment of slaves and her means of putting down the servile rebellions that that treatment incited— it doesn't bear thinking about.

■   ■   ■

Today the vanguard no longer even pretends to believe in the benignity of pagan sex. It isn't against pagan sex. Not at all. It just isn't much for benignity. Thus "theater of cruelty" is not an insult by hostile outsiders. This past summer, in the *New York Times* of all places, Elenore Lester, who likes what is going on in the advanced theater, could write the following:

> Today's near-copulation is likely to give way, in the not-too-distant future, to the real thing, fulfilling a prediction Kenneth Tynan made about two years ago. And after actor-to-actor copulation, will it be actor-to-audience? . . . surely the next step must be programmed rape of the audience.
>
> Of course, sexual relationships are not the only kind possible. . . . Violence is also interesting. . . . Polish drama theoretician Jan Kott observed that, because of all the shocks that are being given by the real world these days, there is a need for real shock in the theater. "We get that from sex and violence," he said. "It is possible to show lovemaking on the stage today, but," he added with a tinge of regret, "it is still impossible to murder." But of course, that was last year.

Someone should tell Mr. Kott about the Roman theater. In a recent Roman history he could read that "the Colosseum was the scene of theatrical performances in which the murders were not fictitious but real. Under Domitian the public was able to see plays in which one criminal plunged his right hand into a fire, and another prisoner was crucified. . . . In this period, too, Tertullian saw a performance of the *Death of Hercules,* in which the actor representing Hercules was actually burned to death as part of the show."

Only yesterday we thought of hippies as flower people. Their apparent gentleness could be taken to prove that if you satisfy the sexual instinct, you will be peaceful and mild. Today they, or their slightly younger brothers and sisters, aren't more frustrated sexually, they're only less gentle. Similarly with college students. Granted, we exaggerate the degree to which they are sexually freer than their parents were when *they* were in college; but if there is a difference between the class of '70 and the class of '40, surely it is in the direction of greater freedom for the class of '70. Yet that isn't a notably unviolent class, and we don't find that its more violent students are also the more repressed sexually. Their violence is of speech and thought and appetite as well as of action.

Soft-boiled modern pagans have for some time been turning to Eastern pagan spirituality—music, meditation, texts, and so on. How long is it, as these things go, since the British in India had forcefully to suppress suttee, the burning-alive of widows? And in the summer of 1968 the Associated Press received the following dispatch from India:

> Prime Minister Indira Gandhi has demanded an example be made of those responsible for the ritual slaying of a 12-year-old boy in Rajasthan state. A contractor is reported to have slashed the boy's neck to appease the gods at the laying of the foundation stone for an irrigation project. In a letter to the Chief Minister of the state, Mrs. Gandhi said that even those indirectly responsible for this "inhuman and barbarous act" should be punished.

The soft-boiled Western pagans may have only a partial understanding of Eastern paganism.

In our day, though, an intellectual or style-setting elite has to be hardboiled. Its violence isn't comic book or television violence—that's for kids and the lower middle class—but something a little more thoroughgoing. There is the Sorbonne philosopher who is reported to have proclaimed, at the time of the French student uprising, that it wasn't enough to develop a philosophy of terror, it was necessary to replace philosophy by terror. There is the American literary review that helpfully ran a front-page diagram of a fire-bomb. (The Black Panthers' attraction for some whites is less clear-cut. The whites may only be personally kinky.) Like the Enlightenment ancestors, the vanguard despises puritanism for its sexual repressions; but while the ancestors condemned puritanism for encouraging cruelty, our vanguard should be condemning puritanism for repressing it.

At this stage of the evolution of modern paganism, where you get your kicks isn't important, as long as you get them. Both bed and Colosseum are groovy. If the Colosseum—whips and chains—is groovier for you, O.K. Do your own thing. In fact, if we could only stop being hypocritical long enough to admit it, maybe the Colosseum is groovier for everybody. Isn't death the ultimate kick? (Someone else's death, that is; but maybe your own, too.) Anyway, nature unfortunately limits the frequency and duration of orgasm. But fortunately, nature doesn't limit the duration or frequency of orgiastic cruelty. You can torture someone for as long as you want. In hardly any time at all you can hurt or kill as many as you want.

If one doesn't want to say "pornographic books," for fear of using a censor's word, one says "sex-and-violence books." *And,* not *or.* Sade wrote a few books in that genre himself.

■　　■　　■

It needn't be said here that "puritanism" is one of those slippery words. Normally we could call D. H. Lawrence a pagan, not a puritan. Dr. Leavis seems to see Lawrence as a puritan—because he is serious not frivolous, radical not graceful, intelligent not clever. Or we think puritanism hated sex. But historically, puritanism is Protestant, and Protestantism had little use for celibacy: the monk Luther married a nun. (Queen Elizabeth wasn't so Protestant that she could quite get used to a married Archbishop of Canterbury.)

Puritan religion isn't only Protestant. So far, to disagree with the conventionally progressive Jewish view, I have been exaggerating the puritanism of the Jewish tradition. That point having been made, it remains to add that of course Judaism isn't Calvinist—or, for that matter, Thomist or Augustinian.

Calvin taught total depravity; and until recently—only a few hundred years ago—all the major Catholic and Protestant traditions agreed on the logically related doctrine of *paucitas salvandorum*. That is to say, the strong consensus of the doctors of a religion that had come to replace Jewish law and vindictiveness by Christian freedom and love was that very few even of the faithful would be saved, the great mass being doomed to eternal punishment in hell. Judaism, so legal and vindictive, doesn't agree. I'm sure it wasn't Isaiah Berlin's intention to speak as a Jew when he denied historical inevitability, a modern secularist counterpart of predestination; but he expressed the central Jewish doctrine, or rather, a central Jewish feeling: often, Berlin said, the irresistible is only the unresisted. The Torah lesson of the Sabbath before Rosh Hashanah ends this way (Deuteronomy 30:19–20):

> I call heaven and earth to witness against you this day: I have put before you life and death, blessing and curse; therefore choose life, so that you may live, you and your progeny. Love the Lord your God, listen to His voice, and cleave to Him; for so you shall have life and length of days....

Nothing predestined, inevitable, or irresistible about that.

So Judaism isn't Calvinist. But it is puritan, in that it likes chastity and doesn't like celibacy. In the historian Jacob Katz's study of the East European Jewish family as it was three hundred years ago, he has shown us Jewish law and thought concretely at work. The rabbis may have been naive about other things, but they weren't naive about the sexual drive. They knew how strong it is. They didn't try to deny it or suppress it or divert it—they just tried to hallow it, in marriage. (Their term for marriage is *qiddushin*, "hallowing.") In the time and place Professor Katz examined, Jews married young. Nor were the rabbis Victorian, imagining that women—or good women—were sexless. Like any law, Jewish law deals with obligations and rights. East European Jews knew that Jewish law obliges a husband to give his wife sexual gratification, and entitles her to it.

Hume, and later Nietzsche, thought ill of Christianity for teaching men humility. Nietzsche was wrong in thinking that the source of that doctrine was Judaism. To be sure, man's humility is Jewish; but it is coupled, kept in permanent tension, with an equally Jewish belief in man's grandeur. In my part of the congregation, these last Days of Awe, the visiting rabbi preached a sermon based on the aphorism of a Hasidic master: "Everyone should have two pockets. In the first he should keep a slip on which is written, 'I am but dust and ashes' [Genesis 18:27]. In the second he should keep a slip on which is written, 'For my sake was the world created' [Mishnah Sanhedrin 4:5]."

In that verse from Genesis, Abraham is abasing himself before the Lord, though the abasement is somewhat *pro forma:* he is questioning the Lord's justice in dooming Sodom. The Mishnah quotation comes toward the end of a long section about the warning that must be given to witnesses in a capital case: a man's life depends on what they say, together with the lives of all the descendants he could have:

> ... one man alone was created in the world, to teach you that if any destroys a single soul, Scripture regards him as if he has destroyed a whole world; but if any preserves a single soul, Scripture regards him as if he has preserved a whole world.... one man alone was created [from whom we are all descended], so that none should say to another, "My ancestor was greater than yours," ... and in order to proclaim the greatness of the Holy One, blessed is He. For a man stamps many coins with one seal and they are all alike; but the King of the kings of kings, the Holy One, blessed is He, has stamped every man with the seal of the first man, yet none is like another. Therefore each must say, "For my sake was the world created." ...

■   ■   ■

The major Torah lesson on Yom Kippur is the eighteenth chapter of Leviticus. Some years ago, I suggested why it had been chosen for reading on Yom Kippur. Mostly it is about unchastity—incest, adultery, sodomy, and bestiality. Unchastity is forbidden not only as wrong in itself but also as an expression of paganism. Unchastity is the piety of paganism: the things that are "abominations" for Israel are the "statutes" and "abominable customs" that "they do in the land of Egypt, where you dwelt, and . . . in the land of Canaan, to which I am bringing you." An equally abominable custom is the sacrifice of children: "You shall not give any of your children to be offered up to Molech. . . ." Bloodshed is likewise the piety of paganism.

Now I see that I stopped just short of understanding that for the rabbis this chapter must be a concentrated scriptural statement of the practical negative theology of Judaism. It is a negative theology because in one rabbinical definition Judaism is that which is not pagan: "[Mordecai] is called 'the Jew' because he repudiated idolatry, since everyone who repudiates idolatry is called a Jew" [Megillah 13a]. On "My statutes and my ordinances, by doing which a man shall live: I am the Lord" (Leviticus 18:5), the Midrash comments: "R. Jeremiah said: Why may one say that even a Gentile, if he fulfills all the Torah, is like a High Priest? Because Scripture says, 'by doing which a man shall live.'"

It is practical because it is not a theologumenon, it is binding law about life and death. "Having voted, they passed this law . . . : Concerning all the transgressions prohibited in the Torah, if a man is told, 'Transgress and do not be killed,' let him transgress and not be killed; except for idolatry, unchastity, and bloodshed" (Sanhedrin 74a). Since this is law—the most important law—normal legal reasoning applies. Is it legally permissible for a Jew, out of supererogatory piety or devotion, to allow himself to be killed rather than violate any other prohibition? Maimonides limits a Jew's right to allow himself to be killed in such circumstances: By insisting on martyrdom rather than making the Muslim profession of faith, a Jew would be acting unlawfully, since Islam is completely monotheistic and aniconic. In this Maimonides agreed with the Midrash:

> R. Ishmael says: Why may one say that if a man is told privately, "Worship idols and do not be killed," he should worship and not be killed? Because the Torah says, "by doing which a man shall live"—not "by doing which he shall die." Should he also obey a public order to worship idols? The Torah says: "You shall not profane My holy name, that I may be hallowed in the midst of the people of Israel; I am the Lord who sanctify you" (Leviticus 22:32). If you hallow My name, I too will hallow My name in you.

Hallowing the Name is *qiddush ha-Shem,* which is also the term for martyrdom.

Paganism/idolatry, unchastity/licentiousness, and murder/bloodshed are for Judaism the unholy triad. (Respectively, they are [1] *avodah zarah* or *avodat elilim* or *avodat gillulim* or *avodat kokhavim umazzalot*; [2] *gilluy arayot,* narrowly incest, literally "uncovering of nakednesses," as in Leviticus 18; and [3] *shefikhut/shefikhat damim.*) The three have an affinity for one another. In Genesis 6:13, "God said to Noah, 'I am determined to make an end to all flesh; for the earth is filled with violence [*hamas;* Jewish Publication Society, 1962: lawlessness]. . . .'" On this the Midrash says: "R. Levi says: *Hamas* is idolatry, *hamas* is unchastity, *hamas* is bloodshed. . . ." Yoma 9b gives a striking conglutination of the cardinal sins: "Why was the First Temple destroyed? Because of three things: the idolatry, unchastity, and bloodshed in it. . . ." Examples from rabbinical literature could be multiplied. Maimonides says, in the *Guide of the Perplexed:* ". . . transgression of the commandments is also called uncleanness [*tame/timme*]. This expression is used with regard to mothers and roots of the commandments, namely [the prohibitions against] idolatry, unchastity, and bloodshed" (quoting Leviticus 20:3, Leviticus 18:24, and Numbers 35:34).

The rabbis—founders of that in the Jewish tradition which is most distinctly and specifically Jewish, to this day—were not simply repeating what the Bible had told them, nor in their legislation were they carried away by some kind of exalted urge for martyrdom. They didn't need to read Ovid or Petronius or Tacitus or Juvenal to know how the pagans were about sex and about blood. They were contemporaries of Roman paganism, sensible men with eyes to see and ears to hear. Besides the law about martyrdom, they also enacted more prosaic laws, like this one: "Cattle may not be left in the inns of the [pagan] Gentiles, since they are suspected of bestiality; nor may a woman remain alone with them, since they are suspected of unchastity; nor may a man remain alone with them, since they are suspected of shedding blood" (Mishnah Avodah Zarah 2:1).

For the rabbis, paganism was idolatry, and they really couldn't understand it. They knew, because the Bible told them, that in the olden times the Israelites had repeatedly backslid into idolatry, and they knew that the contemporary Gentiles were idolaters, but how people could take it seriously was a mystery to them. (Emil Fackenheim considers that problem, brought up to date, in his fine "Idolatry As a Modern Religious Possibility" in the *Religious Situation*.) It seemed reasonable to the rabbis that paganism must be a pretext for something else: "R. Judah said, quoting Rav: Israel [in the days of the First Temple] knew very well that idolatry has no substance to it. They were idolators only to permit themselves public licentiousness" (Sanhedrin 63b).

■ ■ ■

What about pluralism? I know I'm being anachronistic and reading a modern sensibility back into the rabbis' outlook. They insisted on a total Jewish repudiation of paganism, honored Gentiles who abandoned paganism, and longed for the day when the Lord will be King over all the earth; but sometimes I like to think that maybe they also had a quiet weakness for pluralism. I can't fault the rabbis for being harsh to Esau and I'm glad my descent is from Jacob. But the price Jacob paid for his qualities was that he couldn't at the same time have Esau's qualities. Is there no room in God's world for Jacob and Esau, both? I want to think there is, and to think the rabbis thought so, too.

Certain virtues—if that word may be used here—primarily aesthetic, go with paganism: Balinese temple dances, for instance, and Polynesian graces. When in the *Alenu* I join the congregation in hoping for the time when the Lord has removed the idols from the earth and all flesh invokes His name, sometimes I become a little anxious. What will the world be like when everyone's a Jew? Then I calm myself. That isn't likely to happen right away. Right now, Bali and Tahiti are rather more immediately vulnerable to jet airliners than to Judaism.

For a pluralist, that's too bad. As with liberty and equality, so with the unity of mankind and pluralism: in each set the two members don't get on easily with each other, but the intellectual difficulty of holding on to both is nothing compared with the moral difficulty of giving up either.

I suppose the rabbis could have justified a measure of pluralism by appealing to some such verse as Micah 5:4, which—for varied, sometimes contradictory reasons—has been popular with the Jews of modernity: "For let all the peoples walk each in the name of its god, but we will walk in the name of the Lord our God for ever and ever." Not that rabbis could have approved human sacrifice, then or now. For Jews and Gentiles alike, the rabbis wanted none of the practices of the bad old Israelite days, when, more or less like that Indian contractor in 1968, "Hiel the Bethelite [re]built Jericho. With Abiram his first-born he laid its foundations, and with his youngest son Segub he set up its gates" (I Kings 16:34). But maybe the rabbis weren't entirely unhappy that others were so foolish as to think paganism had some substance to it. Maybe they didn't object to pagans preserving un-Jewish virtues or graces in the world. That could be one meaning of the famous answer in Avodah Zarah (54b):

> Philosophers asked the elders in Rome, "If your God dislikes paganism, why does He not abolish it?" They answered, "If the pagans worshipped something the world has no need of, He would abolish it; but they worship the sun and the moon and the stars and the planets. Shall He destroy the world because of fools? The world goes its wonted way, but the fools who have behaved unworthily will be held to account."

(1968)

"Judaism Is Against Paganism"

IT HAS BEEN SAID BEFORE, and needs to be said again: The trouble is not that religion in general has too small a role in American public life or American life simply. The trouble is that a particular religion has too great a role—paganism, the de facto established religion. When dissenters pleaded that it is no business of government to endow art like Robert Mapplethorpe's, all they got for their pains was a derisory token victory and the expectable disdain of the *New York Times*.

Let historicists wince at statements that begin, "Judaism is." Judaism is against paganism.

Ha-yehudi, "the Jew," occurs six times in Scripture, only in the book of Esther and always in apposition to "Mordecai," who is also once "a Jewish man" and once "a Jew." In Rabbi Johanan's exegesis (Megillah 13a), Mordecai is so insistently called a Jew "because he abjured paganism [*avodah zarah*], for everyone who abjures paganism is called a Jew; as is written (Daniel 3:12): '... Jews ... serve not thy gods nor worship the golden image which thou has set up.'"

For the rabbis, as for Scripture, the essence of paganism is unchastity. In Leviticus 18 the unchastities forbidden to Israel are not merely the practices of the Egyptian and Canaanite pagans but actually their laws (*huqqot*=Septuagint's *nomima*): paganism does more than tolerate, it demands unchastity. Rabbinically, only paganism's licentiousness explains its appeal. About Israelite paganism in the age of the First Temple, Rabbi Judah said, citing Rav, that the only reason Israel adopted idolatry was to permit themselves "public licentiousness" (Sanhedrin 63b).

For the most solemn possible abjuration of paganism/ unchastity, therefore, the rabbis ordained Leviticus 18 to be read in the synagogue toward the close of Yom Kippur. (Was it in Queen Victoria's reign that Reform, fearing that Leviticus 18 might bring a blush to the cheek of the young person, banished it in favor of selected verses from 19? The delayed payoff for a heteroclite rabbinate now is that 18:22 need never be heard by its congregations.)

The honorific subtitle of the historian Peter Gay's *Enlightenment* is *The Rise of Modern Paganism.* The Enlightenment's project was liberal—to liberate us for the pursuit of our happiness—but some of what began as liberal has become libertine, and libertinism has brought enslavement and misery more than it has brought liberation and happiness: AIDS, kids who have kids, the vanishing father. First the French Revolution devoured its children, then the Bolshevik Revolution, and now the sexual revolution.

Drugs, too, are a pagan devourer. In Judaism, you are equally forbidden to injure yourself and your neighbor, but in paganism, you own your body and are free to inflict on it any injury you wish.

With less paganism and less of its bitter fruit, the country would be less diseased, less fear-ridden, less ignorant, less poor. Surely all must agree that American Jewry should try to help bring that about?

As the Duke of Wellington said about something else: If you can believe that, you can believe anything.

A *New York Times* editorial being sacred writ, if the *Times* says so then government must endow exhibits that "documented a sadomasochistic homosexual subculture." We have not yet been instructed about endowing exhibits that documented a sadomasochistic Aryan National subculture.

■ ■ ■

In Cincinnati, a curator was tried for obscenity because his museum defended the cause of Art by showing the Mapplethorpe collection. (He was acquitted, the jury deferring to its betters about "What Is Art?") One expert witness testified for the defense that the photograph of a penis with a finger inserted into it "was a very ordered, classical composition" and that another photograph, of an arm in an anus, was formally similar to the photograph of a flower. In the opinion of the *Times*'s photography editor, the curator of a university museum "came closest to the truth when she told the prosecutor ..., 'It's the tension between the physical beauty of the photograph and the brutal nature of what's going on in it that gives it the particular quality that this work of art has.'" The prosecutor failed to ask her a hypothetical question: What would be her expert opinion of a photograph in which there was tension between its beauty and the brutal nature of what was going on in a Nazi torture chamber?

When the aesthetic and the ethical (or moral) conflict, as they do here, paganism sides with the aesthetic and Judaism with the ethical. In the nineteenth century, Matthew Arnold's Hellenism/Hebraism and Samuel David Luzzatto's Atticism/Abrahamism drew that distinction. (In the twelfth century, Judah Halevi's *Kuzari* drew it.) Arnold thought that in his time Hebraism pressed too hard on Hellenism. Now the effortless low paganism that ousted his kind of Hellenism presses much harder on Hebraism, but American Jews do not champion Hebraism in its distress. They champion separationism—separation of church and state elevated almost to the rank of *summum bonum*—and separationism favors paganism.

Responding to the backward who say that a Christ-in-urine is not what government should endow, the Establishment shudders at the censorship of not giving an artist the money he applies for. (Besides, it was only a tiny fraction of the Arts budget.) If, implausibly, the tiny fraction had endowed art for a church or a synagogue, that would have been an unforgivable breach in the Wall of Separation. Whether the money was much or little would not matter, principle would be at stake. The money must be returned, the guilty exposed, watchdogs posted.

It would be funny if it were not so sad.

I first published my objections to the separationist dogma of the American Jewish community almost twenty-five years ago, and I have since called American Jews diehard conservatives. We have seen the unimaginable become real, the impossible become actual, the obdurate become yielding: Berlin Wall down, statues of Lenin toppled, the triumphant religion of Marxism-Leninism in ruins. Can American Jewry, uniquely, hold out against necessary change?

British Jews are always puzzled by what they take to be our fuss about separation. They do not mind at all that their Chief Rabbi is in the House of Lords.

■   ■   ■

In France and its Jewish community, separationism was once even more deeply rooted than in the United States and its Jewish community, but a Chief Rabbi of France once told me how disappointed he was to find American Jews still vigorously separationist. In substance, he said: "Don't they realize how that has fostered irreligion"—he meant paganism—"and how that in turn has fostered crime and every other evil? In France we realize it." I have forgotten what I told him, but I remember wondering what he would have said if he had been Ashkenazi.

Tiqqun means "setting right, repairing, correcting, perfecting." For Jews on the Left who like to give a Jewish cast to their politics, the tradition's *tiqqun olam*, "setting the world right," means whatever is on the Left's agenda, and the problem of paganism never is. In the tradition itself, the *Alenu* prayer (which Solomon Schechter called the Jewish "Marseillaise") has this: "... in hope we wait, O Lord our God, ... for Thee to remove the idols from the earth, the no-gods being utterly cut down, to *taqqen olam bemalkhut Shaddai* set the world right by the Almighty's kingship...." The prayer ends in two verses from Scripture: "The Lord shall reign for ever and ever" (Exodus 15:18) and "And the Lord shall be king over all the earth: in that day shall there be one Lord, and his name one" (Zechariah 14:9). *Tiqqun olam* is *tiqqun* from paganism.

When will the Synagogue Council, the National Jewish Community Relations Advisory Council, ADL, and the two AJC's each appoint its Task Force on Combating Paganism? We should live so long.

Are Jews unlikely to bestir themselves soon to seek relief and deliverance from paganism and its bitter fruit? Then let us hope with Mordecai that "relief and deliverance will come to the Jews from another quarter."

(1991)

Ancients and Moderns

On Leo Strauss

LEO STRAUSS DIED IN OCTOBER 1973, at the age of seventy-four. His name is known chiefly to two groups of scholars whose interests do not normally converge, political scientists and specialists in medieval Jewish thought. For political scientists he was the man who challenged what "everyone" knew was the first requirement of science—that it should be, in Max Weber's language, *wertfrei*, value-free. A scientist—an astrophysicist, say—does not ask whether the things or processes or relationships he studies are good or bad, noble or base, desirable or undesirable. A social scientist is a scientist. He has a choice: on the one hand, objectivity, freedom from or neutrality about values, science; on the other, subjectivity, value preferences, not science. When, inevitably, the scientist thinks of good and bad, he thinks of them not as a scientist but as a human being or a citizen.

To the scientific study of politics Strauss opposed the philosophical study of politics. He had no objection to empirical political science—the study of voting preferences, for instance, and similar humble but useful inquiries. It was against social or political science understood as value-free that he waged battle. He held that what the social or political scientist studies is so entangled with good and bad, better and worse, that value-freeness is impossible. All social scientists deal with values, only

69

some social scientists know they do and others do not know, or say they do not know. Since the ancients taught this, and since the moderns have obscured or denied it, the beginning of wisdom—not the end, the beginning—is to take the ancients seriously again, to entertain the possibility that they were not defeated once and for all in the seventeenth-century war of the moderns against the ancients. Strauss did not persuade anything like a majority of his profession, but his followers include a number of impressive people. For them, it was he who restored political philosophy from death to life. Beyond that, for them he was a great political philosopher in his own right. Among themselves his followers rank him, if not quite so high as Plato and Aristotle, then at least as high as Locke or Burke.

Strauss was also a Jewish scholar. "Jewish scholar" is ambiguous. It can mean a Jew who is a scholar in non-Jewish things or a scholar in Jewish things. Strauss was both, to a unique degree. Only the most eminent Jewish scholars, in the second sense, are fellows of the American Academy for Jewish Research. He was a fellow because of his work on Judah Halevi, Maimonides, and Spinoza. In the world of scholarship as a whole, he was better known for his work on Gentile thinkers, from Socrates to Weber.

The books he wrote as books are *Spinoza's Critique of Religion; The Political Philosophy of Hobbes; On Tyranny: An Interpretation of Xenophon's Hiero; Thoughts on Machiavelli;* and *Socrates and Aristophanes.* The books that consist of more or less separate studies are *Persecution and the Art of Writing; Natural Right and History; What Is Political Philosophy?; Liberalism Ancient and Modern;* and *The City and Man. Philosophie und Gesetz* ("Philosophy and Law") has not yet been translated.

With Aristotle, Strauss taught that to understand the political one must start neither from the depths nor from the heights but from the surface. Since he himself was a political philosopher, let us take his advice and start from his surface.

At the University of Chicago, where he taught political philosophy for many years, Strauss's title was Robert Maynard Hutchins Distinguished Professor. Yet his disciples called him Mr. Strauss. We may infer that in his citizen's capacity he thought himself and wished to be thought a gentleman rather than a specialist or member of a guild, and that in his thinker's capacity he thought himself and wished to be thought a *philosophos*—the form is his—a seeker after wisdom, rather than a professor of (political) philosophy. Of Hermann Cohen he wrote that Cohen was by force of spirit the most impressive professor of philosophy in Germany. That is respectful, and we know that in fact Strauss had enough respect for Cohen to do him the honor of taking serious issue with his thinking about Spinoza and to write the introduction to the translation of Cohen's book about Judaism and ethics. But he called Ernst Cassirer, no less, a philosophy professor rather than a philosopher, and he said that the relation between philosopher and professor of philosophy is like the relation between artist and member of an art department. A German Jew, he was lacking in the German and German Jewish appetite for the title of Herr Geheimrat or Herr Professor or Herr Doktor. What was good for Socrates, Plato, and Aristotle was good enough for him.

■　　■　　■

The first thing anyone who has heard of Strauss is likely to think he knows about him is that Strauss believed that the authors he studied and wrote about—among them Plato and Lucretius and Judah Halevi and Maimonides and Marsilius of Padua and Spinoza and Locke—wrote esoterically, with secret meanings and intentions at odds with what they evidently said and what the authorities told us they said. There was a time when this idea was resisted and ridiculed, but today it is hardly disputed that on the main point Strauss was right, and that certain texts were written to be read, as it were, between the lines.

Strauss describes the process in *Persecution and the Art of Writing:*

> We can easily imagine that a historian living in a totalitarian country, a generally respected and unsuspected member of the only party in existence, might be led by his investigations to doubt the soundness of the government-sponsored interpretation of the history of religion. Nobody would prevent him from publishing a passionate attack on what he would call the liberal view. He would of course have to state the liberal view before attacking it; he would make that statement in the quiet, unspectacular, and somewhat boring manner which would seem to be but natural; he would use many technical terms, give many quotations, and attach undue importance to insignificant details; he would seem to forget the holy war of mankind in the petty squabbles of pedants. Only when he reached the core of the argument would he write three or four sentences in that terse and lively style which is apt to arrest the attention of young men who love to think. That central passage would state the case of the adversaries more clearly, compellingly, and mercilessly than it had ever been stated in the heyday of liberalism, for he would silently drop all the foolish excrescences of the liberal creed which were allowed to grow up during the time when liberalism had succeeded and therefore was approaching dormancy. His reasonable young reader would for the first time catch a glimpse of the forbidden fruit. The attack, the bulk of the work, would consist of virulent expansions of the most virulent utterances in the holy book or books of the ruling party. The intelligent young man, who being young, had until then been somehow attracted by those immoderate utterances, would now be merely disgusted and, after having tasted the forbidden fruit, even bored by them. Reading the book for the second and third time, he would detect in the very arrangement of the quotations from the authoritative books significant additions to those few terse statements which occur in the center of the rather short first part.

Strauss tells us to watch how an esoteric writer uses and arranges quotations. Though he may not exactly have been an esoteric writer himself, it pays to watch him. To his paper "Maimonides's Statement on Political Science," in *What Is Political Philosophy?*, he prefixes a quotation from "Cicero *De divinatione* I": "*Sed quid ego Graecorum? Nescio quo modo me magis nostra delectant.*" ("But why have I been so occupied with the things of the Greeks? Somehow our own things give me greater pleasure.")

This is missing from the study as it appeared first, in the 1953 *Proceedings of the American Academy for Jewish Research*, which is strange. After "Maimonides" in the title, and in emphatic contrast to "the things of the Greeks," "our own things" must mean Jewish things. It is almost as if Strauss were saying that having dealt with Greek thought all his life he was belatedly turning his attention to Jewish thought. But he wrote about the Greeks last: first he wrote about medieval Jewish and Muslim thinkers, then about the early moderns, and last about the Greeks. What is more, in that study Strauss goes on to show that Maimonides' statement on political science is itself Greek. I decided to look into the quotation from Cicero.

Strauss had not made that easy: if the esoteric were easy it could hardly be esoteric. As it took me some time to discover, the quotation is from *De divinatione* I, xxvi, 55, where I further discovered that *ego*, "I," is not the author, Marcus Tullius Cicero, but his brother and foil Quintus. Against the philosophical Cicero, Quintus upholds dreams and portents. The "things of the Greeks" are incidents from Greek history that he uses as argument for divination, "our own things" incidents from Roman history that he would rather use.

Strauss may be hinting at something like this: Our own things, the Jewish things, give us pleasure because we are Jews, but they are not philosophical things. "Divination" is related to "divine." Jewish things, Jewish books, are concerned with the divine. The divine is not philosophical; philosophy knows nothing of the divine.

Like Maimonides, Strauss was a Jew and a philosopher. Like Maimonides, he held that "Jew" and "philosopher" exclude each other. A Jew must believe in revelation, a philosopher cannot. More than Strauss—and more nobly, Strauss would have been the first to say—Maimonides sacrificed the philosopher in himself to the Jew.

On the other hand, Strauss was as different as can be from the academic non-Jewish Jew, so common on both sides of the Atlantic. He stopped well short of sacrificing the Jew in himself to the philosopher—perhaps because he had perceived that Maimonides' sacrifice, of the philosopher to the Jew, was less than a whole burnt offering.

■   ■   ■

Strauss is also known as the enemy of historicism and of the denial of natural right. There is no better introduction to these matters than a story told by Hans Jonas, a friend of Strauss's from their youth in Germany. Jonas begins his "Contemporary Problems in Ethics from a Jewish Perspective" (*Journal of the Central Conference of American Rabbis*, January 1968) as follows:

> To illustrate the plight of ethics in contemporary philosophy, let me open this paper with a personal reminiscence. When in 1945 I reentered vanquished Germany as a member of the Jewish Brigade in the British army, I had to decide on whom of my former teachers in philosophy I could in good conscience visit, and whom not. It turned out that the "no" fell on my main teacher, perhaps the most original and profound, certainly one of the most influential among the philosophers of this century, who by the criteria which then had to govern my choice had failed the human test of the time; whereas the "yes" included the much lesser figure of a rather narrow traditionalist of Kantian persuasion, who meant little to me philosophically but of

whose record in those dark years I heard admirable things. When I did visit him and congratulated him on the courage of his principled stand, he said a memorable thing: "Jonas," he said, "I tell you this: Without Kant's teaching I couldn't have done it." Here was a limited man, but sustained in an honorable course of action by the moral force of an outmoded philosophy; and there was the giant of contemporary thought—not hindered, some even say helped, by his philosophy in joining the cause of evil. The point is that this was more than a private failing, just as the other's better bearing was, by his own avowal, more than a private virtue. The tragedy was that the truly 20th-century thinker of the two, he whose word had stirred the youth of a whole generation after the First World War, had not offered in his philosophy a reason for setting conduct in the noble tradition stemming from Socrates and Plato and ending, perhaps, in Kant.

Heidegger was that giant of contemporary thought. Strauss agreed that he was a giant. Heidegger was also pro-Nazi, and Strauss hated the Nazis not like a philosopher but like the simplest Jew. After the war Strauss ignored Heidegger's overtures and forbade his students to have anything to do with the giant.

In *Natural Right and History*, Strauss's critique of Max Weber's value-free social science is of special interest to the social scientist. For the citizen, what Strauss suggests in the introduction is more striking: that few teachers of political science and American government agree with the central proposition of the Declaration of Independence, "We hold these Truths to be self-evident, that all Men are created equal, that they are endowed by their Creator with certain unalienable Rights, that among these are Life, Liberty, and the Pursuit of Happiness." For the Declaration, all hinges on the Creator. How many of us believe in a Creator? A passionate desire for equality, and to some degree for liberty also, remains with us, but it is without a reasoned basis. Suppose that tomorrow the dominant passion is for despotism. Having debarred ourselves from invoking a Creator, what shall we then invoke for liberty and equality and against despotism? Once we deny the Declaration's Creator and "the Laws of Nature and of Nature's God," we have nothing left.

Strauss shows that wickedness must ensue from denying natural right. Heidegger's denial led to wickedness, and so did the denial of Hans Kelsen, the most illustrious twentieth-century authority on the philosophy of law. In *Natural Right*, Kelsen is quoted from his 1925 *Allgemeine Staatslehre*, where he expresses impatience with the naive and presumptuous upholders of natural right, who could not see what was so clear to him, that despotism is as legitimate a form of government as any other. (In a blandly lethal footnote, Strauss records that a quarter of a century later Kelsen had not changed his mind about the naiveté and presumption of natural-right thinking. This being so, Strauss asks, what possible reason could Kelsen have had for omitting that passage from the English-language translation, *General Theory of Law and State* [1949]?) Nevertheless, Strauss does not say he has proved that natural right, because desirable, is also real.

■   ■   ■

The third thing "everybody" knows about Strauss is that he was conservative. What is conservative? Is it laissez-faire libertarian? Strauss had studied Bible and Maimonides, Plato and Aristotle. In none of these did he find it written that the owner of a coal mine may not be forbidden to employ a pregnant woman to haul laden wagons underground. He despised that kind of conservatism and its theorists—mostly economists of a certain school.

The guiding instinct of Strauss's conservatism, linked to temperament, family, history, and theory, was this: If it is not necessary to change, then it is necessary not to change. Why should he have thought that change is good? In an unpublished but widely circulated Hillel lecture, he recalled that as

a boy he saw his parents and the other Jews of their community taking care of Jewish refugees from Russian pogroms
passing through Germany on their way to America. He never
thought very highly of Kaiser Wilhelm's character or intellect, but at least he could say for Wilhelm's Germany that it
was a *Rechtsstaat,* a state ruled by law: in the Kaiser's empire,
unlike the Czar's, pogroms were not tolerated. Yet not even
the Russian change has been good. After all these years it
appears that bad as the Czars' Russia was for Jews, for philosophers and poets, and for the people, the Leninists' Russia has
been much worse. As to Germany, Strauss had rather less
regard for Weimar than for the Kaiser. Weimar doomed itself,
in his view, by being too irresolute and cowardly to wield the
sword of the law against its enemies, who had openly sworn
to destroy it.

Preferring stability to change is Aristotelian. In the *Politics* 1268b and 1269a, starting from the question whether it
is advisable to erect a statue in honor of a political reformer,
Aristotle has to ask whether it is better or worse for a *polis* to
change the ancestral laws. We have made technological and
scientific progress since the days of our grandfathers. Why
should there not also be political progress? Our ancestors were
the same, ordinary, even foolish human beings that we are:
there is nothing divine about what they have bequeathed to
us. As a matter of fact, they were more primitive than we,
closer to the savage state.

Having said all this, Aristotle does not conclude that the
laws should be changed. The crafts and sciences are one thing,
the law another. Custom and long usage are the foundation of
the law. To change laws is to risk weakening veneration of the
law. The Declaration of Independence, a declaration of revolution, does not disagree. Asserting "the Right of the People to alter
or to abolish it ['any Form of Government'], and to institute new
Government . . . most likely to effect their Safety and Happiness,"
the Declaration immediately concedes that "Prudence, indeed,

will dictate that Governments long established should not be changed for light and transient Causes." The Founding Fathers did not dispute the ancients' teaching—that while prudence is not a theoretical virtue, it is a practical or political virtue.

The ancients thought that the best regime one could reasonably expect, in practice, was an aristocracy. (It was not the best in theory. That was the improbable one in which the philosophers were kings.) For us, now, with education pretty nearly universal, Strauss held that the best regime one can reasonably expect is liberal or constitutional democracy.

Strauss affirms classical conservatism, the doubt about progress. Yet he lets us understand that conservatism is not the last word. Conservatives are not subversive, by definition. Neither are philosophers. Philosophy, however, is subversive, at odds with the loyal citizen's absorption in the *polis.* Then it must be that philosophers are unsubversive only actively.

It is widely accepted that a belief in natural law is conservative, and that this is why the liberal nineteenth century abandoned the belief. Strauss shows that it was conservatives who abandoned natural law, in reaction against eighteenth-century revolutionary appeals to it—the Declaration of Independence, the Declaration of the Rights of Man. To natural law, conservatives opposed history: the rights of Englishmen; the laws, customs, and traditions of the Germans. Out of the conservative opposition to natural law arose the Historical School. And out of that opposition arose, by way of the Historical School's development or degeneration into historicism, Heidegger and Kelsen, who, each in his own way, ratified nihilism. Conservatism, unsubversive by definition, could be subversive in fact.

A conservative reveres the tradition and continuity of his country. What he overlooks is that every country was founded, and that every founding was by force and fraud: Romulus and Remus; William the Conqueror (or his Saxon predecessors); the American Revolution. Every continuity begins in discontinuity.

■ ■ ■

Strauss denies, or at least doubts, what we take for granted: that the moderns (Machiavelli, Bacon, Descartes, Hobbes, and so on) have superseded the ancients (Plato and Aristotle, mostly) and that this is good. He does not say that the ancients can be reinstated as if the revolution of the moderns had not happened. Modern science, which was originally part of modern philosophy, makes it unlikely that there can be a simple return to ancient philosophy, or philosophies. But a line leads from the abandonment of classical thought to the contemporary political scientists' reserve about the Declaration of Independence. A line leads from Machiavelli to historicism and its dissolution into nihilism or fanaticism, two sides of the same coin; to the greatest philosopher of our time supporting Nazism; to our most illustrious jurisprudent chiding the folly, presumption, and naiveté of those who would refuse legitimacy to despotism.

In 1974, Strauss may be more favorably received than in 1954. At least from *Philosophie und Gesetz* (1935), he was always skeptical of the fundamental modern project (as he called it), first set forth by Bacon: the conquest of nature for the relief of man's estate. To the ancients, theory is separate from and higher than practice. To the moderns, theory is for practice, science is for technology. In the last quarter of the twentieth century, the conquest of nature is less axiomatically desirable than Strauss could have imagined when he began to question the fundamental modern project. Perhaps the victory of Bacon the practical over Aristotle the theoretical should have been a shade less total? Perhaps there is something to be said for classical sobriety and limited expectation? (Did anyone tell Strauss about Toynbee's chic arraignment of the Bible for aggression against nature?)

■ ■ ■

There are many excellent teachers. They have students. Strauss had disciples. His disciples are known as Straussians. Straussians of the first generation are those who studied with him, and their students are the second generation. By now there may well be a third generation. Aristotelians are adherents of Aristotelianism, Thomists of Thomism, Marxists of Marxism, Freudians of Freudianism. Straussians call themselves Straussians, but they deny that there is a Straussism. One can see what they mean. Although close to a doctrine, Strauss's teaching is less palpable than those *isms*, less sturdy, less unequivocal as to theory and more renunciatory as to practice. Perhaps the Straussians are constituted not so much by a unifying doctrine as by the direct personal influence of an extraordinary man? That does not account for the second and third generations.

Whether of the first, second, or third generation, a Straussian is or was a young man or woman who loves to think, a reasonable young reader, an intelligent young man or woman. Such a person can respond to Strauss's yes-and-no, no-and-yes, giving and then taking away, taking away and then restoring. For some, the Straussian austerity can be exhilarating. It can be understood as an invitation to join those privileged few who, having ascended from the cave, gaze upon the sun with unhooded eyes, while yet mindful of those others below, in the dark. With grave agreement Strauss quotes Albo, 250 years removed from Maimonides, who calls his master the great eagle that delights to soar upward, ever closer to the sun.

Straussism also helps Straussians to do good work, which they could not do otherwise. As an example, because I have consulted it recently, I offer Allan Bloom and Harry Jaffa's *Shakespeare's Politics*, especially the chapter on *The Merchant of Venice*. Not many political scientists are Straussian, but of the dozen or so articles in one issue of the *American Political Science Review* (March 1974), three, and those not the least interesting, are by Straussians—young, to judge by their rank of assistant professor, and therefore unlikely to have studied under Strauss himself.

In the first Straussian generation there is a fairly high proportion of Jews. The reasons for this are unclear. Of course, by all accounts Strauss was a great teacher. Like his Greek and Jewish masters, "gladly wolde he lerne and gladly teche." But there must also have been a political or ideological attraction. Unlike other Jewish students, were the Straussians already conservative, or on the way to becoming conservative? Or did conservatism follow discipleship? There were Left Hegelians. There have been no Left Straussians.

Young and old, Jew and Gentile, all agree that Strauss's being a Jew was at the center of his thought and feeling. At the University of Chicago his lectures at the Hillel Foundation were events. In a university that prided itself on intellectual distinction, he was widely regarded as most distinguished; and this formidable Jew evoked respect for Jewish tradition and existence—not least among the Jews, teachers and students alike. On the whole, Jewish Straussians are still respectful, but still distantly. In general they think religion to be a good thing—politically, of course, and for others: Strauss says that liberal education used to be for gentlemen and religious education for the masses. The philosopher's education began where the gentleman's left off.

If the Jewish Straussians were really serious, if they really thought that what a philosopher says and how he says it and how he appears to the nonphilosophical make or should make a difference, would not more of them go to the synagogue? Strauss had stopped going to the synagogue. From his own point of view, should he have? More exactly, should he not have resumed going when he became a master, with disciples? Should he not have offered up a little of that sacrifice—of the philosopher to the Jew in him—that he valued so highly in Maimonides? For the greatest philosopher a noble lie, though inferior to a noble truth, was yet noble.

Strauss was not a believing Jew, but the only religion he could take seriously was Judaism. He himself said that while Judaism—*the* revelation—cannot refute philosophy, neither can philosophy refute Judaism. Philosophy, which rejects faith, is therefore itself a kind of faith. If for him the alternative to philosophy always remained Judaism, that was primarily because he had been brought up in a religious Jewish home. For the children and grandchildren of detached Jewish Straussians, the alternative to philosophy would not be Judaism. For them the alternative would necessarily be Christianity—perhaps by a detour through Eastern religions. Strauss had no difficulty in choosing between Judaism and Christianity, and he wanted the fruitful tension between Judaism/Jerusalem and philosophy/Athens to endure. (His definitive formulation of this, "Jerusalem and Athens," was published in *Commentary*, June 1967.) If this Athenian had lived a more Jerusalemite life, he would have set an even stronger Jewish example than he did. That would not have been inconsistent, or unprincipled. He began to study Maimonides when young and never stopped, to the day of his death. He held that Maimonides was deeper than Spinoza.

■　　■　　■

What did Strauss achieve? How significant was he? History, as they say, will give the answer. Xenophon's achievement and significance have always been seen as rather limited, but if Strauss's reinterpretation prevails they will be seen differently. One thing is indisputable, that Strauss combined to a preeminent degree the qualities that Talmud scholarship knows as those of the *baqi* and of the *harif*—the first, of copious, wide, deep, and exact knowledge; the second, of sharp and subtle analytical prowess. I have counted more than thirty authors that he treats at some length, from antiquity to the twentieth century—and such authors! (And always read in their own languages—in Greek, Latin, Hebrew, Arabic, Italian, English,

French, and his native German.) He may have been the most learned man of our time in the great writings that it is worth being learned in, of poets and historians as well as philosophers; and to his learning were joined acuteness, penetration, intuition, zest, and a certain serious playfulness.

In St. John's College, Annapolis, where Strauss was scholar in residence, a young man spoke *in memoriam:*

> Once, when our conversation ended with Mr. Strauss counseling me to make good use of my youth by studying, I asked for ... the subjects worthy of the most study.... Mr. Strauss suggested a curriculum built around the study of four books. True to form, he named only three of them—Aristotle's *Ethics,* Aquinas's *Treatise on Law,* and Kant's *Fundamental Principles of the Metaphysics of Morals.*

What the wise man says to each who may have it in him to become a seeker after wisdom depends on the particular constitution and needs of each soul. Strauss's enumeration of the books is true to form. His choice is enigmatic. Why Aristotle when Strauss loved Plato more, and which of the books on ethics? Aquinas because the young man is a Christian, or of a Christian family? Why Kant, when Strauss probably agreed with his friend Jonas that Kant's philosophy is outmoded?

What is the mysterious unnamed book? Hardly the Bible. Something by Machiavelli, I suggest, perhaps the *Discourses.* Strauss professes to be shocked by Machiavelli's shamelessness, but it is Strauss who reminds us that shamelessness is a moral or practical vice, not an intellectual or theoretical one. He even reminds us that shamelessness, like impiety, is absent from Aristotle's list of the moral vices.

Strauss tells us that the classical political philosophers teach about the governance of an established *polis,* while Machiavelli teaches about the founding of a city or a dynasty. A founder is superior to an inheritor. But who is a founder?

Moses was a founder. Long before him, the first pharaoh was a founder. How about the Egyptian who expelled the alien Hyksos rulers and reestablished—refounded—a native Egyptian pharaohnate? Was he not in his way as much a founder as the pharaoh who founded the first dynasty? For Machiavelli, just as the ruler who has founded a city or a dynasty is superior to other rulers, so must the thinker who has founded the doctrine about the founding of cities and dynasties be superior to other thinkers. Machiavelli was a founder—of modern political thought. I am persuaded that Strauss regarded himself, and was confident that future generations would regard him, as a refounder: the thinker who expelled (who undermined the taken-for-granted superiority of) the alien, intrusive teaching that had conquered political thought, and who restored, partly, the authentic, classical teaching or teachings. Could Strauss have been a secret Machiavellian? In any event, by the Machiavellian equation he can regard himself as not inferior to Machiavelli, the founder of the modern teaching. By the same equation he may even regard himself as not altogether inferior to Socrates—Socrates!—the founder of the classical teachings.

■   ■   ■

It is fitting to conclude by reverting to Strauss the Jew, the German Jew. In *Philosophie und Gesetz* he takes credit for telling Franz Rosenzweig the story about Hermann Cohen that Rosenzweig made famous: how Cohen once explained his God-idea to an Orthodox Jew; how the Jew then asked, And what about *bore olam*, the Creator of the world?; and how Cohen's only answer was to weep. Strauss was a friend of Gershom Scholem and Ernst Simon, who went up from Germany to Jerusalem fifty years ago (and are among the few contemporaries, along with Harry Austryn Wolfson, he cites in his footnotes). One difference between him and them was that his family was Orthodox, unassimilated, small-town provincial.

This may help to explain why, unlike Rosenzweig and even some German Jewish Marxists, he was never impressed or attracted by Christianity.

In being as Jewish as he was, and as conservative, Strauss was wholly distinct from those we think of when we think of Weimar culture or the intellectual migration: no chapter is devoted to him in the books about these. Of high degree in the culture and the migration was the Institut für Sozialforschung, the so-called Frankfurt School, which included such luminaries as Franz Neumann, Theodor Adorno, Max Horkheimer. Martin Jay, the author of *The Dialectical Imagination: A History of the Frankfurt School and the Institute of Social Research*, tells us ("Anti-Semitism and the Weimar Left," *Midstream*, January 1974) that the members of this brilliant and admired school, and especially the inner circle, mostly "came from Jewish backgrounds." Even after the war these brilliant men continued to deny the intensity, and almost the existence, of prewar German anti-Semitism! Anyway, they knew that anti-Semitism was not especially important, a symptom of something about capitalism; or else that it was a capitalistic device. Always they insisted that their Jewish backgrounds had nothing to do with their politics, or their school, or their dialectical imagination. In short, they used their brilliance to blind themselves to the most obvious facts.

To those who are moved by the exhortation, "change the world" does not mean "change the world for the worse." A Marxism that is not optimistic about the unity of theory and practice is a contradiction in terms. Yet toward the end, while Adorno had not renounced Marxist theory, he had renounced optimism about Marxist practice. His death was hastened by a Marxist woman student's lewd, jeering, cruel, public humiliation of the old Marxist philosopher and teacher, in his lecture hall.

Strauss, a Socratic, was not an optimist even as to theory. His health had long been frail. When he died, he was still learning and still teaching, encompassed by a more than filial reverence and care. "Honor is the portion of the wise" (Proverbs 3:35).

For a Greek Jew, or a Jewish Greek, something from Aristotle (*Nichomachean Ethics* 1100b–1101a) may be an equally suitable epitaph:

> ... no one of the blessed could become wretched. For he will never do hateful or base things ... since, in our opinion, the truly good and wise man bears all vicissitudes in a fitting manner ... ever acting most nobly....

(1974)

Spinoza and Mendelssohn

A FEW SUMMERS AGO a Jewish scholar was in Germany, doing research in the family papers of a former colonel in the Wehrmacht. When he was through, the scholar prepared to leave and thanked his host. "Not at all, Professor," said the colonel, "not at all. But before you go, perhaps you would be kind enough to answer a question. Tell me, do Jews still pray in—what do you call them?—synagogues?"

The curiosity was understandable in a descendant of Moses Mendelssohn.

No such story is possible about a descendant of Mendelssohn's rival for the title of father of Jewish modernity, Spinoza. Spinoza never married. That in itself gives Mendelssohn the better claim to fatherhood, for since the question is one of history—which is to say, the succession of generations—we naturally prefer the claimant who was also a father literally.

Always a Jew, never an ex-Jew, Mendelssohn was the leader of the Jewish community—defender and teacher of the Jews. Reform invokes and Orthodoxy still uses him: the Orthodox annotators of the Hertz Pentateuch frequently cite his *Be'ur*. In one degree or another, therefore, we are all his spiritual descendants. Is he responsible for his actual descendant having been a German army officer in 1939–45? Almost certainly not.

Almost—for if we judge Mendelssohn with a rigor suitable not to ourselves but only to the highest and best, we may ask whether for him that should have been altogether impossible to foresee. If Spinoza had lived in Germany rather than Holland, and if he had had children, and if one of our contemporaries were an Oberst von Spinoza, we would have less right to ask whether Spinoza should have been able to foresee that.

Mendelssohn wrote in German—the first memorable Jew to do so. (In those days the German Jews spoke Yiddish.) A century earlier, Spinoza had written not in the language of his country, Dutch, but in Latin—the first memorable Jew, or ex-Jew who had not become a Christian, to do so. By the eighteenth century, the national tongues had superseded Latin not only for literature but also, or as near as makes no difference, for scholarship, philosophy, and science. (In our time, an introduction to a classical text may still be in Latin, and very rarely a work of Bible scholarship. The introductions to Nestle's New Testament and Rahlfs's Septuagint are in Latin but also in German and English, and to Kittel's Biblia Hebraica in Latin but also in German.) In the seventeenth century, Bacon and Hobbes wrote in Latin and English, Descartes and Leibniz (a German) in Latin and French. Spinoza wrote in Latin.

Yet unlike the Gentile philosophers, Spinoza had not had a classical education and was not steeped in the Latin literary tradition: his Latin is serviceable rather than elegant, says his English translator. Not even the worldly Sephardim of his milieu gave their children a classical education. Instead the children were taught Jewish things, on the one hand, and things useful for commerce, on the other. (A few ambassadorial types, defenders and apologists of the Jews, wrote in Latin—which they had learned in Spain or Portugal while still outwardly Christian—for reasons like Cromwell's in appointing Milton to write Latin defenses of regicide England.) To the Jews of

Christendom, Latin had been *leshon kemarim,* the language of the idolater-priests; and it has been said that in Spain the Jewish dislike of Latin contributed to the ascendancy of Spanish.

Spinoza's circumstances, outlook, and interests differed from those of the Jews, medieval or contemporary. For him the ecclesiastical character of Latin was less marked, if only because he lived after the Reformation and in a Protestant country, where the vernacular was also the church language. Latin was the language of the international republic of learning, and that was more important to him than to the Jews, then or earlier. He did not leave Judaism and the Jews to become a Christian, or even a Dutchman. He left to become a citizen of the world—the world of philosophy. Latin must have been more than merely useful to him, it must have been positively attractive. It was universal not local or particular, ecumenical not parochial. In good faith the ex-Jew could take Latin's universality as evidence that choosing to be a citizen of the world was neither illusion nor opportunism. After Latin had been abandoned, Schopenhauer was to be harsh about that chauvinist betrayal of the international republic. (Now some American medical journals publish abstracts of their articles in Interlingua, an artificial language largely based on Latin that has been devised for communication among scientists across linguistic borders. Normally not a very cheerful soul, Schopenhauer would nevertheless have appreciated the joke: first we abandon the millennial interlingua, then we have to invent Interlingua.)

■　　■　　■

Two objections can he made against exculpating Spinoza on such grounds. The first is that an assertion of Latin's universality is itself provincial and chauvinist. What is or was Latin to the non-European, non-Western world? Even in Europe, what is or was Latin to the peoples whose very alphabets are not Latin but Greek or derivatively Cyrillic? (Until a hundred years ago Romanian, though a Romance language, was written in Cyrillic. The change to our alphabet was a Westernizing gesture.) This objection is anachronistic. In Spinoza's time, what was not West European hardly counted intellectually.

A variant is that in Western Europe itself, Latin was not evenly universal. After all, Latin is closer to Portuguese than to Danish. The language of an ode to Venice, of no great literary merit but of a daunting ingenuity, is both Latin and seventeenth-century Italian; and Gaston Paris used to begin his lectures on Old French at the Collège de France by declaring, *"Nous parlons latin"*—in speaking French, we speak Latin. True enough, but Latin seems to have been no less at home in the Germanic North than in the Romance South.

The second objection is that nothing in Latin from those days compares to the French writings of Ronsard and Racine or the English of Shakespeare and Milton—which is to say that if we think not of philosophy and scholarship narrowly but of culture broadly, then by Spinoza's day it should already have been obvious that Latin was declining and would soon fall. May it not have been some apprehension of this which persuaded Bacon and Descartes and Hobbes to write in their vernaculars things no less philosophical than the things they wrote in Latin?

If so, the apprehension was easier for a Christian or ex-Christian than for the ex-Jew. Spinoza assigned a much lower place to the imagination and the work of the imagination, poetry, than to reason. So did those other philosophers. (So did Plato and Maimonides.) Still, Spinoza was—he had to be, one may say—more single-minded and uncompromising about it than the Gentiles. For him, brought up a Jew, poetry was the Bible, and the Bible was contrary to reason. Because none but the few could lead lives guided by reason, the many needed the Bible—poetry, revealed religion's carrot of the hope of heaven and stick of the fear of hell—to keep them from murder and tumult. But the Bible, revealed religion, also bred sectarian war and the persecution of philosophers. Hence Spinoza's advocacy of the secular state, in which the citizen's adherence to one or another revealed religion must be a private matter, of no interest to the state provided that the citizen also subscribed to the civil religion, which taught virtue and duty. (In the eighteenth century as well, freethinking *philosophes* like Voltaire would remain convinced that there could be no such thing as a polity of atheists and that the common people required a civil religion, complete with belief in an afterlife.) The philosopher and ex-Jew would not be safe, could not live in honorable security, would never cease to be an outsider so long as reason and philosophy had not tamed the imagination and poetry.

For Christian or ex-Christian philosophers too the Bible might be, while necessary for the many, dangerous and merely imaginative and poetic; but it was not identical with poetry, nor was poetry intrinsically quite without value even for the few. Gentile philosophers also knew and might still enjoy Ovid and Arthurian romance and Petrarch. Besides, they knew and enjoyed Lucretius, from whose example they had learned that poetry need not be the certain enemy of reason and philosophy but could be a powerful ally. Nor would Christians or ex-Christians experience all the urgent intensity of the ex-Jew's desire to transcend the status of outsider.

Consequently, apart from any consideration of fluency, it is not to be wondered at that Spinoza abstained from writing in a vernacular, while those others did not. And he was consistent. He did nothing for which even a Spinoza, whom we have the right to hold to standards of the utmost rigor, must answer to us. His seeming preference, in the *Tractatus Theologico-Politicus*, for Christianity over Judaism? It is only a seeming preference. Philosophical eyes, which knew how to read a political philosopher, could see that Spinoza had little regard for either, and probably less for Christianity. He could hardly know that after him philosophy would value the imagination and poetry. He could hardly know that he was to be the last great philosopher, except his younger acquaintance Leibniz, to write in Latin. Some may say that he ought to have understood what was portended by such things as the Royal Society's publication of its *Philosophical* (= scientific) *Transactions* in English. However that may be, Spinoza could hardly have foreseen Romanticism.

To Mendelssohn, a hundred years later, the linguistic nationalisms of the learned might by themselves have sufficed to reveal how hollow was the internationalism of that famous international republic. Mendelssohn lived at the beginning of Romanticism, when it could no longer be taken for granted, even by those who earlier would have supported Spinoza and Hobbes, that reason was everything and poetic imagination almost nothing. (John Stuart Mill, sickening on a diet of Bentham, would recover by taking Wordsworth and Coleridge.)

With the change in the status of the imagination and poetry came a change in the status of the folk. The Romantic doctrine that *das Volk dichtet,* the folk is a poet, would neither have surprised Spinoza nor raised his estimate of the folk. He stood in the tradition that had long known the folk to be ruled by the imagination: it was ruled by the imagination because it was incapable of reason. In a Romantic age, *das Volk dichtet* meant an enhanced respect for the folk. That did not contradict Romanticism's exaltation of the solitary genius. The Romantic solitary genius was not Descartes, alone in his chamber and spinning thought from his unassisted intellect. The Romantic genius, though solitary, yet had an infinity of connections, subterranean and unconscious, with the folk which had borne and nurtured him. Though the genius's poetry and art were higher than folk poetry and art, his were connected with theirs undeniably, however obscurely. Somehow he represented them and spoke for them. Well into the twentieth century, the Artist as a Young Man could say, "I go . . . to forge in the smithy of my soul the untreated conscience of my race."

For ex-Jews this was to cause difficulties. Religion a private matter? At most, only if religion were understood narrowly. If understood to stand also for much else that is imaginative and poetic and traditional, how could it be private? How could it be kept distinct from culture and memory? In what country are the national literature and history not taught in the schools? If ex-Jews had to take the folk's imagination seriously, what were they to make of the Grimm brothers' tales, in which Jews are hateful, evil, uncanny, alien? How could ex-Jews *honorably* identify themselves with the folk whose spirit revealed itself in such tales? Could it be enough to say you were a Jew no longer? In Weimar Germany, both ex-Christians and ex-Jews could register as *konfessionslos* (of no formal religious affiliation), but the term was commonly understood to mean "ex-Jew." (In the United States, when respondents check "none" in answer to a question about their religion, the proportion of Jews among them, or of would-be ex-Jews, exceeds the proportion of Jews in the population.) The folk was Christian. To be related to the folk, you had to be Christian, or at least ex-Christian.

■   ■   ■

The ex-Jew Spinoza was never Christian; the ex-Jewish Mendelssohns were. Thirty and forty years ago German Mendelssohns whose families had been Christian for generations had some unpleasant moments—and, it is said, recourse to genealogies unflattering to the chastity of ancestresses—before they could be certified as Aryan, fit for service to the Third Reich. Long before Nuremberg there had been difficulties. Felix Mendelssohn, wrote Wagner in his *Judentum in der Musik*, was an estimable Christian gentleman of the highest musical gifts, but he was not a great German composer, or a great composer simply. He could not be. He had no roots in the folk. Of course Wagner, genius that he was, was also a disgusting man and a vile anti-Semite.

The German-speaking Jews were never more than one or two in a hundred of all German speakers. Toward the beginning of their history was Heine, perhaps the greatest nineteenth-century writer of German, who had a premonition of what was to come. Toward the end was Kafka, perhaps the greatest twentieth-century writer of German. Kafka had questions about his relation to German. He asked himself whether it was fitting for a Jew to call his mother *Mutter*, in German, when the Yiddish is *mamme*. Yet he had heard German from his mother, not Yiddish. His situation was complicated by his belonging to the Jewish minority of the German-speaking minority in mostly Czech Prague, but if he worried about German it was less because of present Czech than past Yiddish. The Jews had left behind their own folk quality without being able—without having the right to be able—to enter into another. The problem was folk quality, not citizenship.

But that had to do with German culture, and of Western cultures the German was least modern, most linked to a medieval, folkish past. It was otherwise with French culture. Of the one, Barbarossa and the Grimms' tales and Wagner were emblematic; of the other, 1789 and the Declaration of the Rights of Man. Yet there is that passage in Sartre's *Anti-Semite and Jew:*

> To the anti-Semite, intelligence is Jewish; he can thus disdain it in all tranquility, like all the other virtues which the Jew possesses. They are so many ersatz attributes that the Jew cultivates in place of that balanced mediocrity which he will never have. The true Frenchman, rooted in his province, in his country, borne along by a tradition twenty centuries old, benefiting from ancestral wisdom, guided by tried customs, does not *need* intelligence. His virtue depends upon the assimilation of the qualities which the work of a hundred generations has lent to the objects which surround him.... To be sure, this sensibility ignores eternal truths or universal values: the universal is Jewish.... The principle underlying anti-Semitism is that the

94

concrete possession of a particular object gives as if by magic the meaning of that object. Maurras said the same thing when he declared a Jew to be forever incapable of understanding this line of Racine: *"Dans l'Orient désert, quel devint mon ennui."*

But the way is open to me, mediocre me, to understand.... Why? Because I possess Racine—Racine and my country and my soil. Perhaps the Jew speaks a purer French than I do, perhaps he knows syntax and grammar better, perhaps he is even a writer. No matter; he has spoken this language for only twenty years, and I for a thousand years. The correctness of his style is abstract, acquired; my faults of French are in conformity with the genius of the language.

"The universal is Jewish." French Jews liked to think that the universal was French, and German Jews that it was German. The French Jews were somewhat less self-deluded, France having had the Revolution and the Declaration; but if most Frenchmen did not hate the universal so much as Sartre's anti-Semite, neither, surely, did they love it so much as the Jew. A Nazi said that when he heard the word "culture" he reached for his revolver. He did not necessarily mean that he scorned opera (especially Wagner) or even that he was waging war against *Kulturbolschewismus*. He may have meant that the word "culture" was a likely sign of a Jew speaking. Jews (and ex-Jews) did not want to recognize that for others, the words "culture" and "universal" may have been likely signs of a Jew (or ex-Jew) speaking.

Of course Nazis would take it as probable that a universalist was really a dirty Jew. Marxists could not—except that Soviet Russia is where "cosmopolitan," together with synonyms like "passportless wanderers," has officially been a bad word, meaning "dirty Jew." The Little Russian Cossack hetman Bogdan Khmelnitsky massacred Jews (and Poles) in Spinoza's time. Soviet Russia thinks so well of him that a city and, if memory serves, a decoration have been named after him. Stalin canonized him.

For Jews and even for Spinozaic ex-Jews it is not much compensation that in Marxist teaching Spinoza figures as a precursor. It will still be hard for them to find room in Russia.

It ought to be less hard for Mendelssohnian ex-Jews. They have been pretty good at that sort of thing.

(1974)

Past and Present

No Hitler, No Holocaust

FOR SOME YEARS AFTER the Bolshevik Revolution, young people in the Soviet Union could leave school thinking that Peter the Great was the name given to economic modernization and political centralization in late feudal Russia. Their teachers' insistence on impersonal historical forces had turned a person into a personification, an abstraction, a metaphor.

Hitler has been disappearing behind abstractions. If he is mentioned at all, it is likely to be as a metaphor.

In 1982, two articles with "Holocaust" in their titles appeared in *Commentary*, Henryk Grynberg's "Appropriating the Holocaust" (November) and Hyam Maccoby's "Theologian of the Holocaust" (December). Each mentions Hitler only once, and only in a quotation: Grynberg quotes the President's Commission on the Holocaust, "the Jews were Hitler's primary victims"; and Maccoby quotes Emil Fackenheim, "Jews are forbidden to grant posthumous victories to Hitler."

In Jacob Katz's "Was the Holocaust Predictable?" (May 1975), on the other hand, Hitler is real. Katz says "Hitler" twenty-eight times, "Führer" twice, "one man" once, and "this man" once. I wish he had not stopped just short of saying, explicitly, "No Hitler, no Holocaust."

No Hitler, no Holocaust. And if there had been no Churchill?

99

Thoughts like these trouble us both intellectually and emotionally. Intellectually, believing that Hitler nearly destroyed our world, or that Churchill saved it, can seem close to believing with Carlyle—of whom Jews, especially, are bound to be leery—that history is but the biography of great men. It can seem close to taking literally Pascal's meditation on Cleopatra's nose. Many of the best historians in the past generation or two have held biography, the concern with the particulars of the life of this personage or that, to be rather quaint, a form of gossip. Nor have they a much more exalted opinion of narrative ("what happened") history. For them what counts is geography, demography, technology, *mentalités*. They see great men and events affecting the human race little more decisively than Cleopatra's unsnubby nose did.

Understanding Bishop Berkeley's philosophy to deny that physical objects are real, Samuel Johnson said, "I refute it *thus*," and kicked a stone. Did some of the new historians refute their own philosophy by taking care to vote when Mitterrand and Giscard contested the presidency of France?

If it is wrong to hold any one man responsible for the fateful dementia of World War I, it is not wrong to hold the one man Lenin responsible for the Bolshevik Revolution. He was no more of his time and place than any other Russian, yet only he, in his particularity of heredity and environment, of constraint and freedom, did what he did. By himself he could not have made the Revolution, but without him it would not have been made and we would be living in a different world entirely. Lenin was not the sufficient cause, but he was the necessary cause.

And so with Hitler. Hitler willed and ordered the Holocaust, and was obeyed. Traditions, tendencies, ideas, myths—none of these made Hitler murder the Jews. All that history, all those forces and influences, could have been the same and Hitler could as easily, more easily, not have murdered the Jews. He could more advantageously have tightened the screw of oppression. That the Jews were not being murdered, that they were only being humiliated and exploited, would not have caused his followers to grumble, let alone to rebel.

Anti-Semitism was a necessary condition for the Holocaust; it was not a sufficient condition. Hitler was needed. Hitler murdered the Jews because he wanted to murder them.

Nor does anti-Semitism explain the men who pulled the triggers or released the gas. Let us suppose that Hitler's Viennese years had made him as anti-Slavic as anti-Semitic, or maybe even more. Or let us suppose that on account of German memory, anxiety, and ambition Hitler had decided that rather than murder the Jews, or before murdering them, he should subjugate the Slavs, starting with gas chambers and execution squads to rid himself of the educated. Would there have been any lack of men to carry out such an order? The thing would have been done, as in large part it was done. Maccoby recalls "Himmler's notorious speech to SS officers in which he lectured them on the moral imperative of stifling their feelings of nausea about the mass killings" of Jews. If Himmler had lectured the SS officers on the moral imperative of steeling themselves to their heroically hard duty of extirpating the Slavic peril, they would have been as dutiful about Slavs as they were about Jews. The obedience of Himmler and the SS was to Hitler, not to anti-Semitism. Himmler was anti-Russian as well as anti-Semitic, but when Hitler made his pact with Stalin the SS cooperated cheerfully with the NKVD.

That one man made so much difference may be even harder to accept emotionally than intellectually. The disproportionate frightens us. We need to believe that causes are proportionate to effects. We want to think that our world is a cosmos, and here is evidence that our world is a chaos. We feel bad enough knowing about the Holocaust, but if we have to accept that one man decreed the Holocaust we can feel still worse. We would rather talk about socioeconomic stresses and strains, political backwardness, group psychopathology, religious hatred, racism.

All those things were indeed there, and Hitler was indeed affected by them—affected, not determined. Those things necessarily meant trouble for the Jews; they did not necessarily mean Holocaust.

■　　■　　■

Applauding Fackenheim's resolve to "reject all facile deterministic explanations—such as the attempts to interpret the Holocaust in terms of economics, or xenophobia, or the vicissitudes of German history," Maccoby nevertheless yields to his own determinism. He tells us that we must understand "the Christian background of the Holocaust." For him anti-Semitism is inseparable, all but indistinguishable, from a timeless, unchanging Christianity: "The Jews in the [Christian] scheme are . . . the earthly agents of the cosmic powers of evil. . . . When a community [viz., Christendom] has been taught over the centuries that it is . . . virtuous to persecute them [viz., the Jews], it is only a step (albeit a large one)" to that speech of Himmler's.

This is like saying "it is only a step (albeit a large one)" from an uncomfortable fever of 100° to a lethal fever of 107°. The step is not from less to more, it is from one kind to another kind altogether. "Only a step (albeit a large one)" papers over a chasm.

I know a man who was a young lawyer in Germany when he was forced to close his office and prepare to emigrate. When his secretary cried, he said, "Don't worry. This sort of thing happens to us every two or three hundred years." He meant being cast down from the heights to the depths, for which there were precedents aplenty in Jewish history. He could not imagine the Holocaust. It lacked precedent.

Maccoby knows, of course, that "the Holocaust . . . had not yet happened in world history." Why did it finally happen, and only in the fifth decade of the twentieth century? He adduces "the continuance into the post-Christian era of deeply-implanted fantasies about the Jews" and "the release afforded by Nazism from all vestiges of the restraint imposed by traditional Christian morality, which had hitherto acted as a counterweight to [anti-Jewish] Christian mythology." But is not "the release ... from ... traditional Christian morality" in a "post-Christian era" only another way of saying that not Christianity but the weakening or supersession of Christianity was responsible for the Holocaust?

A further proof of Christianity's responsibility, he says, is that "unsophisticated ... people in Europe" later reasoned that after all, the Jews "are the Christ-killers, aren't they?" But simple people may have said that out of a simple need for theodicy, the vindication of God's justice. Jews call this *zidduq haddin*, at burials declaring with the Bible, "The Rock, His doing is perfect." In Israel itself simple Jews from Muslim lands have been known to say that the Ashkenazim who perished in the Holocaust must have been very sinful for God to punish them so.

When people who are not simple say such a thing, we have a more serious problem. For the late Rav of Satmar and his disciples, the Holocaust was a visitation upon the whole house of Israel for the rebellion of too many of its sons and daughters against God and His commandments, and for their attaching themselves to the Devil (the "Other Side") and his Zionism. Satmar is not simple, only implacably antimodern. In a modern such a theodicy is particularly hard to stomach. I shall never forget my revulsion, and everyone else's, when to a group of Jewish theologians and writers a professor of philosophy intoned, in an exaggerated East European (mis)pronunciation of the Hebrew, his solution to reconciling Holocaust with God's justice: the penultimate verse of the psalm that a Jew recites more often than any other, the 145th: "The Lord watches over all who love Him, but all the wicked will He destroy."

■   ■   ■

Christianity was hostile to the Jews and Judaism, but when Christianity ruled and was strong, Jews knew subordination, expulsion, even massacre, not Holocaust. If one sentence can summarize Church law and practice over many centuries, it is this: the Jews are to be allowed to live, but not too well.

Obviously, this does not mean that most Jews fared worse than most Christians: think of twelfth-century England or nineteenth-century Russia. Or take literacy. About medieval Western Europe, G. G. Coulton concluded that the average Jewish layman was more literate than not only the average Christian layman but also the average priest, the Christians' specialist in literacy. "Not living too well" is the sort of thing implicit in Casanova's saying that for a doctorate in law he wrote a dissertation on the prohibition of building a synagogue higher than a church. The dissertation may have been fictitious but the prohibition was real.

Muslim countries prohibited Jews from riding horseback. In Jerusalem I once asked a mounted policeman for directions. To talk to him I had to crane my neck, I had to look up to him. A pedestrian has to look up to an equestrian. For Muslims it was unnatural to look up to a Jew, and not only for Muslims. To Christians, Saladin was a foeman worthy of Richard Lion-Heart's steel. After the eviction of the last Crusaders from the Holy Land, Christians of all sorts, Western and Eastern, Latin and Greek and Syrian and Armenian and Coptic, became used to Muslims on horseback protecting the Christian holy places and keeping the peace between the Christian sects. But Jews on horseback? Jewish police protecting Christian holy places and keeping the peace between the Christian sects? A Jewish state in the Holy Land? Unnatural. It occurred to me then that such feelings might help to explain the coldness toward Israel of Christians like the late Bible scholar Father Roland de Vaux, and maybe of the Vatican.

In general harsh in his judgment of Christianity, on one point Maccoby is too tender. It was not "traditional Christian morality" that kept Christendom from killing Jews. Charlemagne did not doubt his Christian morality when he proved the truth of Christianity to the pagan Saxons by killing them. Some centuries later, Charlemagne's successors likewise did not doubt their Christian morality when they disproved the Albigensian heresy by killing the Albigensians. In World War II the Ustashi, Croatian Catholic Christians, murdered as many Serbian Orthodox Christians as they could, and it now appears that the Ustashi were encouraged by Franciscans, whose patron saint, they tell us, would not hurt a fly. More than "traditional Christian morality" it was "Christian mythology," the special place of Jews and Judaism in Christian teaching, that granted the Jews a special privilege of life. In principle, at least, the Inquisition had jurisdiction not over Jews but only over Christian heretics and apostates, actual or suspected, including ex-Jewish Christians and their descendants.

In the Ashkenazi rite, *Av Harahamim* ("Merciful Father") memorializes the Jewish martyrs killed by Crusaders in the Rhineland. It is a prayer for divine retribution, prefiguring in sentiment, if not in art, Milton's "On the Late Massacre in Piedmont": "Avenge, O Lord, thy slaughtered saints" the Waldensians. Ivan G. Marcus (*Prooftexts*, January 1982) summarizes the twelfth-century German churchman Albert of Aix's denunciation:

> ... when the Crusader rabble was itself decimated in Hungary, that disaster was a sign of God's judgment. The Christians who had violated Church law by forcibly converting, not to speak of murdering, Jews were themselves justly punished.

It bears repeating: the Church law that protected Jews embodied "Christian morality" less than it embodied "Christian mythology."

In modern times, with the dethronement or mildening of Christianity in the enlightened parts of Europe, the Jews' privilege of life was replaced by a right to citizenship. Hitler revoked both.

■   ■   ■

Was Hitler a Christian? He was an anti-Semite, and Maccoby tells us that anti-Semitism lies at the heart of Christianity.

The Jews are old, Christianity is old, hatred of the Jews is old. "Anti-Semitism, -ic, -ite" are so new that they do not appear as entries on their own in the *Oxford English Dictionary.* "Anti-Semite," undefined and dated 1881, only illustrates "anti-." ("Semite" mentions "Hebrews, Arabs, Assyrians, and Aramaeans," not Jews in the present.) "Semitic" includes a parenthesis: "(In recent use often *spec.* = Jewish)." For "Semitism" one definition, illustrated by something written in 1885, is "In recent use, Jewish ideas or Jewish influence in politics and society." "Anti-Semitism," therefore, is only a hundred years old in England and only slightly older on the Continent, where the word originated. Why the new name for an old thing?

The thing was not altogether old.

In World War I some German had the bad idea of saying that the British soldiers were militarily contemptible, so they promptly called themselves the Old Contemptibles. That is not how it was with the anti-Semites. They coined the name for themselves, and "anti-Semitism" for what they believed and propagandized. They needed a new name to distinguish their enmity toward the Jews from the older, religious kind. They did not believe that Christianity was truer and better than Judaism, or that Jews were to be guarded against because of their Judaism: "Say this for the old-fashioned Jews, they are easier to recognize and guard against than the modern kind, who are abandoning their Judaism." Those who used the new name believed something new, that the uncreative, parasitic Semitic race endangered the creative, productive Aryan race. The neologism took root and spread, displacing the older "Jew-hatred." Soon people were also using it anachronistically, so to speak, as by applying it to antiquity.

Aside from the troubling anomaly of the New Christians in Spain, tainted indelibly by their Jewish blood, the rule in Christendom was that baptism, which Christians were exhorted to promote zealously, made a Jew into a Christian; but a Nazi ditty went: *"Ob Jud, ob Christ, ist einerlei, / In der Rasse liegt die Schweinerei"* ("Whether the man's a Jew or a Christian makes no difference, it's his race that's filthy"). Many anti-Semites hated Christianity itself as Jewish. Ludendorff, second only to Hindenburg among the Kaiser's war lords, wanted Germans to throw off Semitic Christianity and return as good Teutons to Woden and his pantheon. Neal Ascherson reports (*New York Review,* November 24, 1983) that Klaus Barbie the boy had been a Catholic but that Barbie the member of the Hitler Youth was "committed to anticlerical neopaganism."

Anti-Christian anti-Semites could play down their anti-Christianity in order to make a united front with Christian anti-Semites, and Christian anti-Semites could contrive not to notice the anti-Christianity of people otherwise estimable for their anti-Semitism. The Christian and anti-Christian anti-Semites agreed that the Jews, having by a swindle acquired French/German/etc. citizenship, were now swindling, corrupting, and lording it over the true Frenchmen/Germans/etc.

Hitler the boy was Christian but Hitler the man was anti-Christian. (Remarkably, this enemy of the liberal Enlightenment scorned Judaism and Christianity not like Ludendorff the Teutonizer but like Voltaire the Enlightener.) Hitler was about as Christian as Stalin the ex-seminarian.

■　　■　　■

Grynberg agrees with Maccoby: "the Holocaust was prepared and caused by Christian anti-Semitism."

Grynberg "left Poland in 1967." The late Sam Levenson used to say that Jewish kids don't go to summer camp, they're sent. That is funny. What is less funny is that in 1967, the year when Israel had the impudence to win the Six-Day War, Jews did not leave Poland, they were pushed out. Gentile Poles were happy with Israel's victory because it was a black eye for Moscow and Moscow's puppets in Warsaw: "Our Jews beat their Arabs." Jews were happy because—well, because they found to their surprise that they were still Jews, a little. The Polish government could not banish all those Poles, but it could banish nearly all the Jews.

Between the two world wars, the ratio of Jews to the total population was higher in Poland than anywhere else except Palestine. Jews were Polish in citizenship, but for the most part not in language or culture. Governments were Christian and nationalist. They were also anti-Semitic, some more than others. In a notorious incident in the 1930s, a Polish government did not readmit Polish Jews whom the Nazis had expelled from Germany, but no Christian Polish government ever expelled Polish Jews.

In 1967 no more than one or two Jews were left in Poland for every hundred in 1937. This remnant was Polish in language, culture, and feeling. The government was Marxist, anti-Christian. Christian Polish governments had not expelled un-Polish Polish Jews, but an anti-Christian government expelled Polish Polish, Marxist, anti-Zionist Jews—as "Zionists."

Grynberg reminds us that the Pope visiting Auschwitz repeatedly apostrophized the slain as Jews. In the Soviet Union the anti-Christian authorities have never consented to recognize the slain of Babi Yar as Jews.

In 1968 the Polish army's journal based a good part of its case against "Zionism" on a denial of the Bible's account of the Israelites' sojourn in Egypt and their Exodus under Moses. Even if we concede the relevance of such antiquarianism, the argument remains odd. Marxists pride themselves on being *wissenschaftlich,* scientific, and modern *Wissenschaft* of the Bible and the ancient Near East, whether practiced by believers or by unbelievers, Jews or Christians, is skeptical of what

the Bible says about Egypt and Exodus. Marxists might therefore be expected to crow that even believers, so long as they
make any claim to *Wissenschaft,* must pooh-pooh the Bible
as history. Instead those Polish Marxists chose to put forth a
bit of anti-Semitica situated not in any pretense to modern
scholarship, nor in any Christian tradition however anti-Jewish, but in a pagan tradition stretching back to Tacitus and
finally to Manetho, an Egyptian priest who lived some centuries before Christianity. Countering the Jews' version of
their history with his anti-Jewish version, Manetho said that
a thousand years earlier the Israelites had left Egypt not tri-
umphantly but shamefully, expelled as lepers.

The main reason why the Polish Marxists repeated this
ancient nonsense, preferring it to traditional Christian anti-
Judaism and to modern Bible scholarship, must be that Marx
himself had repeated it. Only that tradition about Egypt and
Exodus derides the Israelites. Both in antiquity and in modern times it has been used to legitimate enlightened distaste
for the Jews.

Just a few intellectual generations before Marx, mediated
to him by the French Enlightenment of the eighteenth century and radical German Protestant theology of the early nineteenth, were the English deists, of whom Thomas Morgan was
particularly nasty. On one of the Ten Plagues he wrote:

> And perhaps, one Reason why the Egyptian Sorcerers could
> not create Lice, might be because they had none about them,
> and the Israelites were better stock'd; for according to all Antiq-
> uity, Leprosy, Scabs, and Lice, were some of the Plagues with
> which these Shepherds, before their Expulsion had infested
> the Egyptians.

Traditionalist Christians might hate Jews and Judaism, but
none ever jeered at Israelite sacred history and especially its
core, the Exodus. They believed that that history now belonged
to them, the new Israel of the spirit, having passed to them

from the Jews, the old, disinherited Israel of the flesh. Only an anti-Christian could laugh about "Scabs, and Lice" and "Expulsion," and only in reliance upon the anti-Jewish pagans of "all Antiquity."

Having suffered from anti-Christian anti-Semitism, Grynberg condemns Christian anti-Semitism. And though, like Maccoby, Grynberg denounces abstractions, for him too Hitler is hardly more than an abstraction.

■ ■ ■

In a way, it is easier to understand the Christians who blame Christianity for the Holocaust than the Jews who blame it. Historian or theologian, a Christian can feel that for Christians it is morally insufficient to strike the balance dispassionately and judge that Christianity in the twentieth century is not primarily responsible for the Holocaust. But there is more. Perhaps without being aware of it, Christians may be moved to say that Christianity is responsible because responsibility implies power, and they would rather think Christianity guilty and still powerful than guiltless and powerless. Be that as it may, such people recognize an obligation of Christian teachers to lead their fellow Christians in contrition and in confession of sin.

One-sidedness in preaching need not be a vice, and historically Christians have had less cause than Jews to fear being overheard by the Others, the unfriendly majority. When the Israeli commission of inquiry found Israel's government and army indirectly responsible for the killings by Lebanese Christians in Shatila and Sabra, many Jews outside Israel were upset. They thought, "That may be all very well to say in Israel, it's a Jewish state. But here, what will the Gentiles think? Won't they just love hearing Jews say that Jews are murderers!" Catholics amid Protestants may have corresponding reticences, and Protestants amid Catholics, but seldom Christians as such. If Christians overemphasize the guilt of Christianity, that does

them honor. Let them by all means continue—provided, however, that in emphasizing how anti-Semitic Christianity was
in the past they do not deny how anti-Semitic neopaganism
can be in the present. Chastising what is left of Christendom,
some Christians now tend to be if not pro-neopagan then at
least anti-anti-neopagan.

So, precisely because Christians, or most of them, would
rather not hear about Christian anti-Semitism, their teachers
ought to tell them about it. Applying the principle of telling
people what they would rather not hear, what should Jewish
teachers tell Jews? But first, what do we like and what do we
dislike to hear?

John G. Gager's *Origins of Anti-Semitism* is an impressive addition to scholarship. The book's substantive findings
are evenhanded:

> Only in a highly restricted sense can Western anti-Semitism
> be said to originate in pagan and Christian antiquity. The pre-
> sumption of a universal anti-Semitism in antiquity, pagan or
> Christian, has been made possible only by suppressing, ignor-
> ing, or misinterpreting the mass of nonconforming evidence.

That is Gager the scholar, the authority on early Christian
society. Gager the citizen says that as a concerned but disin-
terested outsider to the Jewish-Christian debate—doubtless
meaning that he is not a Jew and no longer is a Christian—he
thinks it necessary to restore balance by emphasizing the good
in pagan antiquity, on acount of the prevalent "belief in a uniformly anti-Semitic pagan antiquity . . . [which] has in different ways served the interests of both Christians and Jews."

It is Gager the citizen that I am not sure I agree with fully.
The reason he suggests for Christians' belief in a uniformly
anti-Semitic pagan antiquity is plausible: "It has served to
absolve Christianity of full responsibility for anti-Semitism
in the West." Less plausible are his finding that Jews share the
belief and the reason he suggests for it: "Pagan persecution is

held to have greatly strengthened the cohesiveness which has enabled Judaism to survive."

A priori, Gager should be right. The Jews' three pilgrimage festivals celebrate redemption from Egyptian bondage and triumph over that primordial, archetypal pagan oppressor, Pharaoh. Moses' Song at the Sea is part of the Jewish prayer book, to be recited every morning of the year. In the book of Exodus we are commanded to remember the Sabbath because of Creation, in Deuteronomy to keep the Sabbath because of our bondage in Egypt. Accordingly, our Sabbath benediction is in commemoration—*zikkaron, zekher*—of both. Purim celebrates victory over the pagan enemy Haman, and Hanukkah over the pagan enemy Antiochus. So much for our celebrations. Our mournings—primarily Tishah be'Av—recall the destruction of the First Temple by the pagan Nebuchadnezzar and of the Second by the pagan Titus.

What an outsider can miss is that the very Jews who rejoice on the feasts and mourn on the fasts can be taken aback when asked to remember that all these enemies were pagan, and that all but Titus were pre-Christian. The unstated assumption, by no means limited to the ignorant and unsophisticated, is that Gentiles = Christians. (I had to keep reminding myself that a Baghdadi Jew's reminiscences about Gentiles were about Muslims.)

Maccoby says that behind "the world's" transparently anti-Jewish denunciation of Israel for killings perpetrated by Christians is, again, Christianity. But even better than Americans he as a European should know that that denunciatory world was mostly the world of leftist parties and journalists, nearly all Gentile but few Christian. After terrorists attacked a Roman synagogue, wounding many and killing a little boy, a remorseful Italian journalist cried out that the media, slipping from anti-Israel to anti-Jewish, had in effect incited the attack. I do not think he was referring chiefly to *L'Osservatore Romano*.

■ ■ ■

Once, speaking in Israel to mostly Modern Orthodox Jews, I said: If the Church had wished, no more Jews than Albigensians would have survived in Christendom. The Church did not want us to live well, but it let us live. In the Hitler years, who would not have welcomed back the rule of the Church? Then I used the Polish example to make the point that anti-Christian anti-Semitism continues to be worse than the Christian kind.

This was received without enthusiasm. "How about Pobedonostsev?" someone asked. Pobedonostsev, the lay procurator of the Holy Synod of the Russian Orthodox Church in the reigns of Alexander II and Nicholas II, believed that the best solution to "the Jewish problem" in Russia would be for a third of the Jews to emigrate, a third to be baptized, and a third to starve to death. (He also despised the West and Catholicism, prizing autocracy and caesaropapism in state and church.)

I answered: Practically every Jew in the world longed for an end to the czarist regime. With the revolution of 1905, Pobedonostsev was dismissed. He died soon afterward. A few years later still, anti-Semites brought Mendel Beilis to trial on a charge of killing a child for the Christian blood that they said Jews use in preparing *matzot* for Passover. The jury in the czarist court exonerated Beilis and set him free.

After forty years and two world wars, in Communist Czechoslovakia, Rudolf Slansky and seven others officially identified as "of Jewish origin," fervent Communists and anti-Zionists, were charged with treason in the service of Zionism, declared guilty, and hanged. Then, in Russia proper, came the Doctors' Plot, in which Jewish doctors were accused of having conspired, in the service of Zionism, Wall Street, and the CIA, to poison the leaders of the Soviet state and the Communist Party. The Jews of the Soviet Union are convinced that only Stalin's providential death spared them to live their wonted life of anxious inferiority.

In the old Russia the Czar and his entourage abetted the Black Hundreds and the other pogromchiks, and the Okhrana, the secret police, concocted the *Protocols of the Learned Elders of Zion,* still potent for evil. But in that Russia the Jews, beset by hostility and hardship, doubt and division, were nevertheless not kept from living a communal and cultural life unsurpassed anywhere, before or since, for variety, intensity, and achievement, from the most traditional to the most revolutionary, in Yiddish, Russian, and Hebrew. And the Jews of the Czar's empire could leave. In their many hundreds of thousands they did leave, a few to prepare the way for the state of Israel and more to become the parents and grandparents of most Jews in the English-speaking countries and Latin America today. The anti-Christian Russia of Stalin and his legatees almost makes the Czar's Christian Russia look good.

Later on, a man told me that I had persuaded some minds but no hearts, because people are not stirred by a demonstration that something is less bad than something else. Besides, he said, the new, anti-Christian anti-Semites are hypocritical. They denounce their quarry not as Jews but as Zionists or rootless cosmopolitans, and somehow they benefit from their hypocrisy. Not so the old, Christian ones. Remember Admiral Horthy, regent of Hungary between the wars, unfriendly to the Nazis. After World War I, when the Young Men's Christian Association sent a relief mission from America to Hungary, Horthy shook the YMCA representative's hand and said, "Glad to meet a fellow anti-Semite." More often than not, the word Christian—*christlich, chrétien*—in the name of a European movement or party meant anti-Semitic.

The man speaking to me had been young in Poland in the 1930s. He said that while he could not deny anti-Christian anti-Semitism, for him only Christian anti-Semitism was real: Jewish benches in the universities, and assaults by the student anti-Semites, and frightened alertness in the Easter season. He was a teacher and did not fail to tell his students what he had seen and experienced.

∎ ∎ ∎

Loyal children of the Enlightenment think that irreligion's ideas are good, so they are slow to admit that its deeds can be bad. As Marxists and *marxisants* can say that the Soviet Union is not truly socialist, so they will say that true Marxism/socialism cannot be anti-Semitic, that it has not failed but has never been tried. (G. K. Chesterton said that Christianity had not failed, it had never been tried.) Do Marx's own words convict him of being a foul-mouthed anti-Semite and racist? Ignore it, deny it, explain it away. ("Newton may have been loony about the numbers in the Book of Daniel, but he was a great genius anyway.") Does George L. Mosse's meticulous examination of the evidence prove that "revolutionary socialism desired to put an end to Jews and Judaism"? Ignore it, deny it, explain it away. Do leftists, in pain, report anti-Semitism on the Left? Forget it. By definition, enemies must be on the Right, the political and above all the Religious Right.

Liberals can exhibit a similar tropism. For many American Jews the enemy is the Moral Majority, never mind that it is pro-Israel and that its morality is close to traditional Jewish morality. Though some may have a less than unshakable faith in prayer—or, for that matter, in God—few things give them greater pleasure than the chance to express righteous indignation when an old-fashioned fundamentalist blurts out that God does not listen to the prayer of a Jew. Probably that fundamentalist is an unreconstructed upholder of a classical Christian doctrine, no salvation outside the Church (or Matthew's "no one knows the Father except the Son, and any one to whom the Son chooses to reveal him"). Probably he would say about the prayer of a Muslim—or a Catholic?— what he said about the prayer of a Jew. That does not matter.

He has furnished an excuse for continuing to locate danger in Christianity, especially the Christian Right.

Devotees of "liberation" theology, and most conspicuously the World Council of Churches, are pro–Third World (except Afghanistan), pro-PLO, anti-West, anti-Israel. In France an esteemed Catholic journal, highbrow and leftist, faults Rome for being backward about pretty nearly everything, with one exception. Because the journal hates Israel, it faults Vatican II for being soft on Judaism. About Shatila and Sabra the prevailing tone was, "What can you expect of people whose religion is Judaism?" We are not to suppose that the journal is bigoted or anti-Semitic. It has great respect for Islam, and Arabs are Semites too, aren't they?

Perhaps we should think of such people rather as Christian leftists than as leftist Christians, because the common element in anti-Israel/anti-Jewish animus has long been not Christianity but leftism. As in the 1930s, when the farcical Red Dean of Canterbury flabbergasted even the cynic who was the Soviet ambassador in London by asking him to convey to Moscow the Dean's felicitations on Stalin's splendid victory at the polls, so today, Christian leftists—and Jewish ones—are fellow travelers of anti-Christian leftists, far more powerful and numerous.

■　■　■

Let me summarize, fill in some lacunae, and draw some conclusions.

- Hitler made the Holocaust because he wanted to make it. Anti-Semitism did not make him make it.
- Hitler was ex-Christian and anti-Christian.
- There was much and there remains some Christian anti-Semitism. Hitler's anti-Semitism was anti-Christian.
- Marxist anti-Semitism also is anti-Christian.

- Anti-Christian anti-Semitism is descended ideologically from pagan disdain for Judaism and the Jews, and emotionally from Christian hatred of Judaism and the Jews.
- In Hitler's time the world capital of anti-Semitism was Berlin. Since then it has been Moscow.
- Jews now have more to fear from anti-Christians than from Christians, and from the Christian Left than from the Christian Right.

(1984)

In the Light
of Israel's Victory

IT'S EASY TO FORGET. Here we are, some months later (October 1967), and the news from Israel is of headache and annoyance, trouble and difficulty. We have almost forgotten the unbelievable victory, and all the more our fear and depression in those weeks before the actual fighting broke out, when Nasser was tightening his noose. Political metaphors from thirty years ago kept running through our minds and conversations. We said, Munich; we said, Czechoslovakia; we said, salami tactics. As the days drew on we asked ourselves, "What are they waiting for? Why didn't they jump on Sharm el-Sheikh right away? The longer they wait, the worse it will be."

Some of us surprised ourselves and each other by our concern. Thirty and forty years ago we wouldn't have felt that way. Not to be parochial Jews was our pride. Now there is less of that kind of antiparochialism than there used to be—not none at all; only less.

In the same way, there is less self-hate than there used to be. The surprise is that some Jews still had to find a reassurance about themselves in the military valor of the Israelis. One would have thought that that been taken care of in 1948, with the Israeli War of Independence. Israel, it then became clear, provided for the Jews of the United States and other countries like it a kind of contemporary pioneer or cowboy ancestry, reassuring us by showing us what we wanted and needed to have shown—that while Jews can be pretty good with a fountain pen and briefcase, they can also if necessary be pretty good with a rifle or a tank.

This summer, an unreconstructed antiparochialist Jewish scholar was sarcastic. The Jews talk a great game of internationalism, he said, but when the chips are down they are nationalist. The answer to this is: not always, only now. Those of his age and mine aren't happy about where our internationalism led us a generation ago. That the Nazis wanted to murder every Jew they could get their hands on was the last thing about Nazism that interested us. For us the big question, the question that called forth all our dialectical virtuosity, was, Is Nazism the final stage of capitalism? The middle-aged don't want to incur *that* guilt again.

As for the young, I think that what happened to them a few months ago was a sudden realization that genocide, anti-Semitism, a desire to murder Jews—all these things were not merely what one had been taught about a bad, stupid past, not merely the fault of elders who are almost a different species. Those things were real and present. Internationalist, antiparochial young Jews had taken it for granted that the Jews are the fat cats of this world and that no concern need be wasted on them. Concern should go to the wretched of the earth. Suddenly the Jews of Israel were seen to be potentially as wretched as anyone can be.

An aside to the Jewish young: Each generation finds its own good reason for not being concerned about the Jews. Now it's that we're fat cats. Maybe so—though not all are—but earlier in the century most Jews were undeniably skinny. That made no difference. From prison Rosa Luxemburg once wrote a friend: "Why do you pester me with your Jewish sorrow? There is no room in my heart for the Jewish troubles." The sorrow and troubles of others had filled all the room in her heart. On this J. L. Talmon has commented: "Twenty-five years later, after the Germans had occupied it, there was not a single Jew left alive in Rosa's native Zamosc, which was also the home-town of I. L. Peretz."

Today internationalism is less automatically an O.K. word or idea than it used to be. What is internationalism today; who is internationalist? Nasser? Nasser called for genocide. Old-fashioned pro-Sovietism? The Soviets were disgusting in the United Nations, cynical, even anti-Semitic. At best they were coarsely philistine, unable to understand that the things they said were repulsive—especially the repeated equation of the Israelis with the Nazis.

In fact, the Soviets' calling the Israelis Nazis was itself Nazi-like. The Nazis told their lies for more than the usual reason, that they hoped to profit from telling them. They told lies because they were sadists. Lying, and above all their kind of lying, is a sadistic gratification: it twists, it tortures, it murders the truth. And this sadistic gratification can have an added, utilitarian advantage. By appalling and terrifying opponents, it can paralyze them. It can scare them into submission, or into the kind of weakness that makes their defeat probable.

Here were Soviet authorities harping on Nazism and calling Israel Nazi, but in their own country they themselves have consistently repressed the truth about what Nazism did to the Jews. About a year ago, a pathetic little victory was won for liberalism in the Soviet arts: the government allowed a book about Babi Yar to be published. Now even that is in question. The author was careful to say that the Nazis murdered others as well, besides Jews, but he also said that the Nazis found collaborators among the Soviet citizenry. The patriots, displeased with that unpatriotic statement, are charging him with having exaggerated the Jews' suffering—a grossly counter-revolutionary thing to do.

In this country, grumbling about the Jewish masses' desertion of internationalism was heard from a Communist spokesman, a political coprophage of many years' standing.

His kind of internationalism hasn't changed. A few months before Hitler double-crossed Stalin and invaded Russia, the Union for Democratic Action was founded at a meeting where extraordinary speakers spoke. The first was R. H. Tawney, of *Religion and the Rise of Capitalism.* Referring to a neutrality that was then fashionable, he said it reminded him of the provincial lord mayor who, being invested with the insignia of office, promised the townsmen that he would be neither partial, on the one hand, nor, on the other hand, impartial. Reinhold Niebuhr was the second speaker. Of what the Communists called internationalism—in those days they were denouncing the British imperialist war—he observed that not much can be said for the man who believes, "My country, right or wrong," but even less for the man who believes, "The other fellow's country, right or wrong."

■ ■ ■

Arabs, Castroites, and some of the New Left here have been saying that Israel is an artificial state. When intellectuals were the leaders of the Algerian independence movement, before the toughs had banished or imprisoned them, they admitted that Algerian consciousness was new: like the demarcation of the territory itself, it had been called into being by the French rulers and oppressors. Yet today no leftist would argue that Algeria is artificial. Israel is artificial—a country whose people have a consciousness of historical distinctiveness thousands of years old, affirmed in a literature that is ancient and living; a country, moreover, whose citizens identify their fate with its fate, and who were more determined than their government itself to pay the price of war for continued independence.

In 1967 Jews of all kinds, from the most parochial to the most internationalist, were resolved that there should be no more genocide against the Jews—particularly against the Israelis, whose Jewish weight, so to speak, is greater than that of other Jews. We thought of the Syrians in Haifa or Tel Aviv and felt sick. Compared with the Syrians, the Egyptians are calm and reasonable.

The change was best seen in France, and precisely among the French Jews of old stock. One of these people has said about himself and the others like him, "We aren't assimilationist, we're just assimilated." In 1917 they (or their parents) were dismayed by the Balfour Declaration. They were zealous, spirit-of-'89 Frenchmen.

What was supposed to be in the French interest they held to be in theirs, and they would never oppose their government out of mere Jewish interest. In 1967 they opposed their government. The French government was neutral against Israel and the old-stock French Jews were for Israel. Experienced in what genocide against Jews is, they would have no more of it. About thirty years ago Maurice Samuel debated a Reform rabbi of the old school. The rabbi: "Mr. Samuel, how would you feel if you were an Arab?" Mr. Samuel: "Rabbi, how would you feel if you were a Jew?" Which doesn't mean that we're anti-Arab or don't want to be friends with the Arabs. We would like to help them and be friends with them. But how? They won't even talk to us. We feel for them in their humiliation, but what can we do? Our charity would only compound their humiliation.

In short, the Jews seem to be changing a little; but not as it may have been thought we would. For example, if by Zionism is meant agreement with Zionist ideology, we are no more Zionist than we used to be. Two or three days before the shots were fired, a midwestern professor told me about a plan he had for airlifting Israeli children to the United States so that they would be out of danger when war broke out. He was sure that he could place five hundred children in his city. That was a personal undertaking. In France it was the official Jewish community that got ready to receive Israeli children. According to Zionist ideology, this was topsy-turvy: Israel is supposed to be the refuge.

■   ■   ■

How then shall we describe the change that seems to be taking place among us? What has been happening is a slow bringing into consciousness of a disillusionment that has been going on for a long time now with the characteristic outlook of modern, enlightened Jews. It is a shift from the general to the particular, from the abstract to the concrete.

The disillusionment is greatest with our old idea that our enemies aren't on the Left—which is to say, that all our enemies are on the Right. For most practical purposes, that is where our enemies were in the nineteenth century. The French Revolution had equality for the Jews as a corollary. We were for the Revolution and its extension, and the Right was against. Now the location of our enemies is not quite so simple. We have enemies on the Right, but also on the Left; and sometimes it is hard to distinguish between Right and Left. Sometimes our enemies on the Right and Left are happy to cooperate with each other against us.

Among all Arab countries, the one least our enemy is Tunisia, in the moderate center. Bourguiba jailed the ringleaders of a mob that wanted some fun with a pogrom. In Morocco the right-wing Istiqlal called for a purge of Jews from the civil service. So did the head of the left-wing labor movement, until the king jailed him. Nasser is supposed to be of the Left. After the war his newspapers went back to publishing the *Protocols of the Elders of Zion*.

Actually, there was a more than negligible amount of anti-Semitism on the Left in the nineteenth century, as the historian and economist Edmund Silberner has shown. August Bebel had to warn the German workers that anti-Semitism is the socialism of fools, and a reasonably firm anti-anti-Semitism doesn't date from much before the time when Jean Jaurès was able to persuade the French Socialists, against important opposition, that the Dreyfus case wasn't just an internal squabble of the bourgeoisie. As for the *Protocols,* their Stalinist version was the scenario of the Jewish Doctors' Plot, which only Stalin's death kept from being staged. In Stalinist Czechoslovakia the scenario was staged in court, and Slansky and others were hanged. Of those who weren't hanged but only imprisoned, the survivors seem to have been rehabilitated—that is the technical term—but only personally and individually; the government and the party have to this day not retracted the *Protocols*-like (and even racist) accusations, propaganda, and testimony that accompanied those trials.

In the summer of 1967 the Soviet authorities started another propaganda campaign that made you wonder whether Stalin wasn't alive and in hiding, in the Soviet office of Jewish affairs. The article in the pro-Soviet *Nouvel observateur* that Theodore Draper quoted in *Commentary* (August 1967) represents "a high Soviet official" as saying:

> ... some of our leaders began thinking of taking the risk of limited military action on behalf of Egypt within the framework of a "prudent challenge" to the United States. However, this solution was finally rejected. (As elsewhere, the pressure of Jewish opinion made its weight felt in the USSR right up to the leading circles.)

There speaks the anti-Semite, who knows that the inmost secret of things is the Jewish conspiracy. This high Soviet official and Marxist can imagine no other reason for his leaders' avoiding an insanely rash adventure than "the pressure of Jewish opinion." In the Soviet Union, the pressure of Jewish opinion—a melancholy joke.

India is generally held to be of the Left. In the United Nations, India came up with a remarkable theory of international relations. India said to Israel: "If someone is strangling you, you have no right to shoot in self-defense. You have a right to shoot only if shooting is the method your killer has chosen." What India didn't say, because it hardly needed to be said, was that this applied to Israel alone. Certainly India wouldn't adopt it for herself, as in her relations with Pakistan. Whoever supposed that hypocritical, self-righteous moralism was essentially Western, because a byproduct of biblical monotheism—"the Judeo-Christian tradition"—must have been wrong. Look at India.

In the United States, later, the Student Non-violent Coordinating Committee—what's in a name?—brought this forth: "Zionists lined up Arab victims and shot them in the back in cold blood. This [a blurred photograph] is the Gaza Strip, Palestine, not Dachau, Germany." Then followed a few kind words about the Rothschilds. (The fascist National States' Rights Party's *Thunderbolt* said the same things, at the same time.) SNCC anti-Semitic? Of course not. In answer to questions, it explained that it doesn't oppose all Jews, "only Jewish oppressors"—including, besides Israel, "those Jews in the little Jew shops in the [Negro] ghetto." Say what you will about Marxism-Leninism-Maoism-Fidelism-Fanonism, what other mode of analysis would have been able to trace the causes of Negro oppression so unerringly to the real centers of economic and political power in international colonialism-imperialism and American capitalism—Israel and the little Jew shops? The New Left hasn't much use for such old monuments as Bebel. Of what pertinence can it be to the young that the middle-aged remember a Nazi Left—the Strassers and their gang—which was anticapitalist and anti-(British) imperialist? Mostly, the New Left is back on the pro-Nasser and anti-Israel track.

■　■　■

If we are becoming disillusioned with the Left, that could mean we are becoming more conservative. Hence, perhaps, some of our Gentile neighbors and friends' irony at our expense during the excitement. The irony wasn't necessarily malicious. In general, it was a way of saying: "Welcome back to common humanity. Your old enthusiasms always seemed strange to us, but your present enthusiasm we can understand very well. Naturally, a Jew would be worried about Israel's danger and rejoice over its victory. That is the point. You Jews are becoming more natural."

More natural, yes; conservative, not quite. In England the Conservatives were said to be the stupid party. (But if the Liberals were so clever, why are they dead?) In the United States the conservatives are the stingy party. The Jews still belong to the generous party, as is proved by the uproar in Wayne, New Jersey, where we were accused of being liberals, always voting for more liberal school budgets. The Jews of Wayne didn't attempt to deny it. They said the purpose and the effect of the statement were anti-Semitic, not that its substance was false.

What then are we becoming? To use symbols from the English political tradition, let us say that having been Radicals, we are slowly moving toward the Whigs (left-wing Whigs, of course). Or, to use an American symbolism of persons, we may say that having been partisans of Jefferson, we are growing more friendly to Lincoln.

Maybe it is as Whigs that we are learning new respect for old wisdom—such as that admonition of Oxenstierna's: "My son, if you only knew with how little wisdom the world is ruled." To the degree that we are not incapacitated for living in a practical world, we have always known that to be true, and we have made allowances for it in our own affairs and the affairs of government. We have done what engineers do. We have assigned to future events a Murphy factor—a margin of safety to guard against the accident and error and silliness that are bound to befall any human enterprise. (Engineers, told that a bridge should be able to bear a load of N tons, design it to bear $3N$ tons.) But here was a case where even an extravagant Murphy factor was not enough to guard against the surprise of human stupidity. Nasser deliberately goads the Israelis into acting militarily. He knows that a shooting war is about to break out, that it must break out. He isn't quite sure whether his men or the Israelis will pull the trigger first, but he knows that someone is about to pull it. Having done all this, and knowing all this, he is caught with all his planes on the ground.

There is the folk wisdom: too smart is dumb. General de Gaulle was too smart. A machiavellian, he overlooked Machiavelli's caution against being caught practicing machiavellianism in broad daylight. "Put not your trust in princes": everyone knows that governments will break their word when it suits them. But de Gaulle went too far. Who will now be prepared to give him even the small amount of confidence that earlier might have been given to him? Having so publicly betrayed Israel, how can he expect anyone else to believe him?

An old illusion was that war is good, to which moderns and liberals responded with the illusion that any peace is better than any war. It has been a long time now, at least since Rupert Brooke, that anybody has been able to hear that line of Horace's, *dulce et decorum est pro patria mori*—sweet and fitting it is to die for your country—without gagging or giggling. The proper stance has been black humor: *Catch-22*. But rather less so for the Israelis. Theirs was no artificial state, no absurd Moloch. Its citizens were willing to die for it because they knew that if it died, so would they and their families and their hopes. Not much alienation there. One almost envies them.

It is an old, sad truth: a state acquires its legitimacy—the opposite of artificiality—by the blood that its citizens shed in its defense; as the early Christians said, the blood of the martyrs is the seed of the Church. An elite acquires its legitimacy by being prepared to die in a higher proportion than others. Israel's elite died disproportionately. The war dead included many majors and colonels.

■　■　■

Modern, enlightened people, and especially Jews, have generally had a certain amount of contempt for the military enterprise. Our two great culture-heroes, Einstein and Freud, were notably contemptuous. What business is war for an intelligent man? (Note that this is bourgeois. Engels' friends called him "the General" because of his interest in military theory; Lenin annotated Clausewitz; Trotsky commanded the Red Army; Mao made the Long March and said that power grows from the barrel of a gun.) Now, for people like us, the Israeli generals are redeeming the military reputation. It isn't easy to belittle what they did, or to upstage them.

One reads that the Israelis are a major military power in the Middle East. One reads that they have the best tactical air force in the world. Unbelievable. How could they have become such good soldiers? They had no living martial tradition. Peaceable men can become warriors because of love of country, and the roots of the Israeli army today lie in the more or less underground Haganah of twenty and thirty years ago; but while the Haganah could train company commanders, it couldn't train a general staff. Where does the skill of the Israeli generals come from?

It remains true that the military temptation is a certain kind of stupidity. Fortunately the Israelis haven't lost the old Jewish suspicion of *goyim-nakhes*—roughly, "Gentile fun." This expression is to be found in *Ulysses,* Joyce having learned it from his friend Svevo, a modern Jew of the Hapsburg Empire who remembered some scraps of moribund German Yiddish. (The East European phrasing would be *goyish nakhes.*) The first time I actually heard it used in speech was when an Israeli official, of German birth and early education, told me about a visit he had made at the Pentagon's invitation to a crack unit of the United States Army. Mostly he was impressed, but the spit and polish, snappy saluting, marching to the words and tune of a special song—all these struck him as *goyim-nakhes.*

When he said that, I remembered when the idea behind the words had become clear to me—at, of all things, a not very good movie of Walter Scott's *Ivanhoe.* To defend Rebecca against an accusation of witchcraft, Ivanhoe fights the Templar Front de Boeuf. So that was what it was like when knighthood was in flower, I thought—grown men in iron, mounted on horses in iron, hitting each other with axes and huge swords, the metal clanging on metal making the whole thing sound like a machine shop. Isaac of York in the stands, looking scared and disgusted, seemed to me the only adult there. Maybe it is to avoid *goyim-nakhes* that the Israeli army affects sloppiness and informal manners.

If our respect for fighting and military men has gone up, for talking and diplomats it has gone down. Those were weeks when we couldn't tear ourselves away from the proceedings at the United Nations. At home we compulsively watched television, in our cars we kept the radio on, to work we brought portables. We had no mind for anything else, and it wasn't edifying. You asked yourself how grown men could sit there and pretend to take it seriously. Business was transacted somewhere, off in a corner, but the diplomats had to be physically present at the open sessions, pretending to listen to words—countless words, words innumerable—that were mostly meaningless and often malignant. It appeared to me then that the career of diplomat might not be much superior, for a grown man, to the career of king. What can a diplomat learn from that sort of thing that is better than what the Duke of Windsor says he learned from his experience as Prince of Wales and King Edward VIII? The Duke of Windsor says that he learned never to pass up a chance to sit down, or to go to the toilet.

In America the UN has had few friends more devoted than the Jews. Now we know not only that the UN can be no better than the states of which it is composed—including the so-called nonaligned nations, scurrying about on their little Soviet errands—but also that the organization itself, quite apart from the members, is slightly lower than the angels. "U Thant's war" is unfair—about the most that can be said for him. Ralph Bunche was loyal to Thant—about the most that can be said for *him*.

We relearned the old truth that you can depend only on yourself: Israel had promises and friends, but even if it hadn't wanted to fight on its own, it would have had to. We relearned the old, hard truth that only you can feel your own pain. Who has really cared about the Christian Assyrians? Does anyone know whether any Christian Assyrians are left alive? More Christian clergymen worry about the whooping crane than about the Christian Assyrians. When the last speaker of Old Prussian died, and the last speaker of Cornish, did anyone care? Did any Roman care when the last speaker of Etruscan died?

■   ■   ■

Jews who maintain relationships with the Christian clergy were taken aback by the generally reserved attitude of official Christendom toward Israel in its hour of greatest peril. Why the surprise? Christian ecclesiastics have an interest in the Arabs, whether institutional or theological. Through their eyes the Christians could really not see what through our eyes we saw as most urgently obvious. We saw the incommensurability of Israeli and Arab war aims. We saw that the Arabs wanted to destroy Israel—which is to say, to destroy the Israelis. They saw Israeli prowess and Arab refugees.

What I am about to say, a Jew really shouldn't say to Jews. When we talk with each other about Arab refugees, we shouldn't defend ourselves against charges of heartlessness. We should leave that to our friends. Among ourselves we should remind each other how often we are commanded to love the stranger, not to wrong him or oppress him, and to have one law for him and for the home-born, because having been strangers in the land of Egypt we know the heart of the stranger. Having been refugees, we should know what it is to be a refugee.

But our friends aren't saying it and it needs to be said. Those who had to flee Bolshevik Russia or Nazi Germany were refugees, because there was no other Russian or German country to receive them. The Arabs are, or should be, more like the

Greeks from Turkey after World War I. If the Greeks in Greece had not received the Turkish Greeks, there would have been a Greek refugee problem, but the Grecian Greeks couldn't bring themselves to deny refuge to the Turkish Greeks. After the partition of India there were Muslim and Hindu refugee problems, until Pakistan absorbed the Muslims and India absorbed the Hindus. Neither the Muslims nor the Hindus could bring themselves to deny refuge to their fellows from across the border. The West Germans couldn't bring themselves to deny refuge to their fellows from across several borders. Only the Arabs have been able to do it, for almost twenty years. Therefore they have had a triumph. The Arabs turn their backs on other Arabs and the opinion of the world agrees that the Israelis are at fault. Israel, which receives Jews from the Arab lands, in a de facto exchange of populations, is condemned for the Arab refugees.

From a certain point of view, the suspicion of Israelis about the intention of Israeli Arabs shows greater human respect for them than the liberal urging of people like us for Arab integration into Israeli society. Your suspicious Israeli has enough respect for the Arabs to believe that their sentiments aren't determined by a comparison of earning power under an Israeli and an Arab government.

Now the war has been won and humanitarians have their fears and worries over Israeli oppression refreshed by every news report about the looting of a dozen kerosene stoves. No one stops to think any more what victorious Arabs would have done.

A distinguished Protestant theologian wrote a letter to the editor of the *New York Times* condemning "Israel's assault on her Arab neighbors." All, he said, "stand aghast at Israel's onslaught, the most violent, ruthless (and successful) aggression since Hitler's Blitzkrieg .... aiming not at victory but at annihilation." The most revealing things an intelligent man can say are his foolish things. Using Nazi analogies and direct references ("Hitler's Blitzkrieg"), this man implies that the Israelis are Nazis. He actually says that the Israelis wanted to annihilate the Arabs. A learned man, he knows what "annihilation" means. It means making nothing (*nihil*) out of something, destroying utterly. His emotions make him condemn the Israelis for a war aim that was not theirs but, as he concedes, the Arabs'. It was a letter mailed in haste, and the writer must have wished he could recall it. (He was answered by another Protestant theologian, a former student of his, who was not so much pro-Israel or anti-Arab as anti-anti-Semitic.)

■   ■   ■

The letter was a reaction to a stimulus—a rabbi's persistence, after the Israeli victory, in blaming the Christian churches for their indifference to the probable fate of Israel's Jews. Now, in our more Whiggish mood, we can see that it wasn't reasonable to expect American ecclesiastics to take our peril as seriously as we did.

These are only innocent Americans. For them, what Hitler did is true but not real. Having failed to understand what Hitler did in fact, they could hardly be expected to understand what the Arabs only wanted to do. Europeans understood better—clergymen and leftists together. To be sure, Bertrand Russell and Ralph Schoenman were indignant about Israeli aggression; but they aren't European, never having experienced a Nazi occupation. Jean-Paul Sartre wasn't anti-Israel. In the Communist countries, and even in the Communist parties in other European countries, the official anti-Israel line was unpopular.

The fluttery censoriousness of certain Christian clergymen comes through nicely in a satire by Michael Frayn, a letter to "My dear Israel" from "Your affectionate Great-aunt Britain," in the *Observer*, London—though Frayn had others in mind, as well:

...I have ... felt obliged to condemn your *unseemly haste* in opening hostilities [and] your insistence on *winning* the war—particularly in such a brash and violent fashion.... to insist upon defeating your opponents is a discourtesy which they may find *very hard to forgive*.... What makes your behavior all the more perplexing is that when the war commenced you enjoyed the approval and sympathy of polite society as a whole. There you stood, surrounded on all sides by greatly superior hostile forces, whose proclaimed intention was to destroy you utterly. Everybody was *deeply touched!* ... We shouldn't have let you down! If things had gone badly, we had ships standing by which could have evacuated *several thousand* Israeli survivors—who would have had the *unreserved sympathy* of the entire world! ...

Now we can be tolerant of this sort of thing. As poker players say, winners crack jokes and losers snarl, "Deal the cards." We can admit to ourselves that this behavior is normal. Are we much better? Think of the Armenians. What did I ever know about the Armenians, or what sorrow did I ever feel for them? I don't suppose I had ever thought about them for ten minutes at a time until in a hospital I met an Armenian who had escaped massacre by the Turks fifty years ago. Yet Jews and Armenians ought to feel that they have a good deal in common—a favorite expression of his was, "We Armenians are a tiny people." When I was a boy what I knew of them came from an incidental remark in one of those Mr. Tutt stories I was fond of—where, of a do-gooding New England maiden lady, it was said with affectionate exasperation that "the starving Armenians" were her favorite cause. The Armenians were massacred and their survivors starved, but the only impression all that left upon me was of something faintly comical. Granted, *The Forty Days of Musa Dagh* was written by a Jew, of sorts; but I have never read it. Why?

Another Whiggish outlook we have now, or have in a more pronounced way, is a respect for statehood. The

enlightened, modern way of looking at things is to scoff at
states and governments, but Israel has shown us they are nothing to scoff at. It has even begun to occur to some of us that
if there had been an Israeli state in World War II, Hitler
wouldn't have been able to murder quite so many Jews—and
not only because they would have had a place to escape to. If
Israel had been a state, and an ally in the war against Hitler,
the murder camps would have been bombed. In the absence
of a Jewish state the grand strategy of Allied victory gave such
a low priority to disrupting Hitler's machine for murdering
Jews that the camps were never bombed. Israel would have
effected a higher priority—not that the strategists and plan-
ners would have been persuaded, but simply that otherwise
Israel could have made too much trouble, as by threatening to
send its planes on independent bombing missions. (The Israelis
could have taken de Gaulle as their model.) With the bombing of camps and railroads, the gassed and cremated would
have been fewer.

We may even be readier than before to appreciate the cultural importance of a state. Modern Hebrew would not be what
it is if it were not the language of a state. As Max Weinreich
has said, a language is a dialect that has an army and a navy.
Before Hebrew was recognized as one of the three official languages of Palestine, about fifty years ago, it had long had a literary, religious, and philosophical vocabulary, but no real
vocabulary for tariffs and police regulations. It was legal status and responsibility that compelled Hebrew to develop.

Something else that we have learned—again—is to appreciate bourgeois democracy. After all, in the United States, in
Great Britain, and in France, Jews can go counter to government when they feel that vital Jewish interests are at stake. In
Great Britain the Jews could be pro-Israel even in the last days
of the Mandate, when the Irgun was hanging British sergeants.
Contrast a Communist state—Poland, which is supposed to
be tolerable. Gomulka was horrified. He had heard that some

Polish Jews were celebrating the Israeli victory with drinking parties. How shocking, in that abstemious country! He warned the Polish Jews about dual allegiance and being a fifth column. What a threat they must represent! Thirty years ago the ratio of Jew to Gentile in the Polish population was 1 to 9 or 1 to 10; today it is 1 to 1,250.

In a bourgeois democracy, Jews may decide for themselves how Jewish they want to be, and when; and that is why they respond with gratitude and devotion. Some time ago a radical sociologist, critical of America and American Jews, said that self-respecting people have no obligation of gratitude for the elementary decencies, which should be taken for granted. Forget the Soviet Union; even Poland shows us that we can't take the decencies for granted. In our circumstances it is ingratitude that would be problematic, not gratitude.

■   ■   ■

Finally, religion. Religion is complicated. It is conservative and revolutionary.

In the past century or two, religion has been criticized for being a conservative force, for helping to avert needed revolution by giving opiates to the oppressed, or promises of pie in the sky. This criticism would have surprised Thomas Hobbes. In his experience and doctrine, the trouble with religion was the ease with which it could become revolutionary. Any jumped-up prentice, having learned to read, might open his Bible and conclude that the established religion was not in accordance with the Lord's will; and then, incited by dreamers and visionaries, he might band together with other presumptuous enthusiasts like himself and overthrow a king, who knew better than they what religion would best insure domestic tranquility.

The Jewish religious situation may be changing. Israeli Jews have generally been the kind of people who are bashful about using the word God, but after the victory many lost that bashfulness for a while. Speaking or writing, Israelis of whom it was not to be expected invoked God quite seriously, thanking Him for their victory and attributing it to His intervention.

It would be too easy to dismiss that as chauvinistic religion. The Kaiser used to say, *Gott mit uns,* and one cause of the revulsion from religion after World War I was that the churches had prayed for victory and had assured the faithful that God wanted their country to win. But most of the Israelis who spoke of God spoke of Him only after the war. (A minority had intensified their prayers and Talmud study.) It was the Arabs who invoked God constantly. A Jew must assume that He did not want the Arabs to do what they wanted to do—for, like Haman, they purposed "to destroy, to slay, and to annihilate all Jews, young and old, women and children, in one day." And we shall be misled if we confuse the diminished Israeli (and Jewish) bashfulness about God with foxhole religion. The Israelis didn't so much petition God for victory as thank Him for it.

I hope I shall not be thought fetishistic about religious objects. By coincidence, in my last article ("Modernity and Religion"), I mentioned *tefillin* in Israel. After the victory it was hard to find *tefillin* to buy in Jerusalem. There was a run on them. Men who had never had them before, or had lost them years ago, wanted to wear their own while thanking God at the newly rewon Western Wall of Old Jerusalem.

In an Orthodox synagogue in New York soon after the war, a friend of mine has told me, the rabbi called upon a young member of the congregation to speak—a student at the Hebrew University who had been one of the foreigners substituting for the Israeli teachers and social workers called into service. Of what he said, my friend remembers this best: "We Orthodox usually distinguish between religious and irreligious Jews, especially in Israel. My experience during the war showed me that this is wrong. Some Jews are more observant and some are less observant." Now of course this is not altogether true.

It exaggerates our religiousness. But if not altogether true, then at any rate it is less untrue than in a long time. With the Israeli war there was a reassertion of an old Jewish feeling about God and Providence, of a kind that we have not seen in many years—in the United States as well as in Israel.

The newspapers here reported that in those days of strain before the shooting broke out, a great scholar who teaches at the Jewish Theological Seminary gave to the United Jewish Appeal a sum of money large in its own right and immensely large for a professor, a member of a class not usually noted for its philanthropic capacity. The letter he sent to the alumni of the seminary was not reported. This was no time, he said in the letter, for any effort short of the maximum; everything depended on exertion and sacrifice. Having put the greatest possible emphasis on human effort, he concluded with a verse from the Twentieth Psalm: "Some invoke chariots, and others horses; but we the name of the Lord our God." That was enough for the rabbis. Naturally, they completed the psalm in their minds: "They will totter and fall down, but we shall rise and stand upright. O Lord, save; may the King answer us when we call." Rabbis can be expected to know this psalm particularly well because it is read on most weekdays, toward the end of the morning prayer. And because psalms, especially the liturgical ones, recall each other even when they contradict each other, in the end emerging into a tension with each other, this weekday-morning psalm, about not invoking chariots and horses, must inevitably have recalled the 144th Psalm, which introduces the evening prayer after the Sabbath. It begins: "Blessed be the Lord my Rock, who trains my hands for war, my fingers for battle."

■   ■   ■

Not long before this, the Reform rabbinate had said it was going to revise the Union Prayer Book. The last revision, made twenty-five or thirty years ago, is considered to be no longer relevant to contemporary needs. Especially does the prayer then inserted for the welfare of coal miners seem a little irrelevant now.

Well, if you're going to make revisions every twenty or thirty years, you run the risk of being irrelevant much of the time. If this year you compose a prayer for the welfare of computer operators, in twenty or thirty years computer operators may be technologically obsolete. In our desire for relevant texts we can produce something like a daily newspaper, and there is nothing so dead as a newspaper from the day before yesterday. The Twentieth Psalm speaks of chariots and horses, which no army has used for some time now. Would it be more relevant to our contemporary needs or sensibilities if the psalm spoke of tanks and planes? Chariots and horses make the point quite well.

The Twenty-third Psalm says, "The Lord is my shepherd." There's an obsolete occupation for you. There are few shepherds in the United States, and them we call sheepherders; yet somehow, to say that the Lord is my shepherd seems to have meaning. Or the 107th Psalm: "They that go down to the sea in ships, that do business in great waters—they see the works of the Lord, and His wonders in the deep." I should imagine that not only a sailor but also a flyer, or even an astronaut, might find this psalm relevant, though it speaks of ships rather than planes or spacecraft.

In fact, the Jewish liturgy of the entire period in May and June, from the beginning of the crisis to the end of the war, suddenly seemed to have the most immediate relevance to our anxieties and hopes—above all, the specifically scriptural parts of the liturgy, both the fixed passages and the Pentateuchal and Prophetical lessons of the annual cycle. (Not to mention the very names of the Israeli captains: Abraham, Isaac, and Jacob; Moses and Aaron; Amos and Isaiah.)

■   ■   ■

Every morning a Jew who prays recites the Song at the Sea, from Exodus: "... when Israel saw the wondrous power which the Lord had wielded against the Egyptians ... they had faith in the Lord and in His servant Moses.... The Lord is my strength and might; He has become my salvation.... The enemy said, 'I will pursue, I will overtake, I will divide the spoil. My desire shall have its fill of them. I will bare my sword, my hand shall subdue them.' ... The Lord will reign for ever and ever!"

On the last Sabbath of May we read the final two chapters of Leviticus, which hold out the blessing and the curse. The blessing: "... I will give peace in the land, and you shall lie down, and none shall make you afraid.... I am the Lord your God, who brought you forth out of the land of Egypt, that you should not be their slaves...." But the curse: "... you shall be smitten before your enemies; those who hate you shall rule over you, and you shall flee when none pursues you"— and worse. On the first Sabbath in June, two days before the shooting began, the Prophetical lesson was from Hosea, with the verses we recite when we bind the *tefillin* as a sign on our hand: "... I will betroth you to me for ever; I will betroth you to me in righteousness and in justice, in steadfast love and in mercy. I will betroth you to me in faithfulness; and you shall know the Lord."

On the next Sabbath, the war over, the second group of chapters from Numbers was read as the Pentateuchal lesson, including the Priestly Blessing: "Thus shall you bless the children of Israel.... 'The Lord bless you and keep you; the Lord make His face to shine upon you, and be gracious to you; the Lord lift up His countenance upon you, and give you peace.'" The Prophetical lesson was the annunciation to Samson's mother, in Judges: "... the angel of the Lord appeared to the woman and said to her, Behold, you are barren ... but you shall conceive and bear a son ... and he shall begin to deliver Israel from the hand of the Philistines."

Then came Shavuot, with the Ten Commandments of Exodus as the Pentateuchal lesson: "I am the Lord your God, who brought you out of the land of Egypt, the house of bondage. You shall have no other gods beside Me...." And, as if to warn us and our brothers in Israel, a seemingly legalistic and priestly passage follows: "Make for Me an altar of earth.... But if you make for Me an altar of stones, do not build it of hewn stones; for by wielding your tool upon them you have profaned them." Here "your tool" is the right translation, but what the Hebrew actually says is *harbekha,* "your sword." The sword profanes. (A horror of impious iron inherited from the Bronze Age?) It was given not to David the warrior but to Solomon the man of peace to build the Temple.

On Shavuot we recited the Hallel. Not much irrelevant about the 118th Psalm: "It is better to take refuge in the Lord than to trust in princes.... Hark, glad songs of victory ... the right hand of the Lord does valiantly.... The stone which the builders rejected has become the chief cornerstone. This is the Lord's doing; it is marvelous in our eyes." And the verse that the fierce Huguenots liked to intone, in Clément Marot's version, as they rode into battle: "This is the day which the Lord has made; let us rejoice and be glad in it."

■   ■   ■

This little religious thing we now have isn't much of a creed, but for many of us it is rather more than we have ever had before. And it is ours. We can recognize it.

Each of us Jews knows how thoroughly ordinary he is; yet taken together, we seem caught up in things great and inexplicable. It is almost as if we were not acting but were being acted through. In the 1961 *Commentary* symposium, one man said we had been a big thing in antiquity and were now only a little thing. That is not so. In Deuteronomy we are told that even then we were "the smallest of peoples." How many are we? The number of Jews in the world is smaller than a small statistical error in the Chinese census. Yet we remain bigger than our numbers. Big things seem to happen around us and to us.

If one may say at all that the Bible argues for the existence of God, it has two kinds of argument. The first is the argument from nature, as in the Nineteenth Psalm: "The heavens declare the glory of God." The second is the argument from history, or from Israel, as in Deuteronomy:

> For ask now of the days that are past, which were before you, since the day that God created man upon the earth, and ask from one end of heaven to the other, whether such a great thing as this has ever happened or was ever heard of? ... Has any god ever attempted to go and take a nation for himself from the midst of another nation ... with a mighty hand and an outstretched arm ... as the Lord your God did for you in Egypt before your eyes? To you it was shown, that you might know that the Lord is God; there is no other besides Him.... Know therefore this day, and lay it to your heart, that the Lord is God in heaven above and on the earth beneath; there is no other.

Those big things that happen to us, those things that are bigger than we, are not always good things. We have not been promised that they will always be good. We have been told about the curse as well as the blessing. In I Samuel the Psalm of Hannah says, "The Lord deadens and quickens"; and Jews continue to declare so, several times a day, in the Standing Prayer.

In this last third of the twentieth century we may be beginning to believe again that the history of the Jews points to some kind of providential order, which—for reasons having to do not with our merits, but at most with the merits of Fathers—has a special place for it.

■　　■　　■

On Shavuot the first chapter of Ezekiel was read—a Prophetical account of revelation to accompany the Pentateuchal revelation of the Ten Commandments. I suspect I was not alone then to be reminded of another passage in Ezekiel (ordinarily not my favorite prophet): "What comes to your mind shall never happen—your thinking, 'Let us be like the nations, like the tribes of the countries, worshipping wood and stone.' As I live, says the Lord God, surely with a mighty hand and an outstretched arm, and with wrath poured out, will I be king over you."

When the Psalmist says "I," the pronoun is singular and plural, individual and collective, personal and referring to the children of Israel—as in that other verse from the last of the Hallel psalms: "I thank Thee, for Thou hast answered me, and art become my salvation."

(1967)

"Never Again!"

Do not be like your fathers....
—Zechariah 1:4

JUDAISM IS A TRADITION. The Jews are a community of mem-ory, which is to say, of tradition. But tradition is what fathers bequeath to sons: a Jewish expression for tradition is "fathers' inheritance," and Jews pray to "our God and our fathers' God." The Bible emphatically and repeatedly commands fathers to teach sons, and the liturgy further emphasizes and repeats that command. Sons, for their part, are told to heed their fathers' instruction.

Remarkably, Jewish sons/descendants are also warned *not* to be like fathers/ancestors. "Like your fathers"—*ka'avotekhem*—is used negatively wherever it occurs in the Bible (in II Chroni-cles 30:7–8, besides Zechariah): "do not be like your fathers," who ignored the Lord's earlier prophets; "and do not be like your fathers," who disobeyed the Lord; "do not be stiff-necked, like your fathers." And similarly with *ka'avotam*, "like their fathers" (which occurs twice in Psalm 78): "let them not be like *their* fathers" and "they were treacherous like their fathers."

So while tradition is the authority and example of fathers, in the Jewish tradition not all fathers are authoritative and

145

exemplary. Isaac is worthy of receiving and bequeathing the blessing because he obeys his father, Abraham, but Abraham was given the blessing in the first place because he disobeyed his father, the idolater Terah. Honor thy father and thy mother—provided that they honor *their* Father, Who is in heaven.

Even when Jews were traditional, then, it was only the right kind of father upon whom a son was commanded to model himself. Since for some time now most Jews have not been especially traditional, the fathers' presumptive right to obedience and imitation has been all the more in question. In the old days a son was supposed to ask whether his father was a God-fearing man; in modern times a son has been more likely to ask whether his father is a man.

"Do not be like your fathers." For a young Jew today this may mean that the generation of the fathers, even those fathers who are themselves not traditional, have not been men, and that it is his duty to differ from them, rebel against them, by being a man. In what way have the fathers not been men? To go back no farther than the beginning of this century, we can instance Bialik's revulsion, in his poem *Ir haharegah*, "The City of Slaughter," for the Jews who would not defend themselves with arms against the Russian government's armed pogromchiks. (That was in Kishinev in 1903. In Kishinev in 1971 the Russian government brought Jews to trial for the crimes of studying Hebrew and wanting to go to Israel.) Everyone used to know that Jews were good businessmen and no farmers at all, and now Israelis will tell you, more proudly than regretfully, that they are good farmers and bad businessmen. The Jews who did not fight the pogromchiks were storekeepers—"businessmen"—rather than farmers. Israel was the effort of Jews who agreed with Bialik to transform themselves.

It is easy for young Jews to see in their fathers a negative model ("Uncle Jake"). It is easy even for fathers to see in their former selves (e.g., true believers in the Soviet Union as the enemies of anti-Semitism) a negative model for their present selves. Fathers and sons can agree: "Do not be like your fathers. Never again!"

■   ■   ■

"Never again!" must have been used as a slogan long before *nie wieder Krieg!* ("never again war") was popular in Germany, between Kaiser and Führer. Among Jews the currency of the slogan seems to date from the anxious weeks before the 1967 war, when Israel was threatened with destruction. "Never again!" we said, the "again" recalling what Hitler had done, had been allowed to do, to the Jews. Never again, we meant, would we let others fool us or would we fool ourselves about the intention of those who intended to destroy the Jews. Never again would we lean on that broken reed, enlightened opinion. Never again would we do less than all we could do. Never again would we expose ourselves to our own reproaches for having done less.

The "never again!" that 1967 aroused in us (to the surprise of many in whom it was aroused) was not altogether extinguished when disaster to Israel had been averted. It remained, available, mobilizing us in the defense of Jews, or Jewish needs and hopes, wherever else they were attacked or threatened: *imprimis* in the Soviet Union, but in the United States as well. Never again would we incur the guilt, or the guilt-feeling, of 1933–45.

In these times, how do you answer an eighteen-year-old son or daughter who asks you why Jews of America were so well behaved while the Nazis were murdering the Jews of Europe? You can tell the truth, which is that we did not know, or did not believe, how bad things really were; that because there was so much anti-Semitism in the United States we were afraid of increasing it, afraid of giving even more of a Jewish label to the war, by calling attention to ourselves; that we preferred to see the big, unparochial picture, with the liberals among us more comfortable about denouncing the State

Department—we knew how to exempt Roosevelt—for being beastly to de Gaulle than for not losing sleep over the Jews, and the radicals sure that "socialism" would cure everything. We can tell our children that if they had been living then, they would have been as we were and done as we did. But that is a less than satisfactory answer to give them, or to give ourselves. Never again!

A Jewish March on Washington, or more Jewish criticism of Roosevelt, might not have made much difference for the Jews of Hitler's Europe. The difference it would have made is for the Jews of the United States. We would feel less guilty. We might even *be* less guilty.

Moscow now is not Berlin then. The sclerotic Marxism-Leninism, the Great Russian chauvinism, and the Great Power imperialism of the Soviet apparatchiks are not the Nazism of Hitler and Himmler. All this is true. It is also true that Moscow, not Madrid, Athens, or Cape Town, is the present capital of anti-Semitism. The *Protocols of the Elders of Zion* has more credit with—as the expression goes—the ruling circles of Moscow (and Warsaw and Prague) than of other cities, Damascus and Cairo always excepted.

What are the Jews to do? In the Soviet Union some have done wonders. The intensity of Jewish feeling, in a land with none or almost none of the Jewish things that Jews in the United States (or Canada, or Great Britain, or France) take for granted: synagogues, schools, seminaries, books, journals, camps, clubs, organizations, movements, El Al; the courage, bordering on recklessness, in demonstratively challenging a government of jailers hostile equally to Jews and to challenges—that after so many years, in a milieu so unpromising, any substantial number at all should give proof of such virtues, Jewish and human, is not easily to be explained or lightly to be explained away.

Outside the Soviet Union, what we can do is try to make the Soviet authorities pay a higher price than their anti-

Semitism/anti-Jewishness is worth to them. For Hitler the destruction of the Jews was a good so transcendent that no price was too high: his managers and engineers told him his war plants needed more and more workers, and he murdered the Jews who could have worked in those plants; his generals told him he did not have enough trains to carry troops and munitions to the front, and he took away trains to carry Jews to the death camps. By the high price Hitler was willing to pay, he showed the value he put on destroying the Jews. The Soviet authorities know they must pay some price for their enmity toward the Jew; but for them, unlike Hitler, the enmity is not beyond price. If their Jewish policy costs them too much, they may relent. This is the reasoning behind the publicity and demonstrations by Jews outside Russia. Within Russia, the demonstrative Jews reason that if they make enough of a nuisance of themselves, the authorities probably will put them into prison, but possibly will let them go to Israel.

In the first months of 1971 the Soviet Union let more Jews leave than at any time since the early years after the Revolution. This was due above all to Russian Jews themselves. We hope it was due to us, too, a little.

■　　■　　■

In the United States no Jew who cares about the Jews of the Soviet Union thinks we have done enough. (Except that Lubavitcher Hasidim, for instance, who care a great deal, have their own tactics and philosophy, and they think we are provoking Caesar imprudently.) Those who say we have not done enough will often blame our organizations and institutions. These, they believe, are inept, or are lukewarm, or because of rivalry get in each other's way and harm the common enterprise.

Ineptness, lukewarmness, and rivalry are the friction of social machines, which can only be reduced, not eliminated. For the Russian Jews, American-Jewish organizations and institutions have worked with less friction than normal. The dissatisfaction we express with our organizations and institutions is really dissatisfaction with ourselves.

We need no particular bravery, nor any extraordinary intensity of Jewish feeling, to attend meetings, to write a congressman, to send a cablegram to the Kremlin, to demonstrate, to picket. Yet how many of us have done even these things? We are a large share of the consumers of art and culture. In New York we may be an actual majority, week in and week out, of those who go to the theater, opera, symphony, ballet. Not many months ago in New York, connoisseurs assembling in Carnegie Hall to see a troupe of Soviet folk dancers brushed by a picket line that was pleading with them to boycott the performance in reproof of the Soviet government's Jewish policy. Art—specifically, the art of Siberian dancers of Omsk—was greater than political passion, those elevated souls were saying by their deeds; and people like us must strive to bridge, not widen, division. They would not have bought tickets to the performance of a troupe sent by the South African government, or brushed righteously by pickets distributing leaflets against apartheid. I have heard that at a major American university, after a visit by South Africans had been cancelled, one by a Soviet troupe was well attended, despite picketing. Thus did the university community show its disapproval of the excessively Jewish protesters' insensitivity to art and international understanding. Jews are a large share of the culture consumers in universities, too.

But if we are a sorry lot, we are a bit less of a sorry lot than we used to be. That may be because of the example of Israel, or of the Soviet Jews, or of American blacks. It may be because America has changed for the better since the days when it was Hitler who was the Jews' enemy. And it may be because we do not wish to be as we were then, or had to be. Whatever the reasons, we are now less fearful, less inclined to self-censorship, in defense of Jews.

Thirty years ago we insisted that we opposed the Nazis because we were Americans and democrats. We had little choice.

Lindbergh was only the most prominent of those who accused us of enticing America, for narrow Jewish interests, into a war that was none of our business. Today an occasional editorial revives that line—though with anti-Jewish language rather less blunt, and with Russia substituting for Germany as the country with which America (and all the West) must learn to live at peace: why should the Jews be allowed to jeopardize a détente so necessary to all? The revival of Lindbergh coincides with the revival of the Jewish-warmonger line. (Their coinciding, of course, is no more than a coincidence.)

So far, we have been able to persist. We say we will stop when the Soviet Union stops. Let it stop persecuting the Soviet Jews. Let it stop forbidding them to do what they need and want to do in order to be Jews. The Soviet Union must do its part for détente and this includes Jewish freedom for the Soviet Jews.

But the pressures against selfish Jewish protests about the Soviet Union are likely to mount. Everyone is talking of a new coalition in American politics. A new America First movement may be that coalition, with room for Old Right and Old Left, New Left and New Right; and maybe also for a few Jews, as in the old America First. The new America First is likely to resemble the old in uniting upper-class and "responsible" types—more of them than we like to remember—with the slopebrows and the rancorous we remember so well. Lindbergh was pro-German. The second-generation Lindberghs will be anti-anti-Russian.

■   ■   ■

The Jewish Defense League is often thought of as the purest, most unremitting expression of American-Jewish devotion to Soviet Jewry. That is a mistake. JDL was a latecomer. It owes its celebrity, and consequently much of any importance it may have, to the press and TV—especially TV. In part this is for technical reasons: JDL knows how to do and say "newsworthy" things. But in part, also, the press and TV like JDL; they need JDL.

Before Vice President Agnew began to say what he has said, a liberal academic had said something not very different. In 1968 Eric Goldman wrote, in his *Tragedy of Lyndon Johnson:*

> ... in the 1960's ... in the upper-income city neighborhoods and particularly in the suburbs, a new and influential type was emerging, the Metroamerican ... youthful, educated, affluent, more likely to have some minority blood in his veins.... He had ideals.... He was liberal....
>
> Metroamericans were ... especially important ... because of their dominance in the world of books, magazines, radio, and television.

Today "minorities" apparently do not include the Jews, but in those far-off days of 1968 we knew what was meant by "minority blood." Even the Catholics were a minority then: Goldman says that in the eyes of the Metroamericans, John F. Kennedy "was a minority boy who made it to the White House."

For years now liberals and radicals, especially if of Jewish parentage, have been telling themselves and us that American Jews have turned selfishly conservative, or actually reactionary. I can testify to this personally, because I have repeatedly found it necessary to show how wrong this is, as by citing the latest voting data. (In November 1970 the Jews were still voting more liberal than any comparable group, and still giving more liberal answers to the opinion pollsters.) For the press and TV, therefore, JDL could not be more opportune. The dull statistician may tell us the Jews are still disproportionately liberal, but here is JDL saying out loud what the Jews *really* think, showing them up for what they *really* are—as hardhat as the rest of hardhat America.

It is because of the violent and extremist impression of the Jews that JDL wants to give, and others want to receive, that the established Jewish community organizations have felt obliged to insist that JDL is unrepresentative and damaging. Is it not clear that the further decay of restraint and the further growth of what has been termed the cult of utterness will be worse for the Jews than for almost anyone else? And when JDL acts most distinctively JDL-ishly, it does not help the Russian Jews, either.

JDL is said not only to be the voice of a sieged and resentful lower-middle class, but also to be Orthodox. If Orthodox means what is not conventionally liberal or enlightened, then JDL is Orthodox. (Meir Kahane is an Orthodox rabbi.) But its Orthodoxy is of a special sort—one is tempted to say, a folk Orthodoxy. JDL does not look to Rabbi Joseph Soloveitchik, or the decisors, or *rashe yeshivot*, or any of the Hasidic leaders and movements, or Breuer-Frankfurt, or even Mizrachi— no need to mention Agudath Israel, and *a fortiori* the quietist or actually anti-Israel sectaries. The derivation is from Vladimir Jabotinsky; and his attitude toward Orthodoxy, or more generally toward Jewish tradition, had some resemblance to Charles Maurras's attitude toward Catholicism. Maurras was not much of a believer, but as a nationalist he was for French tradition, and that included Catholicism. Maurras attracted many Catholics, and Jabotinsky attracted some of the Jewish Orthodox. If I am not mistaken, a generation ago in Poland young Jews who had abandoned the political quietism in which they had been brought up but who refused to break with Orthodoxy were apt to join Jabotinsky's party in Zionism; and in Palestine—as it then was—apt to join the Irgun Tseva'i Le'ummi instead of the Haganah. (Such rather un-Orthodox Jews as Ben Hecht, in this country, could support the Irgun, too.) When Rabbi Kahane was a boy he belonged to the Jabotinskyite youth movement.

Though most Jews are not for JDL, some defend it—not for what it is itself but as a stick to beat the Jewish Establishment with. Of these, in turn, some dislike the Jewish Establishment because it is too much an Establishment, and some because it is too little Jewish. But that can be a distinction more logical than actual, and the one dislike may shade into the other. Thus the published accusation by "a young Jewish radical": "The Jewish Establishment is so busy serving other people's causes that it neglects the cause of its own people." If he actually is a Jewish radical, he is probably alleging that the Jewish section of the bourgeoisie, insecure and vulnerable, curries favor with its superiors in the bourgeois ruling class by doing their dirty work, oppressing the non-Jewish and Jewish masses alike.

But suppose that the young man is less a Jewish radical than a radical Jew. Then his accusation can mean something different, and can have a thoroughly familiar Jewish ring. Song of Songs 1:6 reads: "... they set me to tending vineyards, *but my own vineyard I have not tended.*" The Targum renders:

> Said the Assembly of Israel to the peoples: "... they taught me to worship your follies and to follow in your ways; but the Master of the Universe, who is *my* God, I have not worshipped, and in His ways I have not followed, and His commands and His Torah I have not kept."

For Yalqut Shimoni, "tending the vineyards" means "honoring the [alien] nations"; and "'my vineyard'—that is the Holy One blessed be He."

According to the modern development of the old Midrash, we are so busy serving other people's causes that we neglect the cause of our own people; or, the Jewish Establishment is so busy serving other people's causes that it neglects the cause of its own people.

■   ■   ■

In a congregational bulletin the Orthodox rabbi of my community has written:

Permit me to present the hapless figure of Avraham Hershkovitz. He was apprehended boarding an airliner with weapons in his possession. The accusation against him was that he was planning to hijack an Arab airship. In the end, the charge against him was for falsifying a passport application.

Mr. Hershkovitz was held on $50,000 bail ... no Jewish group ... was willing to come forward to raise bail for him. One lone Jewish individual refused to let Hershkovitz spend Pesach in jail and he came forward with the necessary funds....

I do not write to defend the plans and machinations of Mr. Avraham Hershkovitz, but why is a party for the Berrigans kosher and one for Hershkovitz *trepha*?

Now that Hershkovitz has been ... sentenced to five years for falsifying a passport application, where are the voices to cry out ... that the sentence may possibly be harsh with respect to the actual deed?

(Passover is when the Song of Songs is read in the synagogue.)

What the Orthodox rabbi and the radical Jew, and many in between, have in common is shame and anger that "... my own vineyard I have not tended." The accompanying resolve is "never again!"

(1971)

Theology and Piety

What Do I Believe?

The symposium "What Do American Jews Believe?" posed the following questions:

1. Do you believe in God? Do you believe the Torah to be divine revelation? Do you accept the binding nature of any, some, or all of the commandments?

2. In what sense do you believe the Jews are the chosen people of God? What is the distinctive role of the Jewish people in the world today? Of Jewish messianism?

3. How have, respectively, the Holocaust and the existence of the state of Israel influenced your faith, your religious identity, your observance?

4. In your judgment, which aspects of the contemporary American situation, including the political situation, offer the greatest stimulus to Jewish belief, and which pose the most serious challenge either to Jewish belief or to Jewish continuity?

5. What is your assessment of the current denominational and ideological divisions within American Judaism? To what degree are you worried about Jewish religious unity?

6. Do you see any prospect of a large-scale revival of Judaism in America?

DO I BELIEVE IN GOD? "I accept the universe," Margaret Fuller said. Poor woman, the universe did not long accept her. I accept God. I hope He accepts me.

Is the Torah divine revelation? Without maintaining the photographic accuracy of Exodus 19–20 and Deuteronomy 4–5, I believe that a law was revealed—a numinous word—to our ancestors and transmitted to us.

Gershom Scholem, the great scholar of Jewish mysticism, believed in God but not in Kashrut, unable to imagine Him closely involved with the kitchen. Scholem knew, of course, that the rabbis had warned against trying to calculate the relative weights of the mitzvot: what seems to be a minor one, sparing a mother bird when taking her young (Deuteronomy 22:6f.), entails the same reward of long life as the Decalogue's mitzvah of honoring father and mother (Exodus 20:12 and Deuteronomy 5:16). But that was homily, not law. The law the rabbis decreed is that mitzvot do differ in weight. For only three of the 613 must a Jew allow himself to be killed rather than be compelled to transgress (the prohibitions of bloodshed, unchastity, and idolatry).

Aristotle on the care needed in changing laws (*Politics* 1269a) is still useful: ".... it is proper for some laws sometimes to be altered. But ... it ... needs ... much caution.... Are all the laws to be open to alteration ...?"

Scholem must have overlooked this caution about slippery slopes. Not even so profound an expositor of Jewish antinomianism is likely to have envisioned rabbis adding the bedroom to the kitchen as one more area beyond God's purview.

When the Reform rabbis were considering whether to ordain homosexuals, a professor at their seminary, Hebrew Union College, reminded them that Leviticus 18—the Jewish tradition's choice, over 186 other chapters in the Pentateuch, as the reading for Yom Kippur afternoon—calls homosexual acts an abomination. A member of the majority easily disposed of the objection: "It's pretty late in the day for Scripture to be invoked in CCAR [Central Conference of American Rabbis] debates." First the Talmud went and then Scripture itself; and within Scripture first kosher and *treyf* flesh, fish, and fowl, and then kosher and *treyf* sexual relationships.

Nor is the end in sight. New victims of discrimination will emerge and assert their right to equality. For instance: isn't prejudice against the pedophilic, necrophilic, and the incestuous religious in origin, and isn't discrimination rooted in religious prejudice unconstitutional? Over religious prejudice, rights will win every time.

■　　■　　■

"How odd / Of God / To choose / The Jews." According to the *Oxford Dictionary of Quotations* it was the obscure William Norman Ewer (1885–1976) who wrote this celebrated quatrain. Lou H. Silberman, in his instructive entry on "Chosen People" (*Encyclopaedia Judaica*, vol. 5, coll. 498–502), attributes it to Hilaire Belloc, author of the anti-Semitic *The Jews* (1922). To Jacques Maritain as to other Christian theologians, Protestant as well as Catholic, the Election of Israel is not an oddity but a Mystery.

Silberman ends his "Chosen People" with this: "Modern Jewish thought is still grappling with the problem . . . in a way that does justice both to the universalist values of Judaism . . . and to the specific character of Jewish historical and spiritual experience. . . ." For modern Jews the very notion of Jewish chosenness can be troubling—elitist, ethnocentric. Maybe we would feel more comfortable if, instead of talking about Election and Mystery, we talked about less lofty extraordinariness.

A science-fiction fantasy: when the alien scouts return in their UFO to their home planet, they report the many odd things they have observed on Earth. One of the oddest is the disproportion between how conspicuous certain humans called Jews are and how few they are—fewer than 25 in 10,000. Odder yet is that the 99.75+ percent are called Gentiles because they are not the .25– percent who are Jews.

What is our distinctive mission today? As always, to remain in being as Jews. Our other missions are additional.

Messianism? We must continue to pray for the Messiah's coming, and when he comes we must examine his credentials. In the past we suffered repeatedly from false messiahs. More recently we have been burned by false messianisms.

The Holocaust and Israel are in their opposite ways part of the Jewish disproportionateness and extraordinariness— the larger-than-lifeness—through which I feel Jewish chosenness. At *yizkor* time, when memorial prayers are recited for the dead, I mourn those murdered in the Holocaust; in my thanksgiving for bread and on the Sabbath I pray for Israel.

■   ■   ■

Will American culture and society be good or bad for the Jews?

Jewish self-hate—Jewish anti-Semitism—is less virulent than it was, in part because Gentile anti-Semitism is less virulent. This means that the psychological and social cost of being a Jew and the temptation of abandoning the Jewish religion and community have shrunk. At the same time, so has the tempting attractiveness of the Gentile world.

In the 1930s many of the philosopher Sidney Hook's Jewish students told him that if they had had a choice, they would have been born Episcopalian. Also in the 1930s, Margaret Mitchell—the literary critic, not the novelist—said to Elliot Cohen, who was to be *Commentary*'s first editor, "The trouble with you Jews is that you think you would be happy if only you were Aryan. You have this illusion of Aryan happiness." Such things would not be said now.

On the other hand, a kind of Gresham's Law can operate in culture as in finance. It isn't easy for a demanding, disciplined culture to compete with the loose, indulgent culture that prevails in America (and the rest of the Western world, not excepting Tel Aviv).

■   ■   ■

Much that is done and said in the name of Jewish religion, here as in Israel, is in effect anti-Judaic. Still, indifference and outright hostility worry me more. In some circles where Jews are no strangers, "religion" is a dirty word.

As to the possibility of a large-scale revival, "Is any thing too hard for the Lord?" More probably, there will be—to echo Ninotchka's sinister justification of Stalin's purges in the eponymous film, "Therrre will be fewerrr but betterrr Rrrussians"—fewer but better Jews. On the demographic side, they will intermarry less than we do now and may procreate more.

"*Hatikvah,*" the Zionist and Israeli anthem, proclaims, "Our hope is not lost." That is in answer to the contemporaries of Ezekiel (37:11), who, more than 2,500 years ago, had despaired, crying, "... . our hope is lost. ... ."

Hope is a Jewish virtue.

(1996)

ENCOUNTER BOOKS

900 Broadway

Suite 400

New York, New York 10003-1239

www.encounterbooks.com

Please add me to your mailing list.

Name

Company

Address

City, State, Zip

E-mail

Book Title

Going to Shul

IN THE PAST MONTHS, since my father died, I have been in the synagogue twice a day to say the Kaddish. Other congregations would regard mine as observing bankers' hours, but its morning schedule nevertheless requires arising in the dark and cold, especially in the winter. For afternoon-and-evening prayer the hour varies, depending—at least in principle and in Orthodox synagogues—on the time of sunset, but going every evening is not easy, either.

Which is why not even the devout necessarily frequent the synagogue every day, contenting themselves with private prayer, particularly on weekdays. It is the man who is saying the Kaddish who must have a *minyan*, public worship. In most American synagogues nearly everyone you see at prayer during the week is a mourner, together with most of those who are there from the beginning on Saturday morning. Inconvenience also helps to explain the tenth-man problem, quite apart from the big explanations we like better: the difficulty of belief, the difficulty of prayer. In few synagogues where the speech is English and the faces shaven is it unnecessary to have a list of volunteers who can be telephoned in an emergency in order to round out the required number of ten.

■   ■   ■

In the Middle Ages it was thought that saying the Kaddish for a year was especially helpful to the dead if they had been wicked. Since no one wanted to imply that his father or mother had been wicked, today we say the Kaddish for eleven months. I do not know what proportion of Jewish men observe the full eleven months, but I suspect it is fairly high, especially when put beside our known propensity for staying away from the synagogue.

If this is so, why? Well, feelings about death, especially the death of a parent; guilt and anxiety, and the need to relieve them; ritual—all these can be interpreted along conventional Freudian lines and have been, often. For Freud, religion was a kind of public, collective neurosis. I take this idea seriously. It tells me better than anything else why the very inconvenience of saying the Kaddish morning and afternoon-evening every day for eleven months, and thereafter on anniversaries—normally at least two in a man's life—becomes a virtue, perhaps an attraction. It is expiatory, it is almost punitive, and we have been taught that guilt seeks punishment.

It is more, of course. Much has been said in dispraise of Jews who obey the rules of the Kaddish though otherwise they hardly ever pray at all. The contempt is unwarranted: the Kaddish must meet their needs better than anything else in the synagogue. And these are not only needs of the kind we have learned about from Freud, but also needs for style and tradition. Freud said that the collective neurosis of religion spares us the trouble of developing individual, personal neuroses. With the Kaddish, Judaism spares each Jew the trouble of developing for himself a style—etiquette, ritual, mode of expression, symbolic action—at a time when he wants it and when he knows he cannot devise something personal that will be as good.

If each of us were accountable for his own ritual of mourning, who would escape censure? Who would escape his own censure? The Jewish rites—the burial, the seven days at home, the Kaddish—have the advantage of being a tradition, a style. We need assume no responsibility for them, as we would for any personal or private symbolic action, nor can there be any question of their appropriateness. They are appropriate almost by definition, because of their antiquity, their near-universality, their publicness—*quod semper, quod ubique, quod ab omnibus.* Yet their publicness, so far from making them exterior and impersonal, makes them all the more appropriate to the particular relationship between mourner and mourned: the Kaddish I now say for my father, he said for his; and so back through a recession of the generations that exceeds what my imagination can grasp. Acting as my father acted, I become conscious that I am a link in the chain of being. Nor am I hindered from expressing particular, local, present emotion.

One of the things a Jew is supposed to say about someone who has died is the prayer that Abigail said for David (though in his lifetime and in his presence), that his soul may be bound up in the bundle of life. Saying this is of a piece with the rest of our ritual. Whatever its efficacy may be for the dead, it binds *me* up in the bundle of life, situates *me* in the procession of the generations, frees *me* from the prison of now and here.

Although we have been born when it is hard to believe in immortality, the Kaddish helps us to believe, a little. I know that it makes me think of my father often, more than forty times a week; and it will keep reminding me of him after I have stopped saying the Kaddish daily, when I hear someone else say it and I make the appropriate response. To think of my father, to recall him, is to hold off his mortality—and because ritual is eloquent, to hold it off still one generation further. Where has Daddy gone? To *shul*, to say Kaddish for Grandpa. By doing what allows my children to ask this question and receive this answer, I also allow myself to hope that my own mortality will similarly be delayed.

■　　■　　■

A Kaddish-sayer and *shul*-watcher can learn something even if his experience, like mine, has been limited to not many more than a dozen synagogues, Orthodox and Conservative, mostly in or near New York.

With our past and present confusingly simultaneous, many of us are not in the category we should be in. Of the elderly and immigrant, for instance, it is to be expected that they will use a Polish-Russian Ashkenazi pronunciation of Hebrew; of the middle-aged, the standard Ashkenazi that was taught in our Hebrew schools a generation ago; and of the young, the more or less Israeli, more or less Sephardi pronunciation that is now taught in most schools—for instance, *yitbarakh*, "may (he/it) be blessed": standard Ashkenazi, *yisborakh*; Polish-Russian, *yisborekh, yisburekh*. With eyes closed, you can usually know the man by his Hebrew. Usually—but I have opened my eyes after hearing *yisburekh* to see a youngish man who could be in advertising or public relations. And as with pronunciation, so with the atmosphere and the ways of a synagogue. In any synagogue you are apt to find people who by all the rules belong more properly in a different one.

Jews who are Americanized (or Anglicized, or Gallicized; before Hitler, Germanized) want restraint in their synagogues, in the officiants as well as the laity. The virtuoso cantor, I had thought, came into his own at a certain time in history, when Jews from the traditionalist villages were moving to the big cities of Europe and America, and he disappeared when their children learned that his kind of singing was out of place in a church. I have not heard really gaudy *hazzanut* anywhere recently, but I have heard other survivals from the bad old days where there was no reason to expect them: a kind of falsetto throating; stretching or repeating some words and swallowing others; singing as if the text consisted of vowels alone, without consonants.

If bar-mitzvahs are a horror, as everyone says, they are normally not so in the synagogue itself. That may come later, somewhere else. But even so, the accumulation of bar-mitzvahs, two or more a week, week after week, can be too much of a good thing. By now I can do without the high voices, and the slow chanting, and the charge to the boys, and the congratulations to the parents, and the benediction, and the presentation of *kiddush* beakers and prayer books, and the boys' pledges and thanks. If I am querulous, put the blame on lingering shock. Not long ago I heard a bar-mitzvah boy double as cantor when the Torah scroll was being returned to the ark. At that point the cantor summons the congregation with a verse from the 148th Psalm: "Let them praise the name of the Lord, for His name alone is exalted." Instead of *yehalelu et shem*, however, the boy sang *yechallelu ...*, "Let them profane the name ..."! (The identical phrase is in Leviticus, negatively of course: "... that they profane not My holy name," *we-lo yechallelu et shem qodshi.* "Profanation of the Name," *chillul ha-shem* is the rabbinical term for blasphemy specifically or conduct unbecoming a Jew generally.)

Sometimes I wonder about the bar-mitzvah guests. The woman in a sleeveless, near-décolleté dress—where does she get her notions of seemliness? The uncle for whom the Hebrew blessings are practically nonsense syllables but who accepts being called up when the Torah is read—why does he do it? Since his abject stammering is surely as painful for him as for the rest of us, he might at least rehearse the syllables a day or two earlier.

In my wanderings I have discovered an argument, new to me, against the Orthodox segregation of the sexes. It is still true that when women sit by themselves they talk, and in *shul* they have to be shushed—one of the few things our grandmothers have in common with their college-graduate granddaughters. When in a Conservative synagogue and dispersed among the men, the same women seem to talk less than when in Orthodox isolation. After one deafening Sabbath morning near the divider between the men and the women, I could appreciate the answer of the great Rabbi Israel Salanter—I think it was he—when he was asked what should be done with some bricks left over from repair work on a synagogue: "Use them to wall up the entrance to the women's gallery." In a way, that is what Conservative and Reform Judaism have done.

■   ■   ■

I have a research project for a specialist in the social psychology of small groups: examine a daily *minyan*. It is an ideal opportunity for a participant-observer, especially if you have to move about from time to time and so get to see how others are.

Take the *minyan* in the congregation I belong to. When you consider that its members are unhappy about having to be there in the first place and that its composition changes, veterans departing as newcomers enter, its morale is remarkable. On the whole they are not conspicuously pious Jews, but most make it a point of honor to disregard bad weather and hazardous driving to get there on time. Clearly they believe that the *minyan* must go on, that it would be wrong to let the side down.

So strong is this sentiment that it makes some who have finished their eleven months keep coming, if not every day then one or two mornings during the week. That is when it counts, because Saturdays and Sundays are no problem. Getting up early when they want to sleep a little longer, and could, their own daily Kaddish-saying now behind them, they show a devotion and self-sacrifice more to be respected than the writing of a check or the signing of a petition. These men do the inconvenient thing so that the other men, who need the *minyan*, will have it. And though they may be too bashful about this motive even to admit it to themselves, I suspect they do it, too, because of what they think a *shul* should be: a place from which the praises intoned by Israel ascend, as is said of the Shema, "evening and morning, twice every day always, lovingly" —or thrice, if you take the afternoon prayers (which lack the Shema) and the evening prayers to be separate in fact as well as principle.

I have the impression that my *minyan* is something of an exception in its morale. At any rate, I find it more attractive than others I have seen. It has little of the prevalent mumbling combined with sprinting that is another survival from the bad old days. In my *minyan* we sing. Not only that, but also I can actually finish one prayer before the next is begun. We are out at the same hour every day, because it is the starting time that varies, not the leaving time: we start early on Mondays and Thursdays, when the Torah is read, and earlier still on a New Month. With the time for leaving calculated and fixed, we do not race the clock. For the kind of people we are, the singing and the deliberate pace ratify our being engaged in what we recognize as suitable prayer. It may even make us a little more prayerful than we would be otherwise.

Not many of us have or attain *kawwanah*—inwardness, concentration, the merging of the pray-er with his prayer. They say it used to be common. Whether or not that is so, I can hardly recite a verse of six or seven words without my mind wandering. (I can hardly listen to three bars of music at a concert without my mind wandering.) Beside *kawwanah*, decorum and singing and pace and every other occidental propriety are trash. Unfortunately, though, their absence does not guarantee its presence; and if we are going to have to do without *kawwanah*, we may as well have niceness. Let a man be free enough from haste to be at least aware of the meaning of the words he is saying or singing. When he leaves, hurrying to his car, let him not have a bad taste in his mouth.

■　　■　　■

I still catch myself daydreaming about the things I would do if I were rich. Lately, one of those things has been to have my own *shul*, with the legislative, executive, and judicial powers all mine. I would make some radical reforms, of a generally reactionary character.

As among the Sephardim, I would have the reader read every word aloud, from beginning to end, except for meditations intended to be silent or those minatory admonitions that are traditionally muted, like Deuteronomy 11:17 after the Shema. As Maimonides decreed for the Jews of Egypt, I would have the Standing Prayer said only once, aloud. Every biblical text that is more than one or two verses long would be chanted, like the Torah and the Prophetical lessons and the Megillot. (The prayer book includes many psalms, but I have yet to hear one chanted that way.) I would have the musical emphasis that is given to a prayer, or even a phrase, correspond to the doctrinal or liturgical emphasis it ought to have. I do not pray for the restoration of the sacrificial cultus nor does the prayer book I use (on the Sabbath) include a prayer for it; and the Conservative theologians who edited that *siddur* even refrained from translating the biblical prescription for animal sacrifice incorporated in the Standing Prayer for *Musaf*. Yet the congregation is encouraged to sing that very passage, in an almost fondling sort of way: "And on the Sabbath day, two he-lambs ..."

The Sabbath service is on the long side: in my congregation, three hours—not unusual—and in another I know of, four. The other is the Orthodox synagogue of Sons and Daughters of the American Revolution. It may be that the four-hour Sabbath worship is one of the reasons why the Sons and Daughters stay away from their synagogue so religiously.

The length of the synagogue service, on the Sabbath and festivals and even weekday mornings, is only a sign of the contradiction or tension in our worship. On the one hand, the rabbis enjoin us not to make a perfunctory routine, *qeva*, of our prayer. On the other hand, our liturgy consists, with some expansions and additions, of prayer-texts that the same rabbis declared to be *hovah*, obligatory. It is hard to keep the repeated and obligatory from becoming routine. Even in the age of faith, only a small elite could have succeeded.

But to make the service short will not help us much. I have felt most untouched and unmoved in short services, Reform or near-Reform Conservative or Reconstructionist; and my neighbors have seemed to me equally untouched and unmoved. In fact, length has certain advantages. In a way, a long service is like a long poem. You do not want unrelieved concentration and tightness in a long poem; they would be intolerable. Length requires *longueurs*. A good long poem is an alternation of high moments and moments less high, of concentration and relaxation. In our synagogues the heights may not be very high, but the long service does provide some ascent and descent. The short service tends to be of a piece, dull and tepid.

If I shortened at all, it would be at the end rather than the beginning—the *Musaf*, not the introductory hymns and psalms. Time would also be saved by a total ban on bar-mitzvahs (let them go somewhere else), but twenty minutes or so would continue to be reserved for the sermon. The sermon would not be consistently topical, because I can acquire on my own the approved attitudes toward whatever the approved topics may be at any given time, from the approved sources: *New York Times Magazine, Saturday Review*, public-service television. It is less easy to acquire Torah.

My most reactionary radicalism would be reserved for the Friday-night service: back to Orthodoxy, almost all the way. Almost—because I would substitute some other reading from rabbinical literature for *Ba-meh madliqin*, which, besides being boring, is offensive in the reasons it gives for women dying in childbirth. Job should forever have put an end to that kind of theodicy.

■   ■   ■

How to recruit a good congregation of respectable size is a problem I am unable to solve even in a daydream. A bare *minyan* is not quite right for a Sabbath, let alone Rosh Hashanah and Yom Kippur. "In a multitude of people is the glory of a king." For the rabbis, that verse from Proverbs proved that Jews should worship together, the more the better. A large number of worshipping Jews assembled together can generate a kind of heat—analogous to the physical heat that people generate when they are closely assembled—that will affect each one individually. I have heard about it but I have not experienced it. On Rosh Hashanah and Yom Kippur a large number of Jews are assembled where I go, only most of them are not what anyone would call worshipping Jews. They are there, they bring warm their bodies, but they are a kind of inert mass and they deaden rather than quicken the worship. They are an audience—not an especially understanding one—rather than a congregation. According to Ninotchka, Stalin wanted fewer but better Russians. That is a cautionary precedent, but I would still be glad to exchange some Jewish quantity for quality.

Now, as to the prayer books I would use: something on the order of Birnbaum's excellent *siddur* and *mahazor,* but different in having an English facing page that does not give the impression it was written by a hand in a woolen mitten. (For Psalm 24:1, "The earth is the Lord's and the fulness thereof," he has "The earth and its entire contents belong to the Lord.") Conservative variations should be presented, besides the Orthodox text. I would not particularly mind additional readings and meditations from modern work, provided they were additions not substitutions, and provided I could continue to ignore them. Either the modern lends itself with difficulty to what a prayer book should be or editors have usually made the wrong choices—probably both. A warning: if "insight" appears anywhere in the book—except perhaps in the introduction, and preferably not there, either—I will not buy it.

A good *siddur* is particularly useful during those necessary and soothing low-keyed stretches in the service. You may decide, for instance, to read a psalm or a rabbinical prayer more closely than you could if you were trying to keep up with the cantor and congregation. You can read for anything you wish— plain meaning, literary effect, doctrine, allusion or suggestion, historical placing, or even praise and supplication. If there are good notes and a good translation, you have most of the help you need.

For astigmatics like me, make sure the Hebrew characters are large and distinct, and more especially watch those vowel signs: I often have trouble telling a *qamez* from a *segol* or a *patah* from a *zere*. To Hebrew editors and printers everywhere I commend the example of David de Sola Pool in his edition of the Sephardi prayer book, who for short *qamez* uses the left-hand half of the sign. Unlike the Ashkenazi, the Sephardi-Israeli pronunciation distinguishes between long and short *qamez*, and a visual marking of the distinction is something to be grateful for. Without it, in hard or doubtful cases it becomes necessary to see whether the Kittel-Kahle Biblia Hebraica has a *meteg*, for example; and then what if the verse or word is not biblical? But even Dr. Pool is not to be completely relied on in these difficulties, because the Sephardi *siddur* is far from identical with the Ashkenazi. What is more, the Sephardim's tradition is unacceptable about such matters as the length of the *qamez* preceding *hatef-qamez:* for instance, instead of *tohorah,* "purity," they say *tahorah,* and Dr. Pool so points it.

My *siddur* would go to the Sephardim for variety, as in the Kaddish. The Kaddish is a doxology, of which the substantial and historical kernel is the congregation's response: "May His great name be blessed/praised (forever and ever)."

Formally, it is not a prayer for the dead; only the graveside Kaddish mentions the dead, and then not specifically but generally, in its praise of God as the future author of resurrection. The four forms of the Kaddish said in the synagogue—two by the cantor or reader, two by mourners—are, as it were, punctuation marks in the service, setting off one part from the next. As far as "may He establish His kingdom" the Ashkenazi Kaddish is the same as the Sephardi one; but then the Sephardim (and Hasidim) add, "... causing His salvation to spring forth and bringing near [hastening the advent of] His Messiah." Why not take that over into, say, the reader's Kaddish *Titqabbal* or the mourner's Scholars' Kaddish? It would make somewhat more explicit the messianic hope that the Kaddish has expressed from the beginning.

In the *Kedushah*, with the reader repeating the Standing Prayer and reader and congregation saying a doxology built around "Holy, holy, holy," there are slight differences between the Ashkenazi and the Sephardi-Hasidic texts. Every now and then we might want to follow the Sephardi usage, and the *siddur* ought to have it for us. In the *Alenu* we should take from the Sephardim the passage that the Christian censors deleted from our text.

■   ■   ■

The story is told about a Hasid—the same story in its essentials no doubt exists in other religious traditions, too—that people complained of his frequent absence from the synagogue. "I start to go," he told them, "but when I leave the house I see God's world testifying to the majesty of Him who in His goodness renews every day, continually, the work of creation. So I recite some psalms, like 'The heavens declare the glory of God; / and the firmament proclaims his handiwork' and 'How great are Thy works, O Lord! / Thy thoughts are very deep!' And then, by the time I remember where I am and where I was going, it's too late, and I don't get to *shul*. But," he said, brightening, "sometimes I don't get distracted by thinking about God, and then I go."

Does the moral apply to us? Of course, but not entirely. We are different from that Hasid. We do not bless the Creator for His creation, because we have learned that the argument from design is a fallacy. Both for him and for us the synagogue is a distraction, but for us the distraction is unlikely to be from thinking about God.

Another story about Hasidim: In the presence of their sleeping master, two disciples were talking low about how hard it was to resist temptation, and how the *yezer ha-ra*, the Evil Desire, kept running after them. Their master, who had not been asleep after all, opened his eyes and said: "Don't flatter yourselves. The Evil Desire isn't running after you, you haven't reached that height. You're still running after the Evil Desire."

Even when a man has arrived at a high degree of spirituality, we are informed, he has problems. I suppose an analogy might be with the rich, who have problems that the poor are either ignorant or skeptical about, and certainly in no position to complain about. The frail spirituality of the synagogue must be a real problem—for the spiritually rich. Who will believe us, and groundlings, if we pretend that it is our problem and that we have reached that height?

(1966)

Relevance in the Synagogue

EVERYONE, ESPECIALLY THE YOUNG, seems to agree that the synagogue is irrelevant. When Jewish college students (and youthful or wishfully youthful college teachers) are asked whether the synagogue is relevant, they answer no. In all that interests them—peace, race, poverty, the meaning of morality, freedom—the synagogue says and does little that seems to them useful or important. It isn't unexpected that they should say this. Most of them are uncommitted or, as they are sometimes called, un-Jewish.

What may be unexpected is that even those young people who consider themselves to be committed Jews are apt to say the same thing. In effect, they say they are committed Jews, synagogue Jews, not because of the synagogue but in spite of it. They are disappointed when they turn to it for encouragement, help, or advice in those things that to them are most important—which aren't greatly different from the important things of the uncommitted. Members of a self-conscious youth generation tend to have similar ideas about what is important; and particularly now, when you don't have to be young to be convinced of the importance of peace, race, poverty, and the rest.

There is a certain ambiguity in this criticism of the synagogue. Are the young people saying that the synagogue is as irrelevant as the church, or that it is more irrelevant? If the

critics wanted to, they could argue, plausibly, that the synagogue is more irrelevant. They could point to the far-out nuns
and priests, the new-morality and secular city theologians, the
community activism of the mainline Protestant denomina-
tions, the traditional peace and service activities of the Quak-
ers. In image, at least, and probably also to some extent in deed,
the synagogue is substantially to the rear of the churches in
these matters. Yet the critics of the synagogue generally avoid
the comparison. I think they avoid it because they like to make
believe that a big, obvious fact doesn't exist: that America,
though it is a secular society and has more separation of church
and state than practically any other country in the world, is
also a Christian society. I shall come back to this later.

Provisionally, let us regard the criticism of the synagogue
as a criticism of religion generally—that is, one which assumes
an equal unsatisfactoriness of church and synagogue. What is
new about this is that it is made at all. Criticism arises from
expectation. In the *entre deux guerres*, enlightened, progressive people didn't make the criticism. They didn't have the
expectation. They simply took it for granted that religion was
so thoroughly stupid and out of the question that it needn't
be thought about at all. We all say and believe that the world
is more secular than it has ever been. Simultaneously, enlightened, progressive people are more disillusioned with irreligion
and more expectant of religion than they have ever been. If a
New Leftist can bring himself to think of coalition at all, he
will include not the trade unions but the churches.

As for the synagogue, it may be less relevant than it used
to be, but I'm not sure. The social-justice phase of Reform
Judaism in the 1930s seems to have been chiefly a matter of
resolutions by the Central Conference of American Rabbis and
of a certain idea that the Reform rabbinate, or part of it, had of
itself. It doesn't seem to have had much effect on the Jewish
consciousness, let alone on the social reality. Looking back, some
are inclined to think social justice was emphasized then not

only because that was what America was thinking about but also to help the rabbis feel they weren't superfluous. A friend of mine, ordained at a Reform seminary in the 1950s, has told me that a professor once explained to his students: "In those days we had rabbis of two sorts: there were the social-justice ones, and then there were the ones who knew Hebrew." (My friend speaks Hebrew with his children; and he was jailed in the South when jail wasn't yet fashionable.)

As it happens, the synagogue did have serious and important things to say then to Jews about social questions, but those were Jewish issues—notably anti-Semitism. We are thankful to have fewer such problems now, but we still have some: anti-Semitism in the Soviet Union and Poland, the incomplete disappearance of anti-Semitism in the United States, the curious rise of an anti-Semitism on the American Left. About these, young Jews aren't greatly concerned. They are likely to deny, impatiently, that such things exist. That is all so parochial, they say; so limited, so—so Jewy.

■ ■ ■

I have read to Jewish college students poems by LeRoi Jones that *mutatis mutandis* are Nazi, and have asked the students what they think. They look at me with bewilderment and incomprehension. What am I talking about? Why do I want to talk about anti-Semitism? What has it to do with them? Besides, Jones isn't really an anti-Semite. If he hates Jews who exploit, they deserve to be hated.

It is as though Hitler were no more recent than Haman.

For a universalist, anti-Semitism isn't an important problem. There are few Jews in the world, and a universalist will worry about the problems of the many. Yet if you're a Jew, anti-Semitism can kill you though you're also a universalist. It killed Jewish universalists on the other side of the ocean in the other half of the century. If you think anti-Semitism unworthy of your notice, think again.

Much has changed, but here little has changed. Thirty years ago the fathers and uncles of the young critics were equally impatient. For them, anti-Semitism was a symptom, a byproduct, of capitalism. To abolish anti-Semitism you had first to abolish capitalism. You had first to institute socialism. Anti-Semitism was rampant in Germany, where capitalism had attained its pure or ultimate form of Nazism, and in the United States. In the Soviet Union, anti-Semitism had been uprooted and had disappeared. Worrying about anti-Semitism only distracted you from what was really needed, the struggle against capitalism.

As we can see now, that reasoning wasn't exactly scientific. It proceeded from essence, or from definition: capitalism was wicked, producing wicked things, and socialism was good, producing good things. The logic was scholastic—decadent scholastic at that, not greatly different from the logic of decadent scholastic medicine that Molière allows us to overhear: *Quare opium facit dormire?—Quia habet quandam virtutem dormitivam.—Optime!* Why does opium make people sleep?—Because it has a certain power that causes sleep.—Very good!

Today in the United States, students wonder what you're talking about when you talk about anti-Semitism, but in the Soviet Union and Poland they know. In capitalist-Nazi Germany, 600,000 Jews were held to be at the same time Bolsheviks and bankers, assuming those roles in a fearsome Jewish conspiracy to subvert the German nation and the Aryan race. In socialist-Marxist Poland, 25,000 Jews are held to be at the same time Zionists, cosmopolitans, and Stalinists, assuming those roles in a fearsome Jewish conspiracy to subvert the Polish nation and its socialist order.

So the synagogue didn't talk too much about anti-Semitism (Nazi and fascist) then. Maybe it isn't talking enough about anti-Semitism (Soviet and leftist, and generally contemporary) now. But that is hardly the sort of thing that universalist critics normally mean by relevance.

Actually, are the critics saying that they're perplexed, that they don't know what to think or do about peace, race, poverty, and that they want the synagogue to advise and lead them? Not usually. They are saying that the synagogue should tell them what they want to hear, that it should support and strengthen them in what they are already doing. And they want the synagogue to transmit the truths understood by the enlightened to its members, so deficient in enlightenment.

A year or two ago I heard a scholar describe the typical sermon in an up-to-date American synagogue as the rabbi's review of a bestseller. He didn't know what he was talking about, probably not having been in a synagogue in thirty years. The book-review sermon isn't typical anymore. When it was typical, that was because rabbi and congregation wanted to be relevant.

Can there be any similarity between social-action deeds and sermons, on the one hand, and popular book reviews, on the other? It may be said that popular book reviews are only an expression of what religionists themselves, especially such Christian theologians as H. Richard Niebuhr, condemn as culture religion (the anthropologists' culture, not Matthew Arnold's). Such religion, whatever it may call itself, is a tribal idolatry, echoing the prejudices and self-love of the secular community, whereas the duty of true religion is to stand apart and judge. Those who agree that book-review sermons were out of place in the 1930s but insist that social-action sermons are needed in the 1960s would transpose to the sphere of society and politics the distinction often made in literature and art between high culture (Arnold's) and popular culture: book-review sermons are bad, belonging to popular culture; social-action sermons are good, belonging to high social thought.

But escape isn't that easy. Lionel Trilling has shown us how blurred the old distinctions have become. In the old days, high culture was for the happy few, and the man who adhered to high culture could realistically see himself as set apart from the vulgar. That is no longer so. The adversary culture, as Trilling calls it, is now as established as what used to be the official, established culture: in that *New Yorker* cartoon the artist's girlfriend asks him, "Why must you be a nonconformist like everyone else?" Niebuhr's judgment can apply equally to religion that affirms what used to be the established culture and to religion that affirms what used to be the adversary culture; equally to religion that affirms popular politics and to religion that affirms adversary politics.

With Jews, what's more, adversary has long been as popular as popular. Fifteen years ago, how much courage did a rabbi really need, or how much distinctive moral leadership did he exercise, when he criticized Senator Joseph McCarthy to his congregation? This year, how much courage does he need, and how much leadership does he exercise, when he praises Senator Eugene McCarthy?

■　　■　　■

The advice to be relevant comes most vocally from students and teachers. From them, is it good advice? Professor Leonard J. Fein of MIT has written (*Judaism*, Winter 1968):

> Around the country, rabbinic groups and individual rabbis have spoken and speak vigorously on social issues. I applaud their vigor. I believe the community cries out for that sort of leadership. But ... I do not believe that the image of the rabbi as a social-protest activist or as a literary critic is going to inspire either the students or the academic community. The rabbi, as he moves from his specific field of competence—which was, of course, always ... Torah ... —becomes a dilettante.... He must be *au courant* with literature, politics, psychology, sociology, history, anthropology ... and necessarily dilettantish.
>
> A sermon on Black Power ... may be all the information a rabbi's congregants will get ... and therefore he is obliged to give it.... If a student of mine came to me to find out about Black Power, I would either send him up to Tom Pettigrew at

Harvard or I would urge him to take my seminar on race in
America.

... the rabbi, in ministering to the needs of the pants manufacturers, is boring the academic. If he were to minister to the
needs of the academic, he would violate his responsibility to
the pants manufacturers. That is what makes this a dilemma. ...

But it may be worth suggesting what my conception of min-
istry to academics by rabbis might mean. ... The rabbi as Judaic
scholar becomes the peer of the academic, and only as Judaic
scholar ... whether by Judaic studies one means biblical exegesis or Jewish demography. ... I would more readily attend a
sermon on historical analogies to Old Testament literature,
perhaps,—than a sermon in which a rabbi purported to inform
me about Black Power or, I might add, about Vietnam.

Professor Fein implies, but it remains to be said explicitly, that a rabbi speaking about or from Torah can also say
something significant about Black Power or Vietnam—something that only he can say, and therefore that we must hear
from him rather than from Pettigrew or Fein. No rabbi imag-
ines that the Torah gives unequivocal commands about Black
Power or Vietnam; yet, struggling with the problems or
demands of this day, he can be helped by what the Torah says
that is not of this day.

Once, rabbis weren't skeptical enough about the usefulness of sermons. Now they're too skeptical.

The synagogues I go to aren't extraordinary. The rabbis
who preach there aren't the most famous, but they are good
rabbis, and I hear good sermons from them. Usually the sermons instruct me, sometimes they stir me, and sometimes
they move me to do what I might otherwise not want to do or
lack the will to do.

One such sermon was about Negroes and Jews, and was
taken seriously because the congregation knew that the rabbi
takes anti-Semitism seriously, including the anti-Semitism of
black nationalist intellectuals. The rabbi told us our attitude

toward Negroes was wrong. It was that line from *My Fair Lady,* Why can't a woman be more like a man? We ask, Why can't Negroes be more like Jews? We should remember, he said, that in the Passover Haggadah the answer to the questions asked by the child begins, "We were slaves in Egypt." It is easier for slavery to produce a rabble than a people: the Torah tells us that many who left Egypt with Moses were *erev rav* and *asafsuf.* Our ancestors had a revelation at Mount Sinai, and Ten Commandments. After having been so uniquely favored, they went on to the golden calf. If we insist on criticism of the Negroes, the rabbi concluded, it should be not that they are too little like the Jews, but too much.

Another sermon, by another rabbi, related even more directly to Passover. On the face of it, the sermon was unworldly, half ritual detail and half eschatology. The Prophetical lesson on the last day of Passover, from Isaiah, sees a transformation:

> ... There shall come forth a shoot from the stock of Jesse,
> and a branch shall grow out of his root.
> And the spirit of the Lord shall rest upon him. . . .
> . . . .
> with righteousness he shall judge the poor,
> and decide with equity for the humble of the earth. . . .
> . . . .
> The wolf shall dwell with the lamb,
> and the leopard shall lie down with the kid,
> and the calf and the lion and the fatling together,
> and a little child shall lead them.
> The cow and the bear shall graze;
> their young shall lie down together;
> and the lion shall eat straw like the ox.
> The suckling child shall play over the hole of the asp,
> and the weaned child shall put his hand in the adder's den.
> They shall not hurt nor destroy
> in all My holy mountain;

for the earth shall be full of the knowledge of the Lord
as the waters cover the sea.
. . . .
. . . and there will be a highway for the remnant of His people
that remains from Assyria,
as there was for Israel
when they came up from the land of Egypt.
. . . .
. . . with joy you will draw water from the wells of salvation.
And you will say in that day:
"Give thanks to the Lord,
call upon His name;
make known His deeds among the nations,
proclaim that His name is exalted. . . .
. . . .
Shout, and sing for joy, inhabitant of Zion,
for great in your midst is the Holy One of Israel."

The rabbi told us that there is a link between that prophecy and a kabbalistic usage in the Seder. When we break the middle matzah we put aside the larger half for the *afikoman:* first we eat the smaller half and only later do we eat the larger. This is to signify that the future redemption will be greater than the redemption that Passover celebrates, of the Jews from Egyptian slavery. There is yet to come the redemption of all men, and of nature itself, from the slavery of hurting, destroying, and ignorance of the Lord. Our Past Passover (*Pesah de-avar*) is of the lesser redemption. The Future Passover (*Pesah de-atid*) will be of the greater redemption. Celebrating the Past Passover, we long for the Future Passover. Prefiguring the Future Passover, we do the little we can—which is all we can—to lessen hurting, destroying, and ignorance.

The third rabbi has a sermon he repeats from time to time, with variations, about America, the Jews, and Jewish education. In America, he says, more than in any other country where Jews have lived as a minority, we enjoy freedom and opportunity without having to pay the price of abandoning Judaism. What we shall make of ourselves depends entirely on us. Precisely because America is so accepting, many are tempted to forget about Judaism—to want the best colleges for their children while being content with a few years of Sunday school, or not even that. In quality and quantity, Jewish education must begin to match our ever-rising general education. Our responsibility, he concludes, is to assure Jewish education for our children (and ourselves).

None of these sermons is irrelevant. All, in different propositions of universalism and particularism, speak directly to us. They are relevant in the synagogue for the very reason that they wouldn't be relevant anywhere else. If we didn't hear them there, we wouldn't hear them anywhere. The synagogue in which they are preached and the rabbi who preaches them aren't irrelevant.

■ ■ ■

Now to return to what I mentioned earlier: on the whole, the critics ignore the simple, big fact that America is a Christian country. What it amounts to is that they ask the synagogue to behave as if most Americans were Jews. Asking synagogues to pretend they are the majority church doesn't mean asking them to be more relevant. It means asking them to be more irrelevant. (Now, in Israel it would be different.)

Whether as individuals or through our institutions, we enter into programs for dealing with racial inequities as if the relation of white Jews to Negroes were the same as of white Christians to Negroes. But most Negroes are, or have been, Christians. That must be our starting point. What would a Jewish congregation's remedial reading program for Christian Negro children amount to? Wouldn't Negroes see it as Lady Bountiful's condescension? Of that they have had all they want. But might they not feel differently if they were members of the congregation, or invited to become members?

People have been asking why there aren't more black faces in insurance offices or in commercials. The synagogue's critics ought to be asking why there aren't more black faces in Jewish congregations. And if that is for the future, right now there is a real problem that we aren't dealing with as we should be. There are some black Jews in the United States. On the whole, the overwhelmingly white synagogue hasn't done nearly enough to welcome them. If there are black Jews who are also black nationalists, the synagogue hasn't done nearly enough to talk with them.

The coin has two sides. It is true, as the critics say, that the synagogue should do more to condemn the exploitation of Negroes by Jewish merchants (or landlords, or employers). It is also true, as the critics usually don't say, that the synagogue should be indignant about having merchants identified as Jews. Granted, *arguendo*, that those merchants are exploiters and that they are Jews. Are they merchants who exploit or Jews who exploit? And in fact, is everyone an exploiter who is so accused? Everyone? Is everything done against him justified? Everything? The synagogue would ask these questions if the accusers, or those in whose name the accusation was made, were white. It must ask these questions if the accusers are black.

Provincialism can be of time as well as of geographic space or life space. In that sense, some of the synagogue's critics are provincial. They want it to be relevant to our time, but its time isn't ours alone. The synagogue's time is also liturgical time. It corresponds in a way to "seedtime and harvest, cold and heat, summer and winter, day and night"—which "shall not cease," we have been promised, "so long as the earth endures." If one wishes, it is cyclical time rather than linear. (The cycles are short: daily, weekly, yearly.) In the synagogue's rhythm of liturgical time, it is being relevant to nonlinear needs. Not that the synagogue's time isn't linear or contemporary at all; just that it also consists of Sabbath and weekday, feast and fast, morning and evening, before eating and after.

The critics' objections to the synagogue are temporally provincial, too, in making the assumptions of our time. For us these are axioms. We assume that only innovation and "creativity" count, forgetting that most of what we do isn't that sort of thing at all. Mostly, we work to hold the wilderness at bay, to preserve a clearing in the woods, to keep things going: making the beds, stopping the leak, mowing the lawn, delivering the mail and the milk. Eric Hoffer calls this maintenance, and he can be lyrical about it. Without maintenance, what would happen to our houses, schools, buildings, factories, stores, farms? The cyclical time of the synagogue is something like maintenance. It isn't innovative, it is merely sustaining—and altogether necessary, and worthy of honor and respect. If maintenance may be said to be feminine, and innovation (like adventure) masculine, then the synagogue, though classically it has been an institution of men, may be said to be in part a feminine institution. Is that wrong?

A girl says, "You go to the synagogue for a dance or to pray, but you never consider going there [for] social action." No Hebrew school when you were a child; no adult education (including lectures about rights); no meetings to protest Soviet anti-Semitism? And why equate prayer and a dance? If your grandfather and *his* grandfather hadn't prayed in a synagogue, what makes you so sure you would be so zealous for social action? Young Jews are a small fraction of all young Americans, but an appreciably bigger one of all young Americans who worry about and do social action. The synagogue— Judaism—isn't a sufficient explanation of that; but neither is any explanation sufficient which disregards the synagogue. And the social action of Jews doesn't have to take place in a synagogue building.

■   ■   ■

There is another way in which the synagogue could fail us by being too much of our time. We would love democracy shallowly if we didn't realize how problematic it is. If we took democracy as self-evidently best, we couldn't hope to understand what Churchill meant when he said that democracy is the worst of all forms of government—except any other form that has ever been tried. We couldn't understand Bishop Stubbs saying that feudalism would be best, if men were angels and archangels. We couldn't respond to the Shakespeare who says:

> ...O! when degree is shak'd,
> Which is the ladder to all high designs,
> The enterprise is sick. How could communities,
> ....
> But by degree, stand in authentic place?
> Take but degree away, untune that string,
> And, hark! what discord follows; each thing meets
> In mere oppugnancy....

Shakespeare our contemporary, yes. And our ancestor. The synagogue is, it has to be, our contemporary and our ancestor.

Perhaps because of the season, Passover is on my mind; or perhaps because Passover is central to the Jewish experience and imagination. At the time of the revolution of 1848, the leading Jewish educator in Germany was Samuel Ehrenberg (the great-grandfather of Franz Rosenzweig and of his Lutheran cousins). Exulting in the emancipations decreed by the revolution, Ehrenberg wanted to remove from the Haggadah the passage that reads, "Now we are slaves, next year may we be free men." He was trying to make the synagogue relevant. Could anyone have been more irrelevant?

Even politically, it is still too soon for us to stop saying, "Now we are slaves." And beyond politics, not until the Future Passover will we stop being slaves (or enslaved, or slavish).

Despite Israeli independence, for which God be thanked, those Orthodox are right who say that only the Future Passover will abolish the fast of the Ninth of Av, which laments exile. The Jews' physical or political exile may be passing—let us hope so—but the passing of the exile of the children of Adam from Eden is not yet on the horizon. Until then, on Passover let us say that now we are slaves and on the Ninth of Av let us lament exile, and let contemporaries think all that to be irrelevant.

On *Shabbat Ha-gadol*, the Sabbath before Passover, we read the last verses of the last Prophet, Malachi: "Behold, I will send you Elijah the prophet before the great and terrible day of the Lord comes. And he will turn the heart of the fathers back to the sons, and the heart of the sons back to their fathers, in order that I not come and smite the land with a curse. (Behold I will send you the prophet before the great and terrible day of the Lord comes.)" Elijah is the forerunner of the Messiah. Only Elijah or the Messiah can bring about a full reconciliation of fathers with sons; only the Future Passover. In the meantime, hoping for as much reconciliation as we are capable of, we are resigned to some separation.

If the fathers are also taken to represent history (the past, tradition), and the sons to represent contemporaneity (the present, relevance), we must conclude that until the Messiah comes we have to live, uneasily, with both. Since it isn't the characteristic temptation of our generations to slight the present in favor of the past, for us a call to present relevance may not be the needful thing. For us the needful thing may be to remember that relevance, unlike ripeness, isn't all.

(1968)

The Vindictive and the Merciful: God of Wrath and God of Love

I USED TO THINK I was fooling my father, but now I suspect that he knew all along and did not want to make an issue of it. When I was about sixteen or seventeen, I no longer went to synagogue every Sabbath, as I had done when I was a child. Left to myself I would probably not have gone at all; but I was not left to myself, and I went with my father on Rosh Hashanah and Yom Kippur, and occasionally on other holy days as well. I still go. When the time came and I could have stayed away, I discovered I did not want to.

My father prays from his prayer book, but I read from mine. If you read more than you pray, you are left with a good deal of time. Skipping repeated matter, for example, represents a very considerable saving. In addition, experience and temperament lead to the establishment of some fruitful principles of exclusion; thus, it has been many years since I last read liturgical poetry in which the verses are set down according to an acrostic or alphabetic pattern. (Sometimes I am astonished by the number of pages this eliminates.) It did not take me long to realize that I could carefully read everything in the prayer book that appealed to me in about half the time a respectable person is expected to remain in the synagogue. This meant that the prayer book had to be supplemented.

When it first became clear that the *Mahzor* was not enough to see me through, I recognized that I would not have a wide range of choice for additional reading.

The language would have to be Hebrew—out of an obscure sense of the fitness of things, and the ignoble calculation that only Hebrew might not arrest my father's casual glance. The same sense of the fitness of things dictated that the reading should have a certain loftiness of spirit, and even of form. In the course of the years since then, my personal canon has come to include the Bible and post-biblical poetry. Two years ago I added a new volume, a collection by the Israeli writer and scholar S. Y. Agnon, entitled *The Days of Awe: A Book of Usages, Homilies and Parables for Rosh Hashanah and Yom Kippur and the Intervening Days*. It is a fascinating book. Last Yom Kippur I came upon a selection entitled "The Reckoning," taken by Agnon from a Hasidic work, *Marvelous Tales of the Great Men of Israel:*

> Once, on the eve of Yom Kippur, the holy Rabbi Elimelech of Lisinsk, of blessed memory, said to his disciples: "Is it your desire to know how one should act on the eve of Yom Kippur? Go to the tailor who lives on the outskirts of the city."
>
> They went to him and stood before the window of his house. They saw him and his sons praying with simplicity, like all tailors. After the prayer they put on Sabbath raiment and lit candles and prepared a table full of good things and sat down to the table in great joy. The tailor took out of a chest a book in which were written all the transgressions that he had committed during the year, from one Yom Kippur to the next, and said: "Lord of the world, today the time has come to make a reckoning between us of all the transgressions that we have committed, for it is a time of atonement for all Israel." At once he began to reckon and enumerate all the transgressions that he had committed in the course of the year, for they were all written down in this account book. After he had finished the reckoning of transgressions, he took out a book larger and heavier

than the first and said: "Having counted the transgressions I have committed, now I shall count the transgressions Thou hast committed."

Then he reckoned the sorrow and afflictions, the troubles and anguish and sickness and loss of money that during the course of the year had befallen him and the members of his family. When he had finished the reckoning he said: "Lord of the world, if we are indeed to reckon with equity, Thou owest me more than I owe Thee; but I do not wish to be exact with Thee in an exact reckoning, for behold, today is the eve of the Day of Atonement and we must all be reconciled with our fellows; we therefore forgive Thee all the transgressions that Thou hast committed against us, and do Thou likewise forgive us all the transgressions wherewith we have transgressed against Thee." He poured brandy into his glass and said the blessing "by Whose word all things have their being," and said in a loud voice: "*Lehayim,* Lord of the world! We hereby mutually forgive all our transgressions against each other; and all of them, whether ours or Thine, are null and void, as though they had never been." Afterwards they ate and drank with great joy.

The disciples returned to their master and told him everything they had seen and heard. And they said that the words of the tailor were harsh words and excessive effrontery against heaven. But their master said to them: "Know that the Holy One, blessed be He, in His glory and essence, and the whole host of heaven come to listen to the tailor's words, which are spoken in great simplicity; and from his words are created grace and joy in all the worlds."

As I read this story, I was reminded of something I had read recently in *Medieval Panorama*, by the late G. G. Coulton, the eminent British medievalist. Coulton is examining the effects on Christian theology of a literal reliance on the Old Testament, and he does not find them good:

[St. Thomas Aquinas] decides definitely that the joy of the Blessed in Heaven will be increased by the sight of the Damned wallowing beneath, in a Hell which he describes ... at greater length and in cruder terms than Calvin in his *Institutes*. The Blessed will not, of course, rejoice in all these infernal torments *per se*, but incidentally, "considering in them the order of God's justice, and their own liberation, whereat they will rejoice." How can he thus decide, it may be asked, after he himself has pointed out that to rejoice in another's pains may be ordinarily classed as hatred, and that God does not delight in men's pains? These apparently invincible natural considerations are brushed aside by one plain Bible text [Psalm 58:11]: "The just shall rejoice when he shall see the revenge." That vindictive verse of a Hebrew poet, to St. Thomas, outweighs everything else.

For Coulton it was all the vindictive Hebrew poet's fault. This follows from the postulate that the God of the Jews is a God of wrath and the God of the Christians a God of love. It also follows from this principle that Aquinas, like Calvin, was an imperfect Christian—i.e. insufficiently merciful—because he had allowed himself to be too much influenced by the Old Testament spirit.

I am not sure why I so resented this passage. It was not the first or perhaps even the hundredth time I had met a reference to the universal acceptance and unquestionable truth of the contrast between Christian love and Jewish wrath. Few doctrines can lay equal claim to Christian antiquity, as we can see when we view it in its most extreme form, the Gnostic identification of Jehovah with Satan.

I suppose the cause of my resentment is to be found precisely in the fact that Coulton did not have any deep-seated bias against Jews or Judaism. His two great passions were opposition to pacifism and opposition to the Catholic Church, especially the latter; he saw himself as a kind of latter-day Lorenzo Valla, whose mission it was to expose the fraudulent

Donations of Constantine of his own time. So far was Coulton from being an anti-Semite that he says many generous and handsome things about medieval Jewry in his book: the treatment of women, for instance, and the almost universal literacy. Respecting literacy and education, he insists that it would be misleading to compare the average medieval Jew with his Christian contemporary; the only reasonable comparison would be with the Christian priest, and at that Coulton is convinced that the Jew would carry off the laurels. We read in Exodus [19:6]: "And ye shall be unto Me a kingdom of priests, and a holy nation." There has been some groping for an understanding of Judaism as the religion of a priesthood without a laity; Coulton's assertion, in an entirely different context, that medieval Jewry as a whole was in a very significant respect to be considered in the same category with the Christian clergy is highly suggestive. But all this leads far afield; let us come back to our muttons.

■　　■　　■

Clearly Coulton was not the kind of scholar who unthinkingly accepts any religious prejudice, however hallowed by time. The theme of vindictive Judaism and merciful Christianity must have run very deep indeed in his culture for him not to question it. Yet Elimelech of Lisinsk knew the Psalms better than Aquinas or Calvin; and though he had read and pondered the same verse by the same vindictive poet, his God and the God of his tailor does not seem very harsh or unforgiving at all. And since we are on the subject of forgiveness and Yom Kippur, neither does the God of the great Levi Yitzhak of Berditchev, in Buber's account: "He used to say: 'Like a woman who suffers overwhelming pain in childbirth, and swears she will never lie with her husband again, and yet forgets her oath, so on every Day of Atonement we confess our faults and promise to turn, and yet we go on sinning, and You go on forgiving us.'"

I return to Aquinas and Calvin. A few pages after Coulton has told us that if they are cruel it is chiefly because an ancient Hebrew poet was vindictive, we come to a passage about the elect and the damned:

> A minority of human beings were "elect": the majority were not indeed "predestined" to hell, but their damnation was "fore-known": God knew that this was their final destination. The difference here between St. Thomas Aquinas and Calvin is far smaller than men commonly imagine.... At least as far down as St. Alfonso Liguori [1696–1857, not many years earlier than Elimelech of Lisinsk and Levi Yitzhak of Berditchev], it had been almost universally taught by writers in the Roman Church that the greater part of mankind would miss salvation. Some even foretold hell for an overwhelming majority; and others, like St. Alfonso, held that "the more general opinion is that the greater part even of the Faithful are damned." ... Medieval preachers sometimes estimated the disproportion as one in a thousand, or ten thousand, or even more.... *Paucitas salvandorum* [the fewness of those to be saved] ... comes very near to a *de fide* doctrine, in virtue of this universal patristic consent until recent times.

If the faithful have little chance of future bliss, infidels have none:

> Tertullian painted the future vengeance of God upon pagan persecutors in language which still enjoys, after all these centuries, a melancholy notoriety.... St. Augustine even taught that unbaptized infants suffered in hell not only the penalty of losing the Beatific Vision but bodily torture also.... The only Ecumenical Council of the West which dealt with this question was that of Florence, which decreed: "The Holy Roman Church professes and preaches that none who is not within the Catholic Church (not only pagans, but neither Jews nor heretics nor schismatics) can partake of eternal life, but shall go into everlasting fire ... unless they have joined her before death.

The dogma here goes back to St. Cyprian, in the third century: *extra ecclesiam nulla salus*—outside the Church, no salvation. Coulton shows that it was not until Cardinal de Lugo, in the middle of the seventeenth century, when the Church felt that a policy of suppleness was required in the face of a vigorous Protestantism and a nascent freethought, that the plain meaning of the Latin words began to be interpreted more liberally.

The religion of the cruel and vindictive Jews knows nothing about the doom of the majority of the faithful to eternal torment. As for those who are not Jews, the standard doctrine is the Talmudic dictum: "The righteous of the nations of the world have a share in the world to come."

■　　■　　■

It has occurred to me that all this may be only *Dogmengeschichte*, intellectual history with an appeal primarily to theologians and amateurs of theological scholarship. Between the eloquence or silence of learned texts on the subject of damnation or salvation and the actual conduct and emotions of ordinary people, there need not exist any direct relation at all. But that relation does exist, or at least it did. Think of the magnificent third chapter of James Joyce's *A Portrait of the Artist As a Young Man*, in which Stephen makes a retreat with the Jesuits and hears a number of sermons, in particular a sermon on hell. I have read that sermon again, and its sadism disturbs me as deeply as it did the first time I read it.

The entire passage is too long to quote, and excerpts would give only an attenuated impression of its total horror. It includes such elements as these: St. Anselm's vision of the damned so closely packed that they are unable to remove gnawing worms from their eyes; a pestilential stench sufficient, in St. Bonaventure's words, to infect the whole world; corpses putrefying into a jellylike mass of liquid corruption and giving off dense choking fumes of nauseous loathsome decomposition; brains boiling in the skull, bowels a red-hot mass of burning pulp, and eyes flaming like molten balls; nameless suffocating filth; fire kindled in the abyss by the offended majesty of the Omnipotent God and fanned into everlasting and ever increasing fury by the breath of the anger of the Godhead; the damned turning on one another, blaspheming God (!) and execrating and howling at each other, helpless and hopeless; and the devils, who once were beautiful angels and now are as ugly as once they were beautiful (so ugly that after seeing one, St. Catherine said she would choose to walk on live coals for the rest of her life rather than see him again for an instant), mocking and deriding the souls they have seduced. "Now the time for repentance has gone by. Time is, time was, but time shall be no more!"

The words are Joyce's, but the contents are precise doctrine, and the *Catholic Encyclopedia* differs only verbally from the apostate artist. This is the hell to which Christian theology, Catholic and Protestant, assigned the large majority of the faithful, let alone the heretics, infidels, and pagans. Knowledge of this hell was not the esoteric possession of the learned but was insistently preached to all Christians, and was common to all Christians' vision of the life to come. In Joyce the memory of the terror inspired by this vision is reproduced as art. Traces of the same memory are found in folk humor: there is, for example, the story of the Scottish Calvinist divine who preached on the wailing and gnashing of teeth at the Last Judgment; when asked about those who had died without teeth, he answered: "Teeth will be provided."

What centuries of inventive ingenuity must have gone into the perfection of such a vision of hell; what fertile imagination and depraved inspiration! And all is attributed to a merciful God. During the Lenten season of 1949, Pope Pius called for greater homiletic emphasis on hell. "Desire for heaven," he said, "is a more perfect motive than fear of eternal punishment, but from this it does not follow that it is the most effective motive to hold them [the people] far from sin and to convert them to God."

Rabbinic literature knows of hell too, but it is a very rudimentary kind of hell as compared with the Christian one. And the folk was not ridden by the fear of hell. When I was a boy my pious and learned grandfather, *alav hashalom,* used to speak to me often about righteousness and sin, reward and punishment; but I remember his telling me in detail about hell only once, and then it was incidental to a proof of the blessedness of the Sabbath. On the Sabbath the damned have respite from their suffering and even the River Sambatyon, which twists around the precincts of hell, ceases to roar and to hurl up its rocks, as it does on the profane days of the week.

There is an extensive literature, mostly in Yiddish and Hebrew, that began more than a hundred and fifty years ago and consists in an unrelenting attack on the degenerate life and thought of the ghetto. This literature is essentially autobiographical. The writers recall with bitterness the wretched squalor of the *cheder* school, the obscurantism of the religion taught and practiced, the mean behavior that was considered the norm of right living. Nearly every one of them says in so many words that he cannot forgive the ghetto and Orthodoxy—which in their emotions go hand in hand—for a childhood poisoned by many things, and each draws up a detailed bill of particulars. Yet I cannot think of one who speaks of a childhood made unhappy by the fear of hell.

When the Jew thought of the world to come, he thought of Paradise. The learned and those with a taste for learning hoped, with a fair degree of confidence, for the enjoyment of the splendor of the Divine Presence and the study of Torah in the circle of Abraham and Moses. The simple anticipated the simpler joys: sitting on a golden throne, eating the flesh of Leviathan and the Ox of the Wilderness, drinking of the Preserved Wine. It did not cross their minds that a merciful God could send the majority of them to hell.

■   ■   ■

I have no quarrel with the contemporary preference for difficult religion over the soft liberal religion that prevailed a generation and two generations ago. We have seen so much human
evil in our day that even if we cannot quite accept orthodox
theology's God, we can accept its man. Man no longer seems
the naturally good and indefinitely perfectible being of the
philosophes and of liberal religion; he more closely resembles
the finished portrait drawn of him by classical theology with
the indications provided in the Bible—indications like these:
"The imagination of man's heart is evil from his youth" (Genesis 8:24); "The heart is deceitful above all things, / And it is
exceeding weak [or 'desperately wicked']—who can know it?"
(Jeremiah 17:9). What lends additional prestige to this theological portrait is that it is complex. Hobbes could speak in his
Leviathan of "the life of man, solitary, poor, nasty, brutish and
short"; but the Bible knows that not even man's fate is so simple: "What is man, that Thou art mindful of him? / And the
son of man, that Thou thinkest of him? / Yet Thou hast made
him but little lower than the angels, / And hast crowned him
with glory and honour" (Psalm 8:5–6).

Consider the new respect for puritanism as an intellectual and moral system. A generation ago the teachings of Freud
and Tawney, vulgarized *à la portée de tout le monde,* had made
everybody understand that puritanism meant sexual inhibi-
tion and economic exploitation. G. K. Chesterton was thought
to be only up to his usual tricks when he said, in his *Heretics:*
"Many modern Englishmen talk of themselves as the sturdy
descendants of their sturdy Puritan fathers. As a fact, they
would run away from a cow. If you had asked one of their Puritan fathers, if you had asked Bunyan, for instance, whether he
was sturdy, he would have answered, with tears, that he was
as weak as water. And because of this he would have borne tortures." In our day Professor Perry Miller, neither a puritan
himself nor a fantast like Chesterton, takes puritanism very
seriously indeed in *The New England Mind: The Seventeenth*

Century. Correspondingly, with all respect for the memory of the late Dr. Liebman, it is hard to take his Peace of Mind seriously; easy and consoling answers are no longer to our taste.

Nor is puritanism foreign to the Jewish tradition. Hasidism, which dared to suggest a kind of camaraderie with God on Yom Kippur, is also responsible for the *Tefilah zakkah* (prayer for purity), a silent meditation to be read before the communal Yom Kippur devotions. The *Tefilah zakkah* is a passionate declaration of unworthiness and dependence on God's grace—a typical puritan document.

■   ■   ■

All this having been said, I persist in thinking that the Jewish backwardness in the matter of hell is better than the Christian accomplishment. On the evidence of hell, the ancient Christian formula of a merciful Christianity confronting a vindictive Judaism is wrong. A final quotation is in order. It is from an article entitled "On Transgressions and Their Punishment," by Professor Saul Lieberman of the Jewish Theological Seminary, published in the Hebrew part of the two-volume Festschrift presented to Professor Louis Ginzberg on his seventieth birthday:

> Research into visions of hell is not merely a matter for amateurs of mysteries and folklore alone; it has a much wider import. In these visions we sometimes detect men's ideas on justice and on transgression and its punishment. What is more, many of the cruel tortures of the Roman rule were incorporated into the idea of hell from actual practice, and the authors of these visions were really talking about contemporary phenomena.
>
> We can recognize the influence of the hell in this life on the hell in the life to come. Crushing the limbs, cutting out the tongue, burning out the eyes, chopping off hands and feet— all of which are mentioned in the lives of the saints, in the works of the Greek and Roman writers, and in the Talmudic

literature—were carried out in practice by the executioners. Rabbinic literature is accustomed to showing the similarities and differences between the kingdom of earth and the kingdom of heaven. It is right that evildoers who offended the honor of heaven should be punished with no less severity than those who offended the honor of the king of flesh and blood. One is forced to the conclusion that our sages, of pious memory, did not refrain from applying the laws of this world to the other world.

We conclude that the hell of this world certainly influenced the hell of the next world; we must now inquire whether there was not a reciprocal influence, of the next world on this. The Christian rulers were very well acquainted with the visions of hell, either from books or from the sermons of priests. Is there any wonder that these visions made an impression on them? Did not the Spanish Inquisition find a finished and detailed program of cruel tortures ready at hand in their literature of visions of hell? We should not be astonished by the customary medieval punishment of hanging offenders by their feet, with their heads dangling, since this punishment is mentioned in almost every Christian work on hell. What is more, even the punishment of hanging by the feet over a bonfire ... was carried out in medieval practice. Similarly, hanging amidst dogs biting the hanging man is not alien to the Christian visions. Likewise, the authorities did not disdain the obscene torture [of hanging by the virile member] mentioned earlier.

In sum, a large number of the cruel tortures practiced by the wicked authorities passed to the hell of the other world, were refined and perfected there, and returned to this world of falsehood; and they still prevail in this world.

It is not the Psalmist that we should blame for the hells of St. Thomas and Calvin.

(1949)

Religion and Politics

Jews, Episcopalians, Puerto Ricans

... Seeing a man standing opposite him with drawn sword in hand, Joshua went up to him and asked him, "Are you friend or foe?"

—*Joshua 5:13*

WHILE THE SHIITES WERE HOLDING those TWA passengers hostage in Beirut, ABC News/*Washington Post* polled more than a thousand Americans. One question they were asked was whether they agreed or disagreed that "the U.S. should reduce its ties to Israel in order to lessen the acts of terrorism against us in the Middle East." Somewhat more than half disagreed, not wanting the United States to reduce its ties to Israel. About a third agreed, wanting the United States to reduce its ties. The rest had no opinion.

Israel is a major Jewish interest. I postulate that those who did not want the United States to reduce its ties to Israel were more pro-Israel than those who wanted the United States to reduce its ties.

Men, the pro-Reagan (those who approved of "the way Ronald Reagan is handling his job as President"), and Republicans were more pro-Israel than the anti-Reagan (those who disapproved), women, and Democrats:

THE U.S. SHOULD REDUCE ITS TIES TO ISRAEL

	Agree	*Disagree*	*No opinion*
Total	32%	53%	15%
Pro-Reagan	26	61	14
Anti-Reagan	43	45	12
Democrats	37	50	13
Republicans	28	57	15
Independents	29	53	18
Men	26	62	12
Women	37	45	18

For the excess of pro-Israel over anti-Israel sentiment in each of these categories, subtract the percentage agreeing from the percentage disagreeing. From most to least pro-Israel, we get:

Men	$62 - 26 = 36\%$
Pro-Reagan	$61 - 26 = 35$
Republicans	$57 - 28 = 29$
Independants	$53 - 29 = 24$
Democrats	$50 - 37 = 13$
Women	$45 - 37 = 8$
Anti-Reagan	$45 - 43 = 2$

The pro-Israel margin of the pro-Reagan was 33 points higher than of the anti-Reagan; of men, 28 points higher than of women; and of Republicans, 16 points higher than of Democrats. It is reasonable to assume that the pro-Reagan were more conservative and the anti-Reagan more liberal, and that as usual men were more hawkish and women more dovish.

For Jews, it was not supposed to be that way.

In the 1984 National Survey of American Jews (NSAJ), conducted by Steven M. Cohen in the first half of that year for the American Jewish Committee, almost a thousand people answered a questionnaire. They were a representative sample, whose information about themselves closely resembled what was already known about American Jews. For instance, they reported that in 1980 they had given Carter a plurality, Reagan not quite two-fifths, and Anderson not quite a fifth. That is what the networks' exit polls had reported about Jews in 1980.

Jews are one of the more educated and civic groups in America. Only one-sixth of the NSAJ respondents had not gone to college; three-fifths were college graduates, and of these a majority also had at least one graduate or professional degree. Nine in ten said they had voted in 1980.

Concerning each of fifteen American groups or institutions, these Jews were asked whether they thought most of the members of that group or institution were anti-Semitic, or many were anti-Semitic, or some were, or few were, or whether the respondents were not sure. The highest combined most-or-many-anti-Semitic rating was for blacks. The lowest most-or-many-anti-Semitic ratings were for Democrats and liberals.

■   ■   ■

Let us look at the blacks first. When the questionnaire went out, Jesse Jackson and Louis Farrakhan were in the news and on Jews' minds. Asked whether they thought Jesse Jackson was anti-Semitic, of the more than four-fifths who were not unsure, ten respondents said yes for every one who said no.

It is not prejudice that leads Jews to believe blacks are less well disposed than whites, because that is what opinion polls routinely show. At the 1984 Democratic National Convention, a *Los Angeles Times* poll found most black delegates with a favorable opinion of Farrakhan, after he had said what he said about Hitler, Jews, and Judaism.

The 1984 NSAJ questionnaire included a kind of popularity contest. Ten groups or institutions were listed, and the respondents were asked whether their impression of each group or institution was generally favorable, or generally unfavorable, or mixed, or whether they had no impression.

The NAACP was third most popular, after the UJA and rab-bis. Its favorable-minus-unfavorable margin was also third. In a telling reversal, the proportion of respondents with a favorable impression of the NAACP was the same as the pro-portion who thought most or many blacks were anti-Semitic: 54 percent.

Aside from blacks, the groups or institutions rated as more anti-Semitic than average were on the conservative or establishment side: the Pentagon, the State Department, and big business, between 39 and 44 percent most-or-many-anti-Semitic; and Catholics, mainstream Protestants, and funda-mentalist Protestants, 40, 42, and 46 percent.

When it comes to ideologies and parties, Jews think they can tell friend from foe:

MOST OR MANY OF THE
FOLLOWING GROUPS ARE ANTI-SEMITIC

Democrats	6%
Liberals	7
Republicans	29
Conservatives	35

Democrats get a low anti-Semitism rating, while blacks, Christians, and conservatives get high anti-Semitism ratings. What Democrats are left once you exclude blacks, Christians, and conservatives? (More Democrats call themselves conser-vative than liberal.) The Democrats that Jews call friends are an abstraction. The real, flesh-and-blood Democrats gave a lower-than-average pro-Israel answer in the ABC poll.

Republicans gave a higher-than-average pro-Israel answer, but Jews do not regard them as friends. Those diplomas must surely mean—must they not?—that Jews are smart. In the face of the Republicans' being more pro-Israel than average, it takes a special kind of smartness to think them unfriendly—and in the face, too, of such things as the even division of the eight Jewish Senators between Republican and Democratic, although for every Jewish Republican there are five or even six Jewish Democrats.

In *A Treatise of Human Nature,* Hume says: "Reason is and ought only to be the slave of the passions, and can never pretend to any other office than to serve and obey them." Jews have used reason to justify loyalty to old passions that have become anachronistic passions.

■ ■ ■

Many more Americans voted for Reagan in 1984 than in 1980. The Democrats nominated Geraldine Ferraro for vice president because they calculated that she would attract not only women but also Catholics and Italians. Thereupon most women, most Catholics, and most Italians—most Italian Catholic women—voted for Ronald Reagan. The National Education Association and the American Federation of Teachers went all out against Reagan, and most teachers voted for him.

While the 1984 NSAJ confirmed that in 1980 more Jews had voted for Jimmy Carter than for Reagan, it also showed that, "knowing what you do now," most were glad that it was Reagan who had been elected. That was only one reason why the Jewish vote for Reagan was expected to rise in 1984. In the event, what happened was so exceptional that it became a nine-days' wonder. The average of five national exit polls' figures had Jews giving two-thirds to Walter Mondale and a third to Reagan, less than in 1980. In 1985, Steven M. Cohen got over half of his 1984 respondents to answer a new questionnaire, and he has been kind enough to show me the result. They too had gone two to one for Mondale over Reagan.

After the 1968 election I wrote what was eventually to become an anonymous aphorism, that Jews had the incomes of Episcopalians but voted like Hispanics ("Is American Jewry in Crisis?" March 1969). It may no longer be true. First, Episcopalians are not what they used to be. Second, while according to the CBS News/*New York Times* exit poll Jews and

Hispanics voted about the same in 1984, according to the ABC News/*Washington Post* poll the Jewish vote for Mondale was 13 points higher than the Hispanic. Let me rephrase the aphorism: Jews vote like Hispanics, only more so.

The prevailing explanation of the Jewish vote in 1984 is that by election day most Jews felt that the Christian Right, identified with the Republicans, was more of a threat than Jesse Jackson, identified with the Democrats. If only because the Republican convention was later than the Democratic one, on election day the alarm that the Christian Right occasioned among Jews was fresher, less dissipated by time, than the alarm occasioned by Jesse Jackson. Besides, Jews think they need worry less about blacks than about white Christians, because blacks are weak and white Christians are strong: in Cohen's 1985 NSAJ almost nine in ten characterized "American Christians" as "powerful" and "secure." By "Christians," Jews usually mean white Christians.

Anecdotal evidence supports this explanation. A Democratic activist told me about his debates before Jewish audiences in California. As soon as his Republican opponents started to do well, as they often did, he would cry, "The Philistines are upon you, Samson!"—the Christian Right has taken over the Republican Party and must not be allowed to take over the country. That never failed.

A Republican activist told me how impervious Jews were to his questions.

Q: Jackson and Farrakhan?

A: Yes, but they're only black.

Q: Assad and Arafat's friend Jackson's probable veto power over a victorious Mondale's choice of a secretary of state, and what that would mean for Israel?

A: Mondale won't give him that veto. Besides, not to worry, the fact that we're voting for Mondale doesn't mean we really expect him to win. [This is another way of saying, "The Gentiles will protect us by not voting like us."]

Q: The Democratic convention refusing to consider a resolution condemning anti-Semitism and racism, in contrast to the Republican convention applauding Ronald Reagan, George Bush, and Jeane J. Kirkpatrick's denunciation of anti-Semitism and praise of Israel?

A: Yes, well, that Democratic convention thing was bad, but didn't a committee say something or other afterward to make up for it? And what difference do resolutions really make?

My last bit of anecdotal evidence comes from an academic political scientist who has done important work in government. After the election he and I agreed that Jews had voted more from the gut than on issues. Then he told me about his brother, a professor of economics in a great university, who preferred Reagan on the economy to Mondale but proceeded to vote for Mondale. Asked why, this professor in a great university said, "I watched the Republicans on television, and they didn't look like my kind of people."

Just possibly, the plausibility and the anecdotes may be yet another case of what everybody knows to be so that is not necessarily so. Of Cohen's 1985 respondents only one in six or seven had voted primarily against Jackson(ism) or against Falwell(ism). Further, of those who had so voted, more voted for Reagan on account of Jackson (9 percent, higher than a quarter of all Reagan voters) than for Mondale on account of the Moral Majority (6 percent, fewer than one-tenth of all Mondale voters). Or so they said.

They were also asked, "In your view, who would have posed a greater threat to the interests of American Jews: Jesse Jackson (in the event Mondale were elected), or the Moral Majority (as a result of Reagan's victory)?" One-third said Jesse Jackson, more than the quarter that said the Moral Majority. An eighth said neither, almost a fifth said both, and a tenth were not sure.

■   ■   ■

A cartoon that is a favorite with producers and consumers of polls shows a pollster shouting at a man he is interviewing, "Those are the worst opinions I've ever heard!" A number of NSAJ percentages bring that to mind.

There are contradictions or at least ambivalences that I can accept with a smile, probably because they are mine too. For instance, two successive agree-or-disagree questions in 1984:

	Agree	Disagree	Not sure
In general, I support ... welfare and food stamps			
	75%	17%	8%
... Welfare and food stamps have had many bad effects on the very people they're supposed to help			
	64	23	13

Some are harder to accept with a smile. Again, successive items in 1984:

To help reduce deficits and relieve world tensions, U.S. military spending should be cut			
	59	27	14
In order to be a reliable military supplier of Israel, the U.S. should maintain a strong military capacity			
	61	24	15

Successively! Some evoke a kind of pity for the poor little rich girl. At a time when prejudice and discrimination are lower than ever before:

Anti-Semitism in America is currently not a serious problem for American Jews			
	40	47	13
Virtually all positions of influence in America are open to Jews			
	31	58	11

On the other hand:

> The U.S. has offered Jews more opportunities and freedom
> than any other Diaspora country
>
> | | | |
> | --- | --- | --- |
> | 83 | 6 | 10 |

This is at any rate not inconsistent with:

> Capitalism works better than socialism
>
> | | | |
> | --- | --- | --- |
> | 73 | 7 | 20 |

Jewish self-definitions are elastic.

With a quarter of the respondents calling themselves conservative, why did only an eighth oppose government aid for abortions for poor women? In the old joke about a Jew wearing a captain's cap to go with the boat he has just bought, his mother says to him, "By me you're a captain, by your father you're a captain, but by the captains are you a captain?" By the conservatives, how many Jews who call themselves conservative are really conservative? It is easy to be right of the Jewish center and left of the Gentile center.

Similarly, with more than a quarter doubting or denying that capitalism works better than socialism, why did only 1 percent call themselves radical or socialist?

■   ■   ■

The worst opinion was this:

> | *Agree* | *Disagree* | *Not Sure* |
> | --- | --- | --- |
> | President Reagan was basically accurate when he called the Soviet Union an "evil empire" | | |
> | 50% | 35% | 15% |

This was a question about truth. They had the next item for agreeing with the worldly wisdom that *toute vérité n'est pas bonne à dire,* not every truth should be told:

Whether or not President Reagan was factually correct, he displayed poor judgment in calling the Soviet Union an "evil empire"

66   25   9

Of the half who disagreed or were unsure that the Soviet Union is an evil empire, Cohen writes: "Were the President more popular among Jews, the 'basically accurate' statement probably would have received more support." Suppose Jews were asked to agree or disagree with this, in a future survey: "President Reagan was basically accurate when he called the state of Israel a friendly democracy." Would half disagree or be unsure? Would more agree only if Senator Kennedy or Senator Hart called Israel a friendly democracy?

In calling the Soviet Union what he did, President Reagan was saying two things about it, that it was an empire and that it was evil. According to the book of Esther, the Persian Empire extended from India to Ethiopia and comprised 127 provinces, each with its own people and language. The Soviet Union extends from East Prussia to Japan. I do not know the number of its provinces, but the number of languages spoken in it is said to exceed five hundred. Who can deny or doubt that a country like that is an empire? It must have been President Reagan's adjective, evil, that aroused the resistance.

Why, especially among Jews? Besides all the other fine qualities and deeds of the Soviet Union, it is also the enemy of Judaism, Jews, and Israel. In the Soviet Union, Hebrew teachers are sent to prison. Hebrew teachers! There's a gang of desperadoes for you. Yet only half of American Jews could bring themselves to agree that the Soviet Union is an evil empire.

The cause of this oddity is that so many Jews are doves. Admit that the Soviet Union is an evil empire and you may have to admit that it has evil intentions. Certain dovish positions then become harder to hold on to, like cutting the U.S. defense budget. The way out is to deny or doubt reality, to say

216

that the Soviet Union is not or may not be an evil empire. Reason is, and ought only to be, the slave of the passions.

About Israel, Jews tell themselves that they can eat their cake and have it too. In 1984, three in five agreed that "U.S. military spending should be cut" and immediately thereafter also agreed that "to be a reliable military supplier of Israel, the U.S. should maintain a strong military capacity." In 1985, more than half denied both that "major reductions in U.S. defense spending will weaken the security of the U.S." and that such "major reductions . . . will weaken the ability of the U.S. to support Israel." As the Duke of Wellington said to the man who addressed him as "Mr. Jones, I believe?"—if you can believe that, you can believe anything.

In 1985, Cohen asked some questions probing for a kind of Judaic altruism, and he found it. Eight agreed for every one who disagreed that "Jewish values, as I understand them, teach us that we must make economic sacrifices for the poor." In another question, respondents were asked to agree or disagree that "taxes on the middle class should be kept low or reduced." Two in three agreed and only one in six disagreed. Two questions later, they were asked about a Jewish interest in low taxes: "Since more Jews are now middle-class, Jewish interests dictate support for candidates who favor lower taxes and limits on government spending." Agreement dropped to less than half and disagreement rose to three in eight. That is, Jews sympathize with an undifferentiated middle class rather more than with themselves as members of the middle class. In the first, general instance, but not in the second, Jewish instance, it is as if they thought of the middle class as poor, and about the poor they know what the right answer is. It is also true that the first statement sounds like Gary Hart and the second like Jack Kemp.

For Israel, American Jews refuse to sacrifice not economically but psychologically. One question was about agreement or disagreement with the proposition that "even though many

Jews think that some black leaders are anti-Semitic or anti-Israel, American Jews should still try to improve relations with the black community." It was no contest. Very few were unsure, and eleven agreed for every one who disagreed. A later question was about agreement or disagreement with this: "Since the Christian Right has been very pro-Israel, American Jews should overlook their objections to the Christian Right's ideas about America, and work more closely with it to help Israel." Only one in five agreed, a majority disagreed, and a little more than a quarter were unsure. In the 1984 NSAJ popularity contest, only the JDL and the Moral Majority had received a higher unfavorable than favorable rating, with the Moral Majority far more unpopular than even the JDL.

What are "the Christian Right's ideas about America" that Jews object to? One of those ideas is prayer in the public schools. If the 1984 NSAJ showed Jews opposing by more than three to one a moment of silent meditation in the public schools, all the more must they be opposed to prayer in the public schools. But a recent poll has found that five in six blacks and two in five black leaders agree with the Christian Right about prayer in the public schools.

A related "idea about America" that Jews ascribe to the Christian Right is the blurring of the distinction not only between church and state, but also between religion and politics, between preacher and politician. In that respect, too, blacks are closer to the Christian Right than to Jews. A significant proportion of leading black politicians and public figures have been ministers, including Martin Luther King Jr., Mayor Andrew Young of Atlanta, Congressman William A. Gray of Pennsylvania, and the Reverend Jesse Jackson, whose campaign for the Democratic nomination depended heavily on the black churches and clergy.

Yet Jews sensibly do not tell blacks that if they continue to be less than zealous for the separation of church and state or of religion and politics—let alone opposition to quotas—

Jews will not work more closely with them to help Israel. On the contrary, Jews think that it is they who "should still try to improve relations" with blacks. Toward the Christian Right, Jews are less accommodating. In effect they will not deign to allow it to work with them to help Israel unless it stops being the Christian Right.

With all their Judaic sympathy for the needy, American Jews contrive to forget that Israel is very needy indeed—almost friendless, in need of all the friends it can get. Will the American Friends Service Committee, will the bureaucracies of the liberal churches rush in to befriend Israel if the Christian Right stops being friendly? An opening to the Christian Right would subject Jews to the discomfort of thinking new thoughts and doing new things. Apparently Israel is not thought to be worth such a grievous sacrifice.

Saul Bellow has recalled that when he was young, he and his friends once outdid themselves in advanced dialectic. His aunt had less education than they but more common sense. Afterward she said, "Smart, smart, but so dumb!" The English say "too clever by half" and "silly-clever." Americans say, "Too smart is dumb."

■   ■   ■

Jewish dumb smartness is inveterate. Is it also incorrigible? Let us consider the 1984 election again.

Lyndon B. Johnson liked to tell the story of a young man in the Depression who had just graduated from normal school and was being interviewed for a teaching job in a small town in Texas. The chairman of the school board, a Southern Baptist deacon, asked him, "In biology, do you teach Darwin or do you teach Genesis?" The young man answered, "I can do it either way." Did the Jewish vote in 1984 show continuity with old ways, or did it show change? You can interpret it either way.

With delight, liberals greeted the Jewish vote as proving continuity. They saluted the Jews for holding fast to a tradition

of unselfish compassion when the rest of America was marching shameless under the banner of "What's in it for me?" as
well as for holding fast to a tradition of pursuing peace when
the voice of the militarist was heard in the land. They taunted
Jewish (neo)conservatives for delivering only one-third of the
Jewish vote to Reagan.

That is the case for continuity. The case for change is basically this: "What do you mean, *only* one-third of the Jewish
vote? Some 'only'!"

First, something must be said about the self-righteous
hypocrisy of denouncing Reagan voters for pursuing selfish
interest. Democrats lament the dissolution of the New Deal coalition. What was the secret of that coalition's success if not appeal
to the interest of each of its constituent groups? In 1984 it was
the Democrats who were widely perceived as pandering to the
interest of every bloc and caucus that made enough noise, while
the Republicans went out of their way to appear to address the
electorate as Americans simply. Most people who said they were
better off than four years earlier voted for Reagan, and most
who said they were worse off voted for Mondale. I remember
that one poll also reported on people who said that while they
themselves were worse off, they thought the country as a whole
was better off. Of these most voted for Reagan. Even people with
annual incomes under $12,500 voted for Mondale only eleven
to nine over Reagan. What was in it for such Reagan voters?

As to the Jewish vote in 1984, in retrospect it can be seen
that what misled the forecasters was the exceptionalness of
1980. It now seems clear that a big part of the 1980 Jewish vote
for Reagan was the desire of many Jews to punish Carter.
Edward Kennedy beat Carter in the 1980 New York Democratic primary mostly because three in eight voters in that primary were Jews, and they gave Kennedy four votes for every
vote they gave Carter.

Only a third for Reagan in 1984? Jews gave a tenth to
FDR's opponents and Goldwater, and a fifth to Nixon running

against Humphrey. One-third was the previous modern Republican high for Jews, in 1972, when McGovern the unpopular was the Democratic candidate. In 1976, Jews had no particular cause for attraction to Carter or for repulsion from Ford. Voting by party loyalty and habit, they then gave about three-quarters of their votes to Carter. In 1984, they gave less than that to a much more appealing Democrat. Mondale did well with Jews in the primaries. He had been anointed by Hubert Humphrey, whom Jews loved dearly and who in turn had been anointed by Eleanor Roosevelt, whom they loved even more dearly—more dearly, in fact, than they loved FDR himself. Instead of saying that only one-third of the Jewish vote went to the Republican in 1984, you could as well say that only two-thirds went to the Democrat. If continuity is there, so is change.

■   ■   ■

Only from an American perspective has the left-of-bankbook voting of American Jews been an anomaly. From a worldwide modern Jewish perspective it was the norm. Until only the day before yesterday, as historical time goes, it was still true, as Jews had learned over and over, in country after country, that their chief enemies were on the Right.

But that was the day before yesterday, not today. Even for Jews, sooner or later reality can break in and undermine old, cozy beliefs and behaviors. This has already happened in France and Great Britain.

In France, according to Shmuel Trigano and Jacky Akoka (*Jerusalem Letter* of the Jerusalem Center for Public Affairs, May 23, 1985), an exit poll in 1983 showed that

> the Jewish electorate differed from the rest of the electorate in the 1981 and 1983 elections in that it voted more sharply to the Left in 1981 than did the nation as a whole (65 percent as compared to 57 percent) and showed a more pronounced shift to the Right in 1983 (59.7 [?!] percent as compared to 49

percent). . . . The Jewish electorate is characterized by greater than average electoral mobility.

In Great Britain, change has been especially dramatic, as Robert Silver reports (*Economist*, December 15, 1984):

> In 1966, there were 40 Jewish MP's, 38 of them Labour. . . . In 1974, there were 46 Jewish Members of the House of Commons—35 Labour, ten Conservative, and one Liberal. . . . By 1983, the distribution had been radically reversed. There were 29 Jewish MP's—17 of them Conservative. . . .
>
> Recent Labour party conferences have seen the passage of pro-Palestinian resolutions. The party is tainted by association with the New Left where there has recently been disturbing evidence of a revival of anti-Semitic motifs in anti-Zionist literature.

Most French and British Jews, and certainly most Israelis, would not agree with most American Jews that deep cuts in the United States defense budget will neither weaken the United States nor lessen its ability to help Israel, or that Jews can help Israel by spurning Israel's strongest Gentile supporters. American Jews, lucky beneficiaries of a reality less harsh than that of Israelis and French and British Jews, have not yet been forced to stop indulging in the luxury of self-delusion.

It will be a miracle if the luck never runs out. The rabbis forbid us to rely on miracles.

(1985)

Church and State:
How High a Wall?

THE JEWS ARE PROBABLY more devoted than anyone else in America to the separation of church and state. At times, hearing some of us talk about separation, or reading the statements of our organizations, one has the impression that we think ourselves more loyal to the Constitution and more skilled in its interpretation as well—although of course nobody ever says that in so many words. Thoughts protected against expression, as this one is, can be foolish. We are not more loyal to the Constitution or more skilled in its interpretation, we are only more separationist. And with every passing year our separationism comes closer to being part of the "old order" that Tennyson, in those verses that used to be so popular, wanted to see "yielding place to new; / ... Lest one good custom should corrupt the world."

The case for the regnant Jewish ideology or emotion goes this way: Granted, there must be something special in our own experience and memory, and some strong feeling about what is in our interest, to account for our separationist fervor; but we perceive and intend separation to be for the good of all as well as for our own good. Thirty years ago the Jews more than anyone else warned against Hitler and Nazism. Afterward, everybody could see that we had been right, that we had not merely been pleading our own cause when we said that resistance to Hitler and Nazism was not a Jewish interest alone but the interest of all. Similarly now in church-and-state matters.

Because the Jews have had to pay for the lesson—so the case continues—we know that separation of church and state is good and the absence of separation is bad. A country with separation is democratic, tolerant, open, free; a country without separation is despotic, persecuting, closed, unfree. The greater the separation, as in America and France, the more democracy and tolerance; the less the separation, as in Spain, czarist Russia, and the Papal States before the unification of Italy, the less democracy and tolerance. Of course Jews do better in an America and a France than in a Spain or a czarist Russia. Doesn't everyone? In wanting America to be ever more separationist, which is to say ever more American, we want it to be ever better for all. "Religious freedom," in the words of the canon, "is most secure where church and state are separated, and least secure where church and state are united."

■　■　■

A good, strong case—or it would be if not for the vice of faulty enumeration. Where do you put England, Denmark, Norway, and Sweden, with their state churches? No one can deny that Great Britain and Scandinavia are free and democratic or that religious freedom is closer to being most secure there than least secure. Nor can any Jew deny that those countries are, as we used to say, good for the Jews. (Proportionately, more than seven times as many Jews are in the House of Commons as in the population of the United Kingdom.) On the other hand, in the Soviet Union church and state are constitutionally separate, but the Soviet Union is neither free nor democratic nor good for the Jews, and so far from making religious freedom secure—let alone most secure—it persecutes religion.

It may be argued that Soviet persecution does not fairly come under the head of separation and that state persecution of religion is a kind of negative mode of state establishment of religion. Without conceding the argument, let us return to the Soviet Union when we consider secularism and for the moment instead compare state-church England with separationist France. In democracy and freedom, the two are alike (or used to be, before de Gaulle's somewhat authoritarian Fifth Republic); in openness and tolerance to Jews, the state-church country is better than the separationist one. Which is not to say that establishment is better than separation, but only that other things—notably democracy as it is inclined by national culture and tradition—make the issue of separation/establishment quite secondary.

Only two years ago the Ecole Normale Supérieure, the nursery of the French intellectual elite, tried to keep out a qualified Jewish student because he observed the Sabbath. Why, he was asked, should he be admitted to an institution that trains *lycée* professors? A *lycée* has Saturday classes, like all state schools in France. Would not his Sabbath observance prevent him from teaching? The Ecole Normale Supérieure has been traditionally on the side of the French Revolution—republican, anticlerical, anti-anti-Semitic—and since before the university careers of the Reinach brothers and Léon Blum, it has had Jewish students. But unlike the other Jewish students before him, this one was religious. Keeping in mind the distinction between secularist and religious Jews may help us understand something about ourselves in the United States.

For a long time the distinction was blurred in the American Jewish community because in this country, church-and-state issues tend to be school issues. Our separationism goes back to the time when the public school was in many ways a common-denominator or intersectarian Protestant school. In that age of Protestant imperialism, as it has been called, the virtues and standards of America were so widely held to be the same as the virtues and standards of Protestantism that a public school had to be a basically Protestant school. One reason why the founder of American Reform Judaism, Isaac Mayer Wise, was a Copperhead in the Civil War was that he resented the Protestant imperialism of the abolitionists. (Lincoln needed the support of the Know-Nothings and did not condemn them publicly. Elijah Lovejoy, the abolitionist martyr, printed anti-Catholic tracts.) It was Wise who began the unbroken reform tradition of opposing public-school Protestantism in the name of separation. Whether he would have opposed religion-in-general in the schools is unclear. In Germany his masters and colleagues took it for granted that the state should favor religion.

Sometimes Wise's tradition was a well-kept secret among his disciples and successors, because the laity was in no mood to attract attention by protest; yet while Reform rabbis now disagree about God, Torah, and Israel, they still do not disagree about the separationist article of faith, though Protestant imperialism has gone the way of so many other imperialisms. And just as the Irish taught the rest of the Catholics how to be American, so Reform Judaism taught Orthodoxy and Conservatism. Separation became the common platform of the major varieties of Jewish religion in America. (The Orthodox have begun to go their own way, but that is a long story.) Wise would have been happy with no Lord's Prayer in the schools, but only yesterday we were unhappy even with the Regents' prayer, certified desirable by the Lubavitcher Rebbe himself.

As for the Jewish secularists, they have opposed religion in the schools for a simple reason: They are secularists. For a secularist, religion is infantile and infantilizing, the enemy of enlightenment, science, progress, freedom, and peace. The less religion a society or community has, he says, the better it is.

But religionists and secularists do not live apart in the Jewish community. They have in common ideas and, above all, emotions. Few Jews of Central or East European origin or parentage, whether Orthodox or Reform, religious or secularist, have been able to think well of the Church. The Church was Pobedonostsev, with his vision of one-third of the Jews of

Russia converting, one-third emigrating, and one-third dying of hunger. The Church was the threat of pogroms in the Easter season. The Church was the Mortara case, the Dreyfus case, the Beilis case. "Christian" was part of the name an anti-Semitic party would give itself, in Protestant Prussia as in Catholic Austria. To Christians, Theodor Reik wrote when he still lived in Austria, Judaism was uncanny (mostly because of circumcision) and therefore fearsome. To Central and East European Jews, it was the iconic, sacramental, and sacerdotal Christianity they saw about them that was uncanny, and it still is to their children and grandchildren. Until a few years ago, the common memories and emotions and sense of danger tended to obscure the differences between Jewish religionists and secularists. So united was the Jewish front that only occasionally would a mainstream rabbi be bold enough to advise his confreres that they would do well, if only for the sake of public relations, to phrase their separationist statements in rather more religious-sounding language.

In Isaac Mayer Wise's Midwest, the Christian environment was Protestant. For most Jews today, who live in and near the great cities, the Christian environment is apt to be mainly Catholic. Wise's separationism was a defense against what he saw as a Protestant threat; ours is mostly against what we see as a Catholic threat, and especially what we see as the threat of the parochial school.

■   ■   ■

Traditions die hard, even the traditions of the untraditional. A man will say that the United States must rethink its foreign policy from beginning to end because the world has changed. Ask him to rethink his own policy because the world has changed and he will tell you he is no trimmer or opportunist; let the weaklings and conformists veer with the winds of popularity, he will remain loyal to his principles. Everyone thinks he is a dissenter and nonconformist—in good faith, because there are always communities of opinion and fashion in opposition to which he can honestly see himself as one. What he prefers to overlook is that there are also communities of opinion and fashion—or, more honorifically, of thought and style— to which he relates positively, and in that relation his nonconformity can be quite conformist. In our own community, the informal and private one or the organized and public one, separationism is not a bit nonconformist. (It is curious that dissent/dissenter, nonconformity/nonconformist should come to us from the language of English ecclesiastical history.)

As things are today, religionists and moderate secularists have one interest and radical separationists another, and our separationism now serves the radical interest. ("Radical" is generally not an O.K. word, but I cannot think of anything better. "Extreme" is even less O.K., "consistent" is not what I mean, and "fanatical" is insulting.) Whether a secularist is moderate or radical depends on whether his secularism is one of several more or less equal goods or whether it is his chief good; whether it is a means as well as an end, to be judged in part by its usefulness in furthering other ends, or whether it is more like an ultimate end. For the moderate, separationism is a strategy more than a philosophy, and if new conditions call for a change in strategy he will be ready to make the change. For the radical, the strategy goes so closely with the philosophy that change can only be betrayal. As integralist Catholics are convinced (notwithstanding Vatican II) that the marriage of Throne and Altar is God's will, so radical secularists are convinced that root-and-branch separationism is Reason's dictate.

What are the considerations that should induce a moderate secularist, and all the more a religionist, to question his inherited separationism? The first of these may by itself not be strictly probative, at least about America, but it points to something. For secularists the example of the Soviet Union should teach skepticism about the secularist faith itself. The

Soviet Union is the most secularist society in what used to be Christendom (or Islam, Judaism never having controlled any territory to speak of). In that most secularist society, separationism has gone so far as to become persecution of religion; and in that most secularist society, secularism is not the companion or handmaiden of freedom, intelligence, and all the other good things of man's mind and spirit, as secularists once thought it must be. Rather it is the companion or handmaiden of the jailer of art and literature, science and scholarship and philosophy, honest thought and honest feeling. It is not state-church England or Sweden that vilifies and imprisons Brodsky, Sinyavsky, and Daniel, but the Soviet Union, which calls itself the guardian of enlightenment and the scourge of obscurantism. For a Jew it should also matter that nowhere else in what used to be Christendom are Jews and Judaism persecuted.

In America a state church on the English or Swedish model is out of the question, and that is all the more reason why the separation decreed by the Constitution should be defended against mutation into separationism. For separationism can be tyrannical even here. No citizens of this country are more peaceful and inoffensive than the Amish, yet a few months ago agents of the Iowa public schools were photographed pursuing Amish children through the fields to drag them into schools that the parents had rejected for religious reasons. Not long after, in New York, it took a decision by the superintendent of schools himself to allow a high-school boy to cover his head in class. A Board of Education lawyer had ruled that if the boy wore a *kippah* he would be breaching the wall of separation between church and state! (The superintendent's name is Donovan.)

■   ■   ■

Almost as alarming is the growing isolation of Jewish separationism from the social liberalism of which it used to be part. On every side, President Johnson's aid-to-education and antipoverty legislation is recognized as a major advance, and if liberals have a complaint, it is that the legislation does not go far enough. Liberal Protestants, accustomed to suspicion of Catholic designs on the public treasury and critical of Johnson on foreign policy, marvel at his achievement in bypassing the kinds of church-and-state objections—or rationalizations—that invariably killed similar bills in the past. The congressional opponents of Johnson's legislation, who went down continuing to profess indignation over the breach in the wall, were mostly reactionaries and racists.

Together with these stand the radical separationists, although theirs is a true and not a feigned indignation. They are unreconciled to educational benefits being extended to children in nonpublic (mostly Catholic parochial) schools, and to churches being included among appropriate neighborhood institutions for conducting antipoverty programs. As the separationists see it, the child-benefit theory is a mere device for benefiting parochial schools by the back door while evading the (presumed) constitutional prohibition of benefits by the front door, and churches and church-related institutions have no business in antipoverty programs or anything else that gets public money.

What if the benefits cannot readily be extended to children outside their nonpublic school? What if excluding a church or a church-related institution in this or that neighborhood weakens the effort to help the poor raise themselves out of poverty? Your single-minded separationist, after first trying to deny that your questions are real questions, can say nothing. Creditably, American liberalism in general does not accept this kind of hard-heartedness. The separationists make the usual defense in such cases: it is not really we who are hard-hearted but the other fellow, to whom we refuse to pay blackmail and who has maneuvered us into a false position. They may believe this, but whenever I hear or read Jewish separationists weighing the claim of the poor against the claim of separationism, their emotion goes to separationism. Yet we are still fond of thinking ouselves *rahamanim benei rahamanim,* the compassionate sons of compassionate fathers.

If not even regard for the poor moves the separationist to condone back-door dealings and aid, it is easy to imagine what he thinks about the front door. But here, too, his single-mindedness is beginning to isolate him. He cannot bring himself to look upon his favorite doctrine as one of many good things, not necessarily compatible in its fullness with the other good things in *their* fullness, and subject, like all of them, to compromise and give-and-take.

Of late some remarkable voices have been heard for governmental aid to the nonpublic school: the *New Republic* and Walter Lippmann, among others. Their purpose is not to help the Catholic schools but to help American education; or better, to help bring about the conditions in which all Americans can have the best possible education. Since the quality of the nation's life will depend so greatly on education, Lippmann and the others say, education has a more urgent claim on the nation than separationism. This means helping the Catholic schools, because so many children are educated there—about one in every seven. The Catholic schools need money, in quantities that can come only from government, to hire more teachers so that classes will be smaller, to get good teachers by paying good salaries, to improve classrooms, to build up libraries.

The First Amendment does not command, "Thou shalt not give governmental aid to parochial schools," it commands that there shall be no establishment of religion and no curtailment of the free exercise of religion. The rabbis said that the gates of interpretation of the Torah are not closed, and the Supreme Court has shown that neither are the gates of interpretation of the Constitution closed. If the justices think the nation needs education more than separationism, they can easily decide that the Constitution permits aid to nonpublic education. If they think otherwise, then it is the turn of the gates of amendment not to be closed. Having had an amendment prohibiting liquor and another annulling the prohibition, the Constitution can have an amendment allowing aid to religious or church-related schools.

This kind of talk is hardly daring anymore, but to most separationists it is novel and perverse wickedness. That is not liberal open-mindedness. It is more like the outrage of a nineteenth-century, Herbert Spencer liberal confronted with the immoral proposal that the government should take taxes from him to support a school for educating his neighbor's children. There are still such liberals, only for many years now they have been called, by general agreement, reactionaries.

■   ■   ■

To Jews, Jewish separationists like to say that separationism is necessary for our safety and well-being. I think this argument is a second thought, invoked to justify a decision already taken on another ground. Those who invoke it remind me of a businessman who wants to contribute corporation money to a university or a community chest or the symphony orchestra. Possibly he wants to do it because he is a decent, generous man, but he has to justify his decency, to himself as well as to the other officers and the stockholders, by giving businesslike reasons for the contribution: it will be good for public relations, or it will help to make the environment so healthy that the corporation will be able to thrive.

There would be nothing wrong about consulting our interest when we are making up our minds whether to support governmental aid to church schools in the name of better education or to oppose it in the name of separation. If we consulted interest, we would estimate advantages and disadvantages by applying the appropriate calculus. That is how a man runs his business, or he is soon out of business. It is how Mr. McNamara chooses between missiles and manned bombers, submarines and aircraft carriers. But though I follow the Jewish discussions, I recall little that resembles a true weighing of alternatives. We prefer incantatory repetition of the dogma that separationism is our interest.

It is time we actually weighed the utility and cost of education against the utility and cost of separationism. All the evidence in America points to education, more than anything else, influencing adherence to democracy and egalitarianism. All the evidence points to Catholic parochial education having the same influence. (And all the evidence points to Catholic anti-Semitism as no greater than Protestant, and possibly less.) Something that nurtures a humane, liberal democracy is rather more important to Jews than 24-karat separationism.

There is another thing related to the Catholic parochial schools that we ought to weigh in the balance of Jewish interest. Consensus has become a dirty word on the Left and among intellectuals. In parts of the world suffering either from despotism or from chaos, they must envy America for this additional sign of affluence, that here people can afford to depreciate consensus. Outside the American consensus stand the far Right and the anti-Semites. (There is anti-Semitism on the outside Left, too, and among some of the young Jews in it.) It is good to broaden the consensus, to bring inside those who are outside. They change when they come inside.

Why are some people outside? Usually because they have a grievance. They feel they are disregarded and treated unfairly. The sociologists call this feeling *ressentiment;* let us call it sullenness. When statesmanship becomes aware that a social group is sullen, it tries to remove the causes, if that can be done without unacceptable cost to the other participants in the competitive cooperation of political society. In part it is because the Negroes have finally been seen to be sullen, in this sense, that the government is trying to make room for them in the game and bring them into the consensus. Sometimes, of course, a group's price for giving up its sullenness is too high for everybody else, and it has to be left outside—like the Birchers, who just for a start want the political and social game to return to the rules of the 1920s or the 1890s. But it must be conceded that some people, disoriented and bewildered by the passing of the America they were comfortable in, are needlessly being driven into the Radical Right. Some good libertarians are saying that such symbolic victories for separationism as making Bible reading in the schools illegal have been won at too high a real cost—the sullenness of the defeated and the departure of some of them from the consensus.

■   ■   ■

Many Catholics are sullen. For a non-Catholic it should not be unreasonably arduous to pretend for a moment that he has children in a parochial school. Call it role-playing. For the average Catholic, affluence is either a figure of speech or what someone else has: he is less affluent than the average Episcopalian, Congregationalist, or Jew. The taxes he pays to the public schools keep rising. So do his parochial-school costs, but the parochial school continues to fall behind the public school— in the size of classes, in salaries to attract good teachers, in equipment and amenities. He can hardly afford to pay once, but he has to pay twice; and in return his children get an education that he fears may not be good enough. This, when the diploma society is already here and meritocracy is on the horizon, and when his children's chances of making it depend more than ever on the education he can give them.

He asks for aid, and a coalition of Protestants and Jews, far from respecting him for having done the hard thing so long, answer coldly that private education must be paid for privately; if he can't afford it, let him not complain, let him use the public schools. At the same time, he sees that in the cities many in the coalition, whether pants manufacturers or intellectuals, do indeed pay to send their children to private schools. Apparently they believe nonpublic education is like a Cadillac: just as it would be ridiculous to subsidize a poor man's purchase of a Cadillac, so it would be to subsidize his purchase of nonpublic education. He suspects that this uncharacteristic enthusiasm of theirs for the principles of Ayn Rand is due rather to their distaste for Catholic education specifically than for nonpublic education generally.

Then, in self-defense, or out of resentment, or as a means of exerting pressure, the Catholic votes against higher taxes for the public schools, and the coalition is confirmed in its opinion of him. He is narrow-minded. But, tolerant and understanding, and proud of it, they tell each other that it isn't really his fault. It is the priests who make him send his children to the parochial school, the priests who make him sullen about the inevitable, unalterable consequences. *We* do not need a priest to make us prefer a nonpublic school; only *he* does. Tell them of the evidence that the average Catholic parent prefers the parochial school of his own accord; they answer: never heard of it, propaganda. If I were that Catholic parent, I could be pretty sullen.

Catholics, therefore, have a real grievance. To remove the grievance would be just. It would also be statesmanlike, and would help to improve the education of a significant part of the American population. People are coming to see that. In the past few years the public-opinion polls have shown a steady rise in the proportion of respondents favoring governmental aid, until now there are more for it than against it.

■　　■　　■

What then will happen to the public schools? Probably not much more than has already happened. Whoever asks this question must come into court with clean hands. Are his own children in a public school? Are the tax-supported schools of Scarsdale or Highland Park as public as the tax-supported schools of New York and Chicago?

Jews have special reason for being grateful to the public school: it helped make the America of opportunities for newcomers, and it trained us to seize the opportunities. It has also helped to make American culture receptive and inclusive, with everything *that* has meant to us. In return, we are all for the public school. At the same time, we tell each other horror stories about what it has become. If we can, we either send our children to private schools or move to where the public schools are not too public. Meanwhile, out there, some others are less attached than we to the public-school idea and system and are asking rude questions about it, aloud. They are even suggesting that the attachment is a cultural lag, unsuited to the new times.

When this is suggested on behalf of the Catholics, we find it easy to dismiss the suggestion as illiberal. But now it is suggested on behalf of the Negroes, and we cannot so easily dismiss that. Christopher Jencks, for instance (in the *Public Interest*, Winter 1966), argues that the public-school systems of the big cities are so diseased with bureaucracy and inertia that they cannot reasonably be expected to recover and do the job they are supposed to do. In their place, he proposes, the government should give parents the money needed for educating their children; and then the parents, having formed suitable associations, can set up their own schools and hire their own teachers.

Whatever the merits of that particular proposal, Catholics might want to use governmental tuition payments for parochial-school education. What objection could there be then?

■　■　■

To repeat: It is not true that freedom is most secure where church and state are separated; separation and separationism are not the same; even in America, separationism is potentially tyrannical; separationism needlessly repels some from the democratic consensus; it is harsh to those who prefer nonpublic schools for conscience' sake; and it stands in the way of a

more important good (and a more important safeguard of Jewish security), the best possible education for all.

The final reason for rethinking separationism is connected
in some ways with what has been said about tyranny. The reverence of right-thinking people for the Supreme Court and
the Constitution is at least twenty years old now, but I still
find it a bit strange. When I was coming of age, my elders and
betters regarded the Supreme Court as the Nine Old Men and
the Constitution as the horse-and-buggy document that
Charles Beard had debunked—or so it was thought—in his
Economic Interpretation. The cause of the change is obvious
and to be grateful for: the Court and the Constitution (as the
Court reads it) have been more decent and libertarian than
government by plebiscite would be, or than a direct democracy of the people at large. But I continue to be put off when
modern types speak of the Constitution as a fundamentalist
does of Scripture, and when they speak of the Court as Jews
once did of the Sanhedrin in Jabneh.

Especially strange is the concentration on (some of) the
ipsissima verba of Thomas Jefferson, so that an unofficial
metaphor about a wall of separation comes to have the sacred
character of the specifications for the Tent of Meeting. Jefferson's more important words tend to be ignored: his enmity to
the empire of the dead over the living and his caution against
excessive deference to ancestral documents and dicta, including his own. It was Jefferson, after all, who advised posterity
to water the tree of liberty every now and then with the blood
of revolution—at the very least, a more forceful way of saying what Tennyson was to say in those verses I quoted.

It is a truism that the problems of freedom have changed
since Jefferson's time. When we worry now about freedom of
the press, we do not have in mind primarily censorship by government or intimidation by a mob. Those restraints have grown
fewer and weaker, but we are not at all sure we have more freedom of the press. What bothers us is that not very long ago a

man with a few thousand dollars could start a newspaper, and there were many papers. Today it takes millions of dollars, and every year we have fewer papers. Neither censorship nor intimidation has caused the multiplication of one-newspaper cities, but only that everything nowadays is more complicated and expensive. For solving this problem the First Amendment, necessary as it is, is not nearly enough.

In Jefferson's time the press was exactly that—the printing press. Except for earshot speech and handwritten letters, there was no other means of communication. Now we have electronic media, and above all radio and television, which influence opinion probably more than print. In our time, unhindered communication of opinion and information depends on a freedom of the press that includes freedom of radio and TV. But the relation of government to radio and TV has to be totally different from its relation to the printing press.

■　　■　　■

The libertarian's conception of the ideal relation of government to the press is that there shall be no relation at all: government and press have nothing to do with each other, nobody needs a license to publish. In principle there is no limit to the number of newspapers or presses. With radio and TV, on the other hand, the laws of physics impose a limit. Two stations cannot operate on the same wavelength at the same time in the same place, so someone must determine that A shall operate and B shall not. That is, the government; and it is to government that A and B come to plead for a license. A government that respects freedom of the press finds itself having to license the radio-and-TV part of the press. What would Jefferson have thought?

In deciding whether to license A or B, the government has first to decide which of the two will probably better serve the public interest and the needs of society. But these include religion in its many forms. Consequently, when the government examines the record of a radio or TV licensee it must ask, among other things, how he has served his community's religious interests and needs. If it did not ask this question, if it asked everything else but not this, a licensee could exclude religion entirely from his programs; or give his own sect a monopoly of the time he allowed for religion; or set aside all that time for attacking a religion he disliked, or some religions, or religion in general; or sell all of it to the highest bidders. Yet a friend of mine (Marcus Cohn, in *Reporter*, January 14, 1965) considers that the government's asking about the religious programming of licensees breaches the wall of separation:

> While the U.S. Supreme Court has been gradually strengthening Jefferson's "wall of separation between church and state," the Federal Communications Commission has been doing its best to persuade people to go to church.... The commission has held ... that the proposed religious programming of one applicant for a television station ... was superior to another because it afforded "a more positive proposal for providing time to diverse religious faiths." In another case, it gave a comparative—although not a disqualifying—demerit to ... [a] proposed program schedule [because it] failed to include "any strictly religious programs" and thus left a "void in ... overall program structure."

Radio and TV are not the instruments of the state, they are the instruments of society. The state is there, has to be there, only because a technology that Jefferson could not dream of has made rationing the airwaves necessary. If Cohn's principle were followed, the FCC would not be protecting the separation of church and state, as he thinks. It would be promoting the separation of religion and society—something else again.

The late Theodore Leskes, a lamented colleague and an authority on First Amendment questions, was rather more convinced than I of the need for a wall. Nevertheless, when I asked him whether he objected to military chaplains, he answered that he could not object in principle. The army, he said, is a surrogate society. When the army drafts a man it is obligated to make available to him, insofar as possible, what he has had in the civilian life from which it cuts him off—including the opportunity for religious worship and guidance. Otherwise the government's maintenance of a conscript army would mean the government's exclusion of religion from the lives of some millions of young men.

■　■　■

And so with education. As late as the end of the nineteenth century, President Garfield could say that a college education was a log with Mark Hopkins at one end and a student at the other. If no longer entirely true when he said it, it still had a certain verisimilitude. Now it would be absurd—not only about our colleges, but also about our high schools, junior-high schools, and even elementary schools. These demand ever more costly laboratories, closed-circuit TV, equipment for teaching languages, psychological testing, vocational guidance.

When logs were cheap, it was rather widely possible to maintain nonpublic schools of the same quality as the public schools, even without governmental aid. Not any more. No violation of the First Amendment is needed to reduce freedom of the press substantively, by the disappearance of one paper after another; the only thing needed is for economic law to be allowed free play. Allowed free play, economic law would have the same effect on the nonpublic schools, but with an even worse effect on society. The space once occupied by nonpublic education would not be left empty. It would be filled by something we might call uniformitarianism, to coin an ugly word for describing an ugly condition.

In the political and social thought that has least to apologize for, despotism is understood to prevail when state and society are all but identical, when the map of the state can almost be superimposed on the map of society. In contrast, freedom depends on society's having loci of interest, affection, and influence besides the state. It depends on more or less autonomous institutions mediating between the naked, atomized individual and the state—or rather, keeping the individual from nakedness and atomization in the first place. In short, pluralism is necessary.

Given that a shriveling of the nonpublic must fatally enfeeble pluralism, especially in education; and given that the agent of that enfeeblement is the unchecked operation of economic law, the remedy is simple: check it. Let the government see that money finds its way to the nonpublic schools, so that they may continue to exist side by side with the public schools. That will strengthen pluralism, and so, freedom.

Arguments for nongovernmental pluralism have to overcome the obstacle of their popularity with conservative immobilists. From Social Security to Medicare, an unfeeling Right has been quick to warn that the omnicompetent state is upon us. Nobody listens any more; the boy has cried wolf too often. But in the fable a real wolf finally appeared, and for us the state coextensive with society may yet appear. Technology encourages it. The simple fact that there are now so many people encourages it. The time when the state took little of the room of a man's life is gone. Happily, a man can favor the welfare state and still oppose the omnicompetent state.

Can government be expected to subsidize the nonpublic sector, to pay for keeping vigorously alive centers of influence and power whose very existence will limit its own influence and power? If government is democratic, the expectation is altogether realistic. American governments routinely subsidize the nonpublic sector: the deductibility provision in the federal and state income taxes is nothing but an indirect subsidy to nonpublic institutions—community chests, universities, theological seminaries, churches and synagogues. And a most reassuring thing about the poverty program is that

government actually calls into being and finances civic group-
ings of the poor in order that they may make trouble for government—reassuring, because it shows that democratic
government understands that democracy requires government
to have cooperators-rivals.

Historically, establishment has gone with monarchy:
throne and altar, crown and mitre. Separation has gone with
a republic: no king, no bishop. And in fact England, Denmark,
Norway, and Sweden have established churches and are monarchies. Republicanism was once even more of a fighting creed
than separation, but who in Great Britain or Scandinavia is
excited by republicanism any longer? It has become an irrel-
evance, an anachronism. While monarchies have shown that
they can be decent and democratic, republics have shown that
they can be neither. In America separationism may soon be
just as anachronistic, if only because our establishmentarians
are not much more numerous than our monarchists.

Even the rhetoric is coming down with mustiness. "Wall
of separation" may have sounded good once, but if you say it
to a young man now he is as likely as not to think you mean
the wall that separates Berlin. Leave it to a poet: "Something
there is that doesn't love a wall."

(1966)

Religion and the
Public Square

IN 1966, COMMENTARY PUBLISHED an article of mine entitled "Church and State: How High a Wall?" It began, "The Jews are probably more devoted than anyone else in America to the separation of church and state." That is probably still so. The 1984 National Survey of American Jews, conducted for the American Jewish Committee by Steven M. Cohen, showed American Jews to be ambivalent about some things but not about separation.

Thus, in answer to one question in the questionnaire, three in four agreed that they supported "such government programs as welfare and food stamps," while in answer to the very next question, two in three agreed that "such government programs as welfare and food stamps have had many bad effects on the very people they're supposed to help." The successiveness of the questions should have discouraged contradiction and ambivalence: Apparently it did not.

Contrariwise, placing similar questions far apart could be expected to encourage forgetfulness, and therefore contradiction and ambivalence. With church-and-state issues that did not work.

Most Americans favor tuition tax credits for parents of children in private or parochial schools. Question 3 asked about that, and question 41 about tuition tax credits for parents of children in Jewish day schools. The answers to both questions were essentially identical: of those having an opinion, two to one opposed tuition tax credits, and only one in eleven or twelve was unsure. Opposition to "a moment of silent meditation each day in the public schools" was even stronger: more than three to one, with one in eleven not sure.

In 1985, Cohen sent questionnaires to the same people who had answered the 1984 National Survey of American Jews and got more than five hundred returns. One question was designed to test whether the attitudes of American Jews toward abortion are the same in the United States and Israel. It turns out that they are much the same. About four in five said they opposed both American and Israeli governmental prohibition of abortion except in the case of rape, incest, or danger to the mother's life; one in eight favored the prohibition, and one in ten or twelve was unsure.

On the other hand, there is a clear difference in response to "teaching about religion in the public schools." Jews oppose such teaching in the United States more than three to one, while more (though fewer than half) favor than oppose it in Israel.

	Yes	*No*	*Not Sure*
U.S.	20%	70%	10%
Israel	47	38	15

This last may be less inconsistent than it looks. Someone who is against teaching about religion in American public schools but for it in Israeli public schools might try to justify himself in some such way as this: In America children study English literature; in Israel they study Hebrew literature. Though the King James version is an English literary classic, you can teach English literature without the Bible. You cannot very well teach Hebrew literature without the Bible.

Note, however, that only about one in four said yes to teaching about religion in Israeli public schools and no to teaching about religion in American schools. Further, that fully three in eight American Jews oppose teaching about religion even in Israeli public schools shows a certain universalization of American values and practice.

∎ ∎ ∎

From an American perspective it is anomalous that most American Jews vote conspicuously to the left of their bankbooks, because other American religious and ethnic groups do not. From a worldwide Jewish perspective it is not at all anomalous, because at least until recently that is how most Jews in Western countries have voted.

What is the right perspective for viewing the strong separationism of most American Jews? If the alternative to separationism is Throne-and-Altarism, then modern Jews everywhere are all separationists. Yet British Jews, and of late even some French Jews, find it hard to understand why American Jews are so intense in their dislike for such things as silent meditation and teaching about religion in the public schools. American Jews might answer that they have higher expectations of the United States than British Jews have of Great Britain or French Jews of France. In the 1984 survey, five of six Jews agreed that "the U.S. has offered Jews more opportunities and freedom than any other diaspora country." (One in sixteen disagreed, and one in ten was not sure.)

How are we to understand the dominant attitude of American Jews toward, say, the Moral Majority?

1984 Impression of	Generally Favorable	Generally Unfavorable	Mixed	No Impression
ACLU	42%	13%	24%	22%
NAACP	54	12	28	6
Moral Majority	7	69	14	10

Maybe our respondents answered in this way because they are Jews, maybe because on the whole they are educated Americans, and maybe because they are both. In 1984, only one in six had never been to college, three in five had graduated, and more had at least one graduate degree than had a baccalaureate alone. About the Moral Majority, at any rate, the unpopularity-to-popularity ratio of ten to one would probably not be greatly different in any respectable faculty club. Which is to say that to Jews, "Jerry Falwell"—the type, not the actual man—may look like Elmer Gantry as well as Torquemada.

In 1985, Cohen tempted his respondents to do as some neoconservative intellectuals do—to think better of the Christian Right on account of Israel: "Since the Christian Right has been very pro-Israel, American Jews should overlook their objections to the Christian Right's ideas about America and work more closely with it to help Israel." Though the wording took for granted Jewish "objections to the Christian Right's ideas about America," few were mollified. Only one-fifth agreed; more than half disagreed, and more than a quarter were unsure. Particularist considerations—"help Israel"— are not allowed to prevail over loyalty to liberal "ideas about America," whether political or cultural. This loyalty, in turn, is itself not without a certain admixture of Jewish particularism. Liberalism has long been held to be not only good in itself but also "good for the Jews."

■　　■　　■

People use denial or evasion for dealing with conflict between one good and another. Dovishness is a liberal good. The 1985 questionnaire asked for agreement or disagreement with the proposition that "major reductions in U.S. defense spending ... will weaken the security of the U.S." A clear majority disagreed—that is, those disagreeing exceeded the sum of those agreeing and those not sure. The contradictory desires for major reductions in defense spending and for national security are reconciled by denying that they are contradictory.

Denial or evasion is also at work in American Jews' assessment of the effects of religion on society. Asked in 1984 whether they agreed or disagreed with the proposition that "the decline of religion in American life has contributed to a decline in morality," the six in seven who had an opinion divided about equally. It may be that some of those who said they disagreed actually did agree but did not want to say so for fear of giving aid and comfort to the Moral Majority. But the reasoning, if that is the right name for it, could also have gone the other way: the Moral Majority is wrong; the Moral Majority says that the decline of religion in American life has contributed to a decline in morality; therefore the decline of religion in American life has not contributed to a decline in morality.

That is denial. Evasion could take this form: Decline of religion? What decline? The Christian Right and those scary pro-lifers are evidence of a rise rather than a decline of religion. Decline in morality? If by morality you mean chastity, you are probably right, but morality is more than that. It also includes such things as tolerance and lack of prejudice. Since America is more tolerant and less prejudiced now than only a generation ago, you could as easily report a rise as a decline of morality. Besides, it is not as if we were against chastity. In the same survey, three in four agreed that "adultery is wrong"; one in six disagreed, and one in ten was not sure. (This recalls the old rabbinical—or is it generically clerical?—joke about the letter that the hospitalized rabbi receives from the secretary of the congregation: "Dear Rabbi, The trustees have instructed me to send you their best wishes for a speedy recovery, by a vote of five to four.")

■　■　■

After we dispose of the denial and evasion, we are still left with something serious that needs to be explained. The question about the decline of religion and morality is central. Put another way, it might be this: Is religion a Good Thing or a Bad Thing for society? Not every religionist will say that it is necessarily a good thing. Though peace is presumably good and the sword bad, the scriptures of a great religion promise not peace but a sword. Nor will every secularist say that religion is a bad thing. For personally irreligious people such as Emile Durkheim and Max Weber, the very asking about the goodness or badness of religion for society might well have seemed as foolish as asking about the goodness or badness of breathing: No life without breathing, no social life without religion. The very *philosophes* whose battle cry was *écrasez l'infâme* and who privately scoffed at the idea that their deistic deity had considerately provided an afterlife to mortal men and women were also convinced that in order for society to endure, the masses must not be disabused of their belief in an afterlife of rewards and punishments.

Why then the even split between Jews agreeing and disagreeing about religious and moral decline in the United States? Let us imagine a Jew who is apprehensive about the new assertiveness of religion in American life. What might such a person say?

He might start by saying that he was typical rather than untypical in being apprehensive—about the new assertiveness of religion, of course, but also about nearly everything else. A kind of free-floating anxiety is the American Jewish norm. The same people who in 1984 said that Jews as a minority fared better in the United States than anywhere else also, and at the same time, *denied*, by almost five to four, with one in seven or eight not sure, that "antisemitism in America is currently"—currently, not in some all-too-possible future—"not a serious problem for American Jews." At a time when Jews have been more successful than ever before, above all in politics, they deny by almost two to one, with one in nine not sure, that "virtually all positions of influence in America are open to Jews." From the outside, American Jews must resemble the poor little rich girl.

The apprehensiveness of us Jews is not altogether without locus or focus. Mostly we see unfriendliness if not downright hostility more among the rich and powerful than among the poor and powerless. (We make an exception for blacks. In 1984 a little more than half of us thought most or many blacks anti-Semitic.) About Republicans, 29 percent of us thought most or many to be anti-Semitic; about Democrats, only 6 percent; about conservatives, 35 percent; about liberals, 7 percent. Averaging these anti-Semitism ratings, we arrive at something like a 15 or 20 percent anti-Semitism rating by Jews for all Americans (all white Americans?) *in their secular capacity.* In their religious, Christian capacity we think them more anti-Semitic than that. In 1984, 40 percent of us thought most or many Catholics to be anti-Semitic; 42 percent thought so of mainstream Protestants; and 46 percent thought so of fundamentalist Protestants. In 1985, one of the questions asked about American Christians, American Jews, and Israelis was whether each of these groups was "basically like me." Naturally, American Jews got the highest vote, more than three-quarters. Next came Israelis, with something less than half. Only a little more than a third considered American Christians to be "basically like me."

■   ■   ■

And what is this talk about the new assertiveness of religion? (The representative Jew is still talking.) People speak not language in general but a language in particular, and they profess not religion in general but a religion in particular. It is not a new assertiveness of religion that makes Jews uneasy, it is the new assertiveness of Christianity, or of some movements and tendencies in Christianity. Nor is the assertiveness new.

It is simply renewed. Some of us experienced it when we were young.

Warner and Srole's *Social Systems of American Ethnic Groups*, published in 1945, is about a New England city ten years earlier. In the public schools the Lord's Prayer was recited every morning. When the authors asked a Jewish boy what he did about it, he answered that he recited it too, "because when in Rome do as the Romans do." When in America do as the Americans do. Americans recite the Lord's Prayer. Since it is a Christian prayer, the real Americans must be Christian.

Since it is not my prayer, I, the Jewish schoolboy, must be something other or less than a real American.

Morris B. Abram, more conservative now than he used to be, still writes about how "very uncomfortable" he was "as a child in a South Georgia public school system—really a Protestant operation supported by public funds—when the time came to recite the hymns and mumble the prayers." At the end of August 1985 a letter to the editor of the *Washington Post* protested the linkage, or hyphen, in Secretary of Education William Bennett's reference to America's "Judeo-Christian" heritage:

> It is almost as though the users of the phrase believe ... that Jews should not be critical of the users' religious agenda as long as that agenda begins with the prefix "Judeo." ... I grew up as a member of one of three Jewish families in a town of 1,600 in northern New Jersey. Each day in public school we read from the Bible, said the Lord's Prayer and sang "Jesus Loves Me." ... To most of us, school prayer means the prayers of other people's faiths ... and reemphasis of our status as a "minority" religion.

To young American Jews in the bad old days, the assertiveness of religion in American life meant conformity, keeping a low profile, not making waves—prudence at the expense of self-respect. It fostered Jewish self-hate, the internalization of the Other's image of Jews as alien and inferior.

Young Jews today have it better than their grandparents had when young, and one reason may be that the Lord's Prayer is no longer recited in public schools. We are not nostalgic about those days, and we doubt that some of the new asserters of religion in American life are equally lacking in nostalgia.

In 1985, Senator Boschwitz of Minnesota sent to a Jewish list a fundraising letter on behalf of the 1986 reelection campaign of Senator Specter of Pennsylvania. (Both are Republicans and both are Jews.) Boschwitz's letter stressed Specter's part in the legislative fight against mandating or allowing prayer in the public schools and urged his reelection for guarding the wall of separation against those who would breach it. The result in money raised was phenomenal, perhaps a record.

A penultimate word about Orthodox Jews. Qualitatively of great and growing importance in the American Jewish community, quantitatively they are a small minority, fewer than 10 percent. On the one hand, they generally are no less suspicious than other Jews of Christian intentions, though from a different angle—interreligious dialogue, for example. On the other hand, they are less separationist, if only from self-interest. Probably a majority—certainly a plurality—of the parents of children in Jewish day schools are Orthodox and resent the opposition of most other Jews to tuition tax credits.

■   ■   ■

My own views have changed little in the almost twenty years since that *Commentary* article of mine. I have quoted its first sentence. Its last sentence was Robert Frost's "Something there is that doesn't love a wall."

To the position that has been dominant in the American Jewish community for the past forty years or so, Naomi Cohen, in her *Encounter with Emancipation: The German Jews in the United States 1830–1940*, contrasts an earlier position:

Jews usually meant a neutral-to-all-religions rather than a divorced-from-religion state. Indeed, the later concept ... was as abhorrent to Jews as it was to most Americans. Rabbis, long the most influential leaders of the community, taught that religion was a vital component of the good life and, like Christian clergymen, inveighed against the inroads of secularization. Louis Marshall, the national spokesman of American Jews on the eve of World War I, found nothing intrinsically offensive about Bible reading in the public schools, so long as it did not become sectarian.

New is not necessarily improved.

(1987)

Appendix

Milton Himmelfarb:
A Bibliography

BOOKS

The Jews of Modernity. New York: Basic Books, 1973. [*JM*]
Jews and Gentiles. New York: Encounter Books, 2007. [*JG*]

ARTICLES, REVIEWS, ETC.
(In *Commentary,* unless otherwise noted)

"What Do American Jews Believe?" August 1996; repr. in *JG*
  as "What Do I Believe?"
"Judaism and American Public Life," *First Things,* March 1991
  (symposium); repr. in *JG* as "Judaism Is Against Paganism."
"Should Jews Criticize Israel?" *New York Times Book Review,*
  September 30, 1990 (review of David Vital, *The Future of
  the Jews*).
Letter, August 1989 (reply to critics of "American Jews: Diehard
  Conservatives," April 1989).
"American Jews: Diehard Conservatives," April 1989.
"American Jews and Israel" (symposium), February 1988.
"Jewish Perceptions of the New Assertiveness of Belief in
  American Life," in *Jews in Unsecular America,* ed. Richard
  John Neuhaus (Grand Rapids, Mich.: William B. Eerd-
  mans, 1987); repr. in *JG* as "Religion and the Public
  Square."

"Higham's 'Social Discrimination Against Jews...' Thirty Years
Later; A Reminiscence," *American Jewish History*,
December 1986 (review of John Higham's *Stranger in the
Land*).

"Another Look at the Jewish Vote," December 1985; repr. in
JG as "Jews, Episcopalians, Puerto Ricans."

Letter, August 1984 (correction to "No Hitler, No Holocaust,"
March 1984).

Letter, July 1984 (reply to critics of "No Hitler, No Holocaust,"
March 1984).

"No Hitler, No Holocaust," March 1984; repr. in *JG*.

"Are Jews Becoming Republican?" August 1981.

Letter, February 1980 (comments on Ruth Wisse's article,
"Women as Conservative Rabbis?" October 1979).

"Liberalism and the Jews" (symposium), January 1980.

"The Case of Jewish Liberalism," in *Emerging Coalitions in
American Politics*, ed. Seymour Martin Lipset (San Fran-
cisco: Institute for Contemporary Studies, 1978).

"A Haunting Question," in *Perspectives on Jews and Judaism:
Essays in Honor of Wolfe Kelman*, ed. Arthur A. Chiel
(New York: Rabbinical Assembly, 1978).

"Pluralism Ancient and Modern," December 1978.

Foreword to *The Religious Drop-Outs: Apostasy among College Graduates*, ed. David Caplovitz et al. (Beverly Hills:
Sage Publications, 1977).

"Carter and the Jews," August 1976.

Letter, October 1975 (reply to critics of "Liberals and Libertarians," June 1975).

"Jews and Gentiles," *Forum on the Jewish People*, Spring 1975;
repr. in *JG*.

"Liberals and Libertarians," June 1975.

Letter, January 1975 (reply to critics of "On Leo Strauss,"
August 1974).

"Plural Establishment," December 1974.

"On Leo Strauss," August 1974; repr. in *JG*.

Letter, June 1974 (reply to critics of "Spinoza and the Colonel," March 1974).

"Spinoza and the Colonel," March 1974; repr. in *JG* as "Spinoza and Mendelssohn."

"Zero Population Growth," in *Population Control: For and Against* (New York: Hart Publishing, 1973).

"Gentlemen and Scholars," October 1973.

"The Jewish Vote (Again)," June 1973.

"The Greeks, the Romans, and Captain Dreyfus," February 1973.

Letter, December 1972 (reply to critics of "McGovern, Nixon, and the Jews," September 1972).

"McGovern, Nixon, and the Jews," September 1972.

"Sword of the Law," May 1972.

Letter, February 1972 (reply to critics of "Of Fish and People," December 1971).

"Of Fish and People," December 1971.

Letter, September 1971 (reply to critics of "A Plague of Children," April 1971).

"Never Again!" August 1971; repr. in *JG*.

"A Plague of Children," April 1971; repr. in *JM*.

"The Topless Tower of Babylon," December 1970; repr. in *JM*.

"Is History Dead?" August 1970.

"This Aquarian Age," April 1970; repr. in *JM* as "A Pole in Denmark," "Power to the People," and "East Side, West Side."

"Jewish Class Conflict?" January 1970; repr. in *JM* as "Class Conflict" and "Reason Thunders in Her Crater."

"The Individual and Society," in *Central Conference of American Rabbis Year Book* (New York, 1969).

"Hebraism and Hellenism," July 1969; repr. in *JM*.

"Is American Jewry in Crisis?" March 1969; repr. in *JM* as "Crisis."

"The Jewish College Student and the Intellectual Community," *Judaism*, Winter 1968.

"Paganism, Religion, and Modernity," November 1968; repr. in *JM* as "Paganism," and in *JG* as "The Enlightenment: Paganism and Pluralism."

"The Psalms in Translation," September 1968.

"Relevance in the Synagogue," May 1968; repr. in *JM* and in *JG*.

"Translating the Psalms," February 1968; repr. in *JM*.

"In the Light of Israel's Victory," October 1967; repr. in *JM* as "The 1967 War," and in *JG* (with original title).

"Secular Society? A Jewish Perspective," *Daedalus*, Winter 1967; repr. in *Religion in America*, ed. William G. McLoughlin (Boston: Houghton Mifflin, 1968), and in *JM*.

"Varieties of Jewish Experience," July 1967; repr in *JM* as "Modern, Honorable, Masculine," and in *JG* as "Modernity and Religion."

"Are Jews Still Liberals?" April 1967; repr. in *JM* as "Still Liberal."

"Controversy," December 1966; repr. in *JM* as "Reply to Two Critics."

"Negroes, Jews, and Muzhiks," October 1966; repr. in *JM*.

"The State of Jewish Belief," *Commentary*, August 1966 (symposium); repr. in *JM*.

"Church and State: How High a Wall?" July 1966; repr. in *JM* as "The Wall," and in *JG* (with original title).

"Going to Shul," April 1966; repr. in *JM* and in *JG*.

"On Reading Matthew," October 1965; repr. in *JM*.

"The Jew: Subject or Object?" July 1965; repr. in *JM* as "Subject or Object?" and "Wanderers."

"Two Cheers for Hedonism," April 1965; repr. in *JM*.

"How We Are," January 1965; repr. in *JM* as "Like Everyone Else, Only More So."

"Rome and Jerusalem," September 1964; repr. in *JM* as "Our Fundamentalists" and "Rome and Jerusalem."

"Catacombs and Khazars," May 1964; repr. in *JM* as "Catacombs" and "And Many People Shall Come."

"Jewish Sentiment," *Commonweal,* January 31, 1964; repr. in *Federal Aid and Catholic Schools,* ed. Daniel Callahan (Baltimore: Helicon, 1964); repr. in *JM* as "Those Catholic Schools."

"How Many Israels?" January 1964; repr. in *JM* as "The Moroccan Vote" and "The Israelis' Religion."

"The Vanishing Jews," September 1963; repr. in *JM* as "The Vanishing Jew."

"Some Attitudes Toward Jews," May 1963; repr. in *JM* as "Unitarians, Trinitarians."

"Some Recent Jewish Books," April 1963.

"Festivals and Judges," January 1963; repr. in *JM* as "The Twelve Weeks of Christmas" and "Two Decisions."

"Some Recent Jewish Books," October 1962.

"Yom Kippur in Nineveh," September 1962; repr. in *JM.*

"Zionism and 'Belonging' in the United States," *Ammot* (Tel Aviv) and *L'Arche* (Paris), August–September 1962.

"Scholars Convene in Jerusalem," August 1962; repr. in *JM* as "Scholars in Jerusalem."

"Algerian Jews and Other Matters," May 1962; repr. in *JM* as "Two Cities" and "Our Cloistered Virtue."

"Soviet Jews, American Orthodoxy," January 1962.

"Fertility, Social Action, Socialism," September 1961; repr. in *JM* as "Population Implosion" and "Universalist Elite."

"Some Recent Jewish Books," August 1961.

"The Rational Symposiasts and Other Matters," May 1961; repr. in *JM* as "The 1961 *Commentary* Symposium."

"Ben Gurion Against the Diaspora," March 1961.

"Some Recent Jewish Books," January 1961.

"Bloc Voting, Unity, Prayers," December 1960; repr. in *JM* as "The Jewish Vote."

"Some Recent Jewish Books," September 1960.

"Some Notes on Jewish Affairs," August 1960.

"Reflections on the Jewish Day School," July 1960.

"Swastikas, Resolutions, Scholarship," April 1960.

Review of *The Zionist Idea: A Historical Analysis and Reader,*
  ed. Arthur Hertzberg, October 1959.
Review of *Tradition and Change,* ed. Mordecai Waxman,
  December 1958.
Review of *Yisrael ba-amim* by Isaac F. Baer, March 1958.
Review of *Great Ages and Ideas of the Jewish People,* ed. Leo
  W. Schwarz, October 1957.
Review of *Guideposts in Modern Judaism* by Jacob B. Agus,
  January 1956.
Review of *The History of the Jewish Khazars* by D. M. Dun-
  lop, June 1955.
"The Problems of Zionism, World Jewry and the State of Israel"
  (forum), October 1954.
"Jews and Philistines: Reflections on Jewish Culture," *Jewish
  Frontier,* September 1954.
Review of *What Price Israel?* by Alfred M. Lilienthal, Febru-
  ary 1954.
"Our Jewish Community Pattern and Its Critics," August 1953.
Review of *A Partisan History of Judaism* by Elmer Berger,
  February 1952.
"Group Life in America," *The Reconstructionist,* November
  30, 1951.
"Nine Books on Israel," December 1950.
Review of *The Jews: Their History, Culture and Religion,* ed.
  Louis Finkelstein, July 1950.
Review of *Essays in Jewish Biography* by Alexander Marx,
  August 1949.
"The Vindictive and the Merciful," July 1949; repr. in *JG* as
  "The Vindictive and the Merciful: God of Wrath and God
  of Love."
Review of *My Glorious Brothers* by Howard Fast, December
  1948.
Review of *The Maccabees* by Elias Bickerman, June 1948.
Review of *Galut* by Yitzhak F. Baer, May 1948.

"Peace Treaties," in *American Jewish Year Book* (New York: American Jewish Committee, 1948).

Review of *The Emergence of the Jewish Problem: 1878–1939* by James Parkes, December 1947.

Review of *Ritual: Psychoanalytic Studies* by Theodor Reik, September 1947.

"The Study of Man: Jewish History Freshly Appraised," May 1947.

"Germany and Austria," in *American Jewish Year Book* (New York: American Jewish Committee, 1945).

"Refugee Migrations," in *American Jewish Year Book* (New York: American Jewish Committee, 1944).

Index

abortion, 215, 244
Abraham, 54, 146, 201
Abram, Morris B., 250
Adorno, Theodor, 85
Agnew, Spiro, 152
Agnon, S. Y., 194
Agudath Israel, 153
Akhmatova, Anna, 37–38
Akiba ben Joseph, Rabbi, 25
Akoka, Jacky, 221
Albert of Aix, 105
Albigensians, 105, 113
Albo, Joseph, 80
Aleichem, Sholem, 10
Alexander II, 113
Alfonso Liguori, St., 198
Algeria, 122
Alliluyeva, Svetlana, 34, 36, 37
America First movement, 151
American Academy for Jewish
  Research, 70
American Civil Liberties Union
  (ACLU), 245
American Federation of Teachers,
  211
American Friends Service Com-
  mittee, 219

American Jewish Committee
  (AJC), 65, 208, 243
American Revolution, 78
Amish, 229
Anselm, St., 199
Antiochus, 112
anti-Semitism: of Arabs, 34, 116;
  assumptions about, 209–11,
  214–15, 248–49; of blacks,
  209–10; and Christianity,
  106–17, 211, 233; and Frankfurt
  School, 85; as insufficient for
  Holocaust, 101–2; Jewish self-
  hate, 162; in *Oxford English
  Dictionary,* 106; as self-applied
  label, 106; as synagogue topic,
  181; *see also* Nazis
Aquinas, St. Thomas, 196, 197–98,
  204
Arabs, 34, 116, 122–24, 131–33,
  137; *see also* Six-Day War
*Are the Jews a Race? (Rasse und
  Judentum)* (Kautsky), 8–9
Aristotle, 70, 77, 79, 160; and
  Strauss, 83, 86
Armenians, 134
Arnold, Matthew, 30, 31, 63, 183

263